HISTORY

of the

HORN

BOOK

Andrew W. Tuer

HISTORY
of the
HORN BOOK

Andrew W. Tuer

ARNO PRESS
A New York Times Co./New York 1979

First Published 1897
Reissued 1968 by Benjamin Blom, Inc.
Reprint Edition 1979 by Arno Press Inc.
LC79-51026
ISBN 0-405-09035-8
Manufactured in the United States of America

BY COMMAND

DEDICATED

TO

HER MAJESTY THE QUEEN=EMPRESS

TO ALL WHO KNOW THEIR ABC, GREETING.

PREFACE

"I HAVE hitherto thought," writes a correspondent, "that my horn-book was the only one in existence, but now I find there are two—I have one and you have the other."

At the Caxton Exhibition in 1877 were four horn-books, and at the Loan Exhibition of the Worshipful Company of Horners, held at the (London) Mansion House in October 1882, when special efforts were made to bring together as many as possible the total number shown was eight. That something like one hundred and fifty are noted herein is due to the power of the Fourth Estate. Unaided by the Press, the writer would never have heard of a quarter of them. So many horn-books having turned up, others are perhaps lurking in out-of-the-way places. May the reader become possessed of some! And in return for the good wish, perhaps he will send me an account of his spoils.

Some interesting notes on the horn-book, written by William Hone of *Every-Day Book* and *Year-Book* fame, which will be found in these pages, have not before been printed.

vii

History of the Horn-Book

The writer has pestered countless people for information about the horn-book. Mr. Gladstone's reply was unexpected but to the point; he said that he knew nothing at all about it.

"Those others"—the countless courteous persons who have ungrudgingly helped with references, or have generously loaned their treasures, and the *littérateurs* who have been the means of bringing us together—are enshrined in a grateful heart. To them I owe this opportunity of adding a chapter to the history of our national education.

18 CAMPDEN HILL SQUARE,
KENSINGTON.

CONTENTS

History of the Horn-Book

Contents

History of the Horn-Book

Contents

CHAPTER XXV

CHAPTER XXVI

WHOLE-PAGE ILLUSTRATIONS

History of the Horn-Book

☞ Some of the pictures in these pages took prizes in *The Studio* competition for illustrations of horn-book subjects for this work. Miss Levetus took the first prize, Miss Kate Light the second, and Miss France the third.

The head and tail pieces and initial letters are by Miss France (Mrs. Gaskin), C. M. Gere, and R. I. Williams, who has drawn the lion's share. To the late Joseph Crawhall are due the chap-book cut facing page xv. and others.

CHAPTER I

The genesis of the horn-book—Definitions—The earliest record; why so called—Continental tablets—No examples preserved in educational libraries or the libraries of public schools—"Destroy and forget"—Millions of horn-books—Horn-books with numerals—Printing a development, not an invention—Written horn-books—Horn-books in the British Museum, South Kensington, and Bodleian Libraries—Horn-books at exhibitions.

ORN-BOOKS came and departed without acclaim, and between their incoming and outgoing nations had long centuries wherein to wax lusty and decay. In days when human history was unwittingly written in the flints and potsherds which mother earth has so faithfully treasured for us, man's earliest attempts at writing must have been signs and pictures drawn in the sand or roughly scratched on wood or stone. As time advanced, thoughts were more conveniently impressed on the inner bark of trees, and later, on papyrus, and wooden, wax-covered folding *tabulæ*. "Write the vision and make it plain upon tables, that he may run that readeth it." Still later, when papyrus was superseded by parchment and vellum, but in days far behind the invention of paper and printing, the horn-book was the happy thought of an overtaxed scribe, who, heartily detesting the profitless labour of

I

History of the Horn-Book

rewriting the A B C, fastened the skin to a slab of wood and covered it with horn. For in those days, as in these, children were prone to destruction, and without taking into account the innocent mischief resulting from damp and grubby paws, they doubtless turned their master's careful handiwork into boats, or sent it skyward trailing behind their kites.

Dr. Johnson somewhat indefinitely describes the horn-book as "the first book of children, covered with horn to keep it unsoiled." "Horn-book: A leaf of written or printed paper pasted on a board, and covered with horn, for children to learn their letters by, and to prevent their being torn and daubed," is the definition given in Pardon's *New General English Dictionary*, begun by a "schoolmaster at Stratford-le-Bow" (London, C. Ware, at the Bible and Sun, Ludgate Hill, 1758). In his *Dictionary of Phrase and Fable*, Dr. Brewer describes the horn-book as an alphabet book or board of oak about nine inches long and five or six wide, on which was printed the alphabet, the nine digits, and sometimes the Lord's Prayer. "It had," says the doctor, "a handle, and was covered in front with a sheet of thin horn to prevent it being soiled, and the back board was ornamented with a rude sketch of St. George and the Dragon. The board and its horn cover were held together by a narrow frame or border of brass."

One of the most recent definitions is that in *The Century Dictionary* (1894), by Prof. Whitney of Yale, U.S.A. "Horn-book: (1) A leaf or page, usually containing the alphabet, the nine digits, and the Lord's Prayer, covered with transparent horn, and fixed in a frame with a handle ; formerly used in teaching children to read. Hence (2) a book containing the first principles of any science or branch of knowledge : a primer." In Gaelic, *spalag*, which also means a piece of dried bark, is the horn-book itself, while *brad* and *brod* apply only to the letters written or printed on its surface. In his *English-Irish Dictionary* (1732) Hugh Mac-Curtin, who devoted himself to the study of the early history of Ireland, gives *Clairin*, lit. a little board or tablet, as the equivalent for horn-book. Richards's *Geiradur Saesneg a Chymraeg* (English and Welsh Dictionary, Carmarthen, 1798) gives *Y llyfr corn*, the horn-book. If the English reader succeeds in pronouncing that double *l* to the satisfaction of a Welshman, he has done something to be proud of. In the extinct Cornish language the horn-book was *corn lyvyr, levar*, or *liver*.

2

THE PEDAGOGUE.   *Ambrose Dudley.*

History of the Horn-Book

While kindly placing at my disposal advance slips relating to the horn-book, gathered together for that student's treasure-house of the English language, the *New English Dictionary*, Dr. J. A. H. Murray writes from Oxford : " As references become suddenly plentiful at the end of the sixteenth century, it looks as if the *word* could not be much older, or as if the *thing* came in about that time." The truth probably is that the horn-book was invented at an earlier period than this, but that it was not generally used until towards the close of the sixteenth century. The earliest record I can find of a real horn-book faced with horn and not a mere alphabetical tablet—more will be said about early horn-books in later pages—is about 1450. No written, and very few of the earliest printed, horn-books have been preserved, and those left to us have suffered more or less from the effects of wear and tear, and dirt and damp.

The earliest printed horn-books were bulkier than their successors, and were in black letter, but Roman was probably used almost as soon as it was introduced in 1467. Black and Roman type ran side by side until the clearness and legibility of the latter almost entirely drove its elder brother out of the field of letters.

The earliest horn-books or tablets—in some the letters were incised on the wood, in others they were written—had nothing but the alphabet. Devotional booklets for children, opening with the A B C, followed, and the alphabet horn-book and the little A B C books of prayers ran side by side. Then the horn-book itself assumed the devotional form it has since retained, the earliest examples in Latin emanating from the Romish Church. About the time of the Reformation we get the horn-book—of which there were many variants—in its English form.

An old writer—I cannot lay hands on the reference—says that the horn-book is called a horn-book because the back was first ornamented with a rough cut representing an animal's horn, probably next to the reed the earliest wind instrument known to man. A horn-book was so called simply because the printed sheet was protected against grubby fingers by a sheet or thin slab of horn, through which the letters could be read. The captious might say that a horn-book without horn cannot be a horn-book. But with the public a horn-book gradually came to mean an alphabetical tablet of any kind whether horn entered into the construction

5

History of the Horn-Book

or not. So elastic did the meaning become that an A B C book or child's primer was often called a horn-book.

The horn-book proper—of which a sheet of horn forms a component part—is peculiar to English-speaking peoples. It has been extensively used here and in America, but never in other countries. The horn-book that we see in old Continental engravings is simply an alphabetical tablet without the protective horn.

The use of translucent horn having been universal, it is possible, of course, that foreign specimens of the horn-book protected with horn may yet be discovered. It is quite certain, however, that the horn-book, as we know it, was never in general use elsewhere than in England and America.

Some of the early horn-books used in this country were printed in Holland. Caxton was fairly free from foreign competition, but in Wynkyn de Worde's time France and Italy, as well as Holland, produced children's and other books for the English market. The Dutch printer continued to manufacture horn-books for us, and kept the trade to a large extent in his own hands, until they finally disappeared.

In home educational libraries the horn-book is practically non-existent, and the reason is given by Mr. F. Jenkinson of the University Library, Cambridge, who writes : "I am sorry to say we have no specimen of a horn-book of any kind. Until comparatively recent times such things would have been looked upon here as not worth keeping, and now it may be long before one comes in our way." Yet it seems inexplicable that all traces of horn-books used in chantry schools attached to religious foundations have so completely disappeared. In cathedral libraries, at any rate, it would be thought that examples might be preserved, but I have sought for them in vain.

In some, at any rate, of the older public schools the horn-book was certainly used. The writer has badgered the headmaster or librarian of every public school in Great Britain about horn-books, but not one specimen is to be found. In the dozen histories of our public schools which have been examined the word " horn-book " does not once occur. When a thing valueless in itself has served its turn, men seem to vie with each other in destroying all trace of its existence. In its later days the humble horn-book was treated with the full measure of contempt lavished on a thing which

6

History of the Horn-Book

has served its purpose. "Destroy and forget," said everybody, and alas! everybody did. Even the very latest horn-books are exceedingly scarce and things of price. In one of Hone's unpublished notes (see facsimile, cut I) is an allusion to "millions of horn-books." He says: " A large wholesale dealer in stationery and school requisites recollects that the last

Cut I.

order he received for Horn-books came from the country, about the year 1799. From that time the demand wholly ceased : twenty years afterwards in clearing out his warehouses a gross or two were found, and destroyed, as useless articles. in the course of sixty years, he, and his predecessor in business had executed orders for several millions of Horn-books." Just imagine a man's destroying a few gross of what collectors would now give their ears for.

7

History of the Horn-Book

In times when the literary aspirations of the people rose not above ballads and chap-books hawked about by chapmen, flying or running stationers, and what Cotgrave, in 1611, describes as the "paultrie Pedlar, who in a long packe or maund (which he carries for the most part open and hanging from his necke before him) hath Almanacks, Books of Newes,

Cut 2.

or other trifling ware to sell," the horn-book formed a usual and readily saleable portion of the stock-in-trade.

John Britton, in his *Autobiography*, published in 1850, tells us that he was placed with a schoolmistress, presumably in the parish of Kington St. Michael, Wilts, where he was born in 1771. "Here I learnt the Chris-cross-row (the alphabet preceded by a cross +) from a horn-book, on which were the alphabet in large and small letters, and the nine figures

8

History of the Horn-Book

in Roman and Arabic numerals. The horn-book is now a rarity." A very late example (1830-35) of a horn-book with alphabet and numerals is depicted in cut 2. Tablets with numerals frequently figure in old prints, and it is probable that horn-books with numerals only have been more or less used. A specimen of these tablets is shown on a much reduced scale in cut 3 (one of a set of seven prints by an unknown

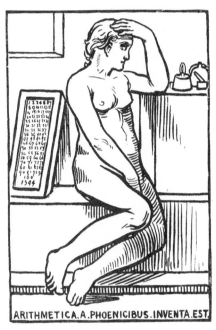

ARITHMETICA.A.PHOENICIBUS.INVENTA.EST

Cut 3.

Cut 4.

Italian artist), in which it will be noted that the invention of arithmetic by the Phœnicians is referred to ; cut 4 forms one of a set of seven prints by H. S. Beham (see p. 156).

It need not be pointed out that printing, of which type-founding forms a part, is a development and not an invention. The art has been improved by many, but was invented by nobody. The writer has said elsewhere : [1] "Who invented and who first used movable types for letter-press printing is a question which will probably never be satisfactorily settled. A library of literature has been written in attempting to answer

[1] *The Saturday Review*, 14th May 1887.

9

these questions, but the solutions seem far off. We know that some printer-genius of an economical turn—or it may have been an engraver—was inspired to have his work cut in such a manner that the blocks could be divided into separate pieces of uniform length, each bearing on its face a letter of the alphabet, which would be the first attempt to form a practicable fount of type. Still earlier, however, words from disused blocks were cut out and patched into new work; therefore, a sort of

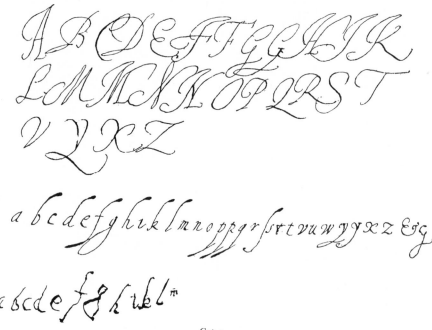

Cut 5.

rudimentary logotype printing preceded even the first crude attempt to use movable letters. In a dissertation, published in 1548, the Swiss writer, Theodore Bibliander (*In Commentatione de ratione communi omnium linguarum et literarum*, p. 80, Zurich, 1548), thought it worth while to record that first they cut their letters on wood blocks the size of an entire page, but because the labour and cost of that way was so great they devised movable wooden types. The fact is, that transition from the use of wooden blocks to separate letters engraved on wood or metal, and finally to cast-metal letters, was due to a slow but irrepressible natural development, the results of which could not have been even remotely foreseen."

It is probable that, after the invention of printing, horn-books were split up into two classes, one with a written copy for teaching writing, and the other with a printed copy for teaching reading. The former, which would be carried about very little, and when in use would be either

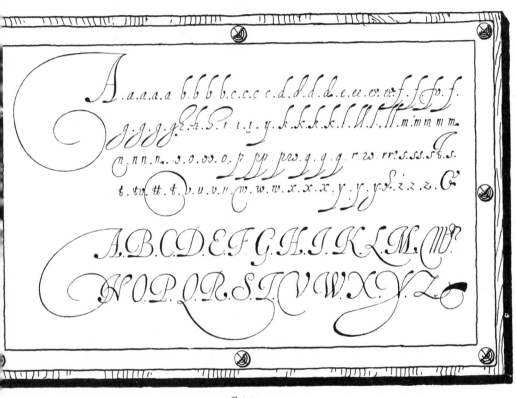

Cut 5*a*.

propped up or laid flat, were probably all handleless. Examples are exceedingly scarce. In fact, none of the old written horn-books of the days before printing have been preserved. The writer has a specimen of the handwriting of Charles I. (cut 5) when a boy. It has a sort of pedigree —valueless, as such things usually are—but there is little doubt that if Prince Charles did not himself pen the double alphabet, some one else did in his time. Working backwards one can imagine and portray the horn-book it was copied from (cut 5*a*), which is a fair reproduction of a lesson set by a writing-master, one Martin Billingsley, in his book on *The Pen's Excellencie, or The Secretaries Delighte*, 1618. That the Prince's writing-master was Billingsley there seems to be no reasonable doubt, for in the dedication of the book he says—

"To the most Excellent Prince Charles, etc.,

Most Gratious Prince.

This humble work of my hands labour, with my hearts love, I first devoted to yō Highnes Gratious Regard, and now (with an addition) for a public good, with yō favourable Patronage, putt forth into the world."

And in his *Preface to the Reader* he says :—

"In the meantime, as this little Booke hath found gracious acceptation at the hands of him to whom it was privately intended . . ."

Of Billingsley we know nothing, except that he dates his book " From my house in *Bush Lane*, neare London Stone, *Decemb.* 22, 1618," and that between this date and 1637 he wrote several works on Penmanship.

The written horn-book, shown full size in cut 6, belonging to Mr. James Falconer of Dundee, is a genuine but late example of the writing-

Cut 6.

A GENTLE DIVERCION
WYTH AN HORN BOOKE
AD: 1560:

E. Macquoid inv.

Percy Macquoid.

master's copy, and evidently forms one of a series. The written paper is fixed on to a thin sheet of iron, the edges of the metal being turned over the horn-covering, as in horn-books, cuts 7 and 8 (see p. 110). The period is

Cut 7.

probably the closing years of the last century. In his unpublished memoranda, Hone says that a friend of his, a Mr. Mackay, learned from a horn-book, and that he also wrote from copies covered with horn, at Exeter.

Something closely approaching to the form of a written horn-book

History of the Horn-Book

appears in *Calligraphia : Or the Arte of Faire Writing. By David Browne. Sanct. Andrewes : Imprinted by Edward Raban, Printer to the Univerſitie there, 1622.* (There is an extended imprint at the end of the

Cut 8.

work as follows :—*Imprinted at Sanct. Andrewes. By Edvvard Raban, Printer to the Vniverſitie there : And are to be ſolde in Edinbvrgh by John Burdon at his Shoppe, beſide the Trone on the South ſide of the Streete, For ſixe Shillinges Sterling the piece.*) On p. 121 is an ornamental

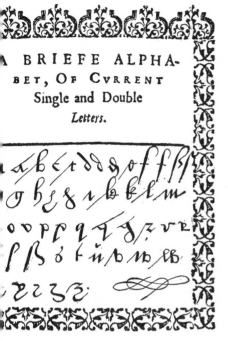

A BRIEFE ALPHA-BET, OF CVRRENT Single and Double Letters.

Cut 9.

border with a printed heading: "A BRIEFE ALPHA-BET, OF CVRRENT Single and Double *Letters.*" When printing the edition a large blank space underneath was left, and therein the author has *written* the alphabet reproduced in cut 9. The writing has faded to a dull dingy brown. On p. 67 there is another specimen of the author's handwriting, bleached by age, within a printed border (cut 10). Both specimens, with many others similarly treated, were intended to be copied by the scholar,

and most minute directions are given as to forming the letters, holding the pen, etc.

In the British Museum are but three complete horn-books, one a spuriosity (see pp. 181, 238, 309, 311, 327, 332). In the South Kensington Museum are eleven (see pp. 262, 332). Bodley boasts of three (see pp. 89, 322, 350), all purchased from the executors of the late Professor Westwood, in whose possession one at least had been for fifty years or more, and had belonged to his father before him.

Cut 10.

17

History of the Horn-Book

Horn-books have often been exhibited. At the Caxton Celebration Exhibition, 1877, the following horn-books were shown :—

Exhibit No. 4214. *Horn-book*, time Charles I. Found at Ashley
Green, Bucks. Lent by A. Smith-Dorrien
(see p. 323).

„ No. 4215. *Horn-book*, probably time James I. Lent by
John Evans, D.C.L., F.R.S. (see p. 313).

„ No. 4216. *Horn-book*, time Charles II. Lent by Sir Charles
Reed.[1]

„ No. 4240. *A new invented Horn-book.* Lent by Sir Charles
Reed (see p. 172).

At the Exhibition of the Worshipful Company of Horners of London held at the Mansion House in London, in October 1882, efforts were made to obtain on loan as many horn-books as possible. The total number that could be gathered together was eight. A newspaper account gave the number as nine, but one of them was " A Horn *Book Cover* of open work," etc., and not, as reported, " A *Horn-Book*, cover of open work," etc. One paper said, " The exhibition is rich in horn-books, there being some half-dozen specimens ; whereas, at the famous Caxton Exhibition, only half that number were forthcoming." The exhibits were catalogued as follows :—

Child's Horn-Book, ante 1600, for teaching letters, the Paternoster, etc.
Found in London, 1882 (cannot now be traced).

A Horn-Book ; being the Alphabet, the Lord's Prayer, etc. Exhibited
by John Evans, F.R.S., etc. (see p. 319).

A Child's Horn-Book. Exhibited by William Gurney (cannot now
be traced).

Two Horn-Books. Exhibited by T. C. Noble (see p. 110).

A Horn-Book. Exhibited by Miss Anne Jeaffreson, Brighton
(see p. 49).

A Horn-Book, large and perfect, with illustrated Alphabet. Exhibited
by the Exors. of Sir Charles Reed (see p. 172).

---

[1] The catalogue entry is incorrect. This horn-book was lent by Mr. Robert White of Worksop and is that described on p. 323 and pictured in cut 131.

History of the Horn-Book

A Horn-Book, found near Chesham, Bucks. Exhibited by Mrs. Smith-Dorrien, Great Berkhamsted (see p. 323).

The interesting silver horn-book, described on p. 43, an heirloom in the family of Lord Egerton of Tatton, was shown at the Tudor Exhibition held in the New Gallery, London, in 1890, and the examples noted in these pages belonging to the writer were in the " Fair Children " Exhibition at the Grafton Galleries in 1895.

Horn-books have occasionally been exhibited and commented upon at the meetings of Antiquarian Societies.

CHAPTER II

HORN-BOOKS must have received many nicknames now lost. In "horny cracker" wit would seem to lurk, inasmuch as a crack on the head inflicted therewith would produce a crackling sound from the horn, which seems to suggest that it might also have been called a Jim-crack. A correspondent who was at school in Portsea says that, in his time, the horn-book was called a "horn-gig." Another name for it was "battledore book." In his *Observations on Dialects in the West of England, particularly Somersetshire* (London, 1825), Jennings gives "hornen-book" as a Somersetshire provincialism. Hornbye (see p. 214) preserves to us "horning-book." Mr. E. F. Shepherd, of Staines, tells me that about 1840 he recollects calling at a roadside inn near Halifax, where he entered into conversation with the landlady's grandchild. I asked her, says Mr. Shepherd, how she was getting on at school. "School!" she replied; "I've never been to school. Granny taught me to read, and here's my horn-bat," which she showed me. It proved to be an ordinary horn-book.

A JIM-CRACK.   *Phil May.*

History of the Horn-Book

Whether it was that the wares were too unimportant, or that every one knew they were kept as an article of common stock which it would not pay to trumpet, horn-books seem to have been little advertised. John Timbs, in his *Things not Generally Known*, mentions an old advertisement (but not its source) of a bookseller dwelling on London Bridge : " Edward Winter at the ' Looking-glass,' Testaments, Primers, Psalters, Horn-books, Grammars," and there is mention of another which sets forth that " Joseph Hazard at the ' Bible ' in Stationers Court near Ludgate sells . . . spelling-books, primers, horn-books, etc."

In the Stockton Corporation accounts (*vide* Richmond's *Annals of Stockton-on-Tees*) there appears " this year " (1737) a payment of 2s. 10d. made to James Marshal for lettering books. His long advertisement in which the horn-book is mentioned is as follows :—" James Marshal, at the ' Bible and Sun,' in Stockton, sells the following Goods, viz. :—Bibles and Common Prayers of all sorts and Sizes, with Cuts or without, in all Sorts of Bindings ; Books of all Sorts ; also School Books of all Sorts, Horn Books, Primers, Guides, Spelling Books, Psalters, Testaments, and all Sorts of Almanacks, etc. He likewise sells all Sorts of Stationery-wares, as Writing-Paper of all Sorts, Printed Paper, Whited Brown and Brown Paper, Pasteboard, Merchants Accompt-Books, Shop-Books, Merchant File-Plates, Pocket Books, Ivory Pocket-Books, Slate Pocket-Books, Copper-Plate Books, Musical Books, Copy-Books with or without Copies ; Letter Cases, Prints, Sea-charts, Maps, Playing Cards, Landskips, Curious Prospects, History Pieces, Drawing-Books, Metzotinto Prints, Pictures, Plays, History-Books, Ballad and Song-Books, Black Lead, Black and Red Lead Pencils, Camel-Hair Pencils, Water Colours in Shells or in Bottles, Indian Ink, Gold and Silver Shells, Slates and Slate-Pens, Sealing Wax, Wafers, Ink of all Sorts, Standishes, Sand Boxes, Pen-knives, Razors, Engravers, Hones, German and Turkey Oil-Stones, Polishing Stones, Pumice-Stones, Rotten Stones, Putty, Emery, Tripoly, Spectacles, Spectacle-Cases, Reading Glasses and Perspective Glasses, Mathematical Instruments, Pocket Instruments, fine Shagreen Tweezer-Cases, Watches, Watch-Springs, Watch-Keys at Six-pence each, the best sort at Eight-pence, Watch-Chrystals at Six-pence each, Regulating Papers for Watches, Cast Brass for Clocks, Bells and Clock-Springs, Right London Lacker, White Varnish, Leaf-Gold, Leaf-Silver, Violins, Flutes, German-Flutes, Hautboys, Fiddle-Sticks, Strings,

History of the Horn-Book

Cases, and Bridges ; Reeds for Hautboys, and several curious Colours for Printing, not sold at any other Shop in Town. At the same place is sold Daffy's Elixir, Dr. Anderson's (or the true Scots Pill) Bottles for preserving the Teeth. He likewise trucks for old Books or Watches and Goose Quills. Also at the same Place Books are bound after the best manner. *N.B.*—Several other Articles, which are not mentioned here, are also Sold : also, Books lent out to read per Quarter or per week, the value of the Book being laid down when borrow'd."

One would think that something about horn-books would be found in children's singing games, but Mrs. Alice B. Gomme, an authority on the subject, tells me the only one she can recollect in which the A B C is introduced is that beginning, " Fool, fool, come to School."

In learning the A B C from the horn-book and in reading, a fescue (L. *Festuca*, O.E. *Festu*), or pointer, which might be a straw, pin, pen, piece of wire, quill, feather, or pointed piece of wood or bone, was long used to direct children. Sometimes the child held it, sometimes the teacher. " It may be worth while to observe," says Halliwell in his Folio Shakespeare, " that the fescue was an important instrument in the process of instructing from the horn-book."

Early references are fairly plentiful. Thus in "*Areopagitica*, a Speech of Mr. John Milton, for the Liberty of Vnlicenc'd Printing To the Parlament of England, London, Printed in the Yeare 1644," p. 20, we find : " What advantage is it to be a man over it is to be a boy at school, if we have only scapt the ferula, to come under the fescu of an Imprimatur ? "

> Not with a fescue to direct me,
> Where every puny shall correct me.
> > Breton's *Melancholike Humors*, 1600.

> The feskewe of the Diall is upon the Chrisse-crosse of Noone.
> > Wentworth Smith, *Puritan*, iii. 47, 1607.

> Why mought not he, as well as others done,
> Rise from his *fescue* to a Littleton ?
> > Hall's *Satires*.

" Some thieves are like a horne-booke, and begin their A B C of filching with a pin."—Taylor's *Workes*, 1630.

In a cut (11) on the title-page of Hornbye's *Horn-book*, published in

1622 (see p. 213), a schoolboy, who is being taught to read from a horn-book, is pointing to the letter B with a fescue.

> 'Tis not to find a fescue, sir, among the Rushes :
> To pick out a lesson in your crisse-crosse row of compliments,

is from *The New Academy, Or the New Exchange.*   By Richard Brome,

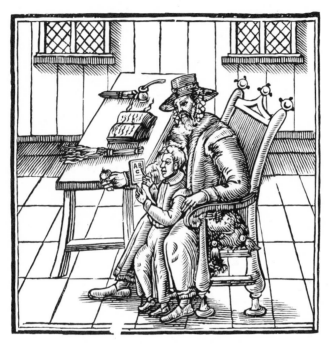

Cut 11.

London, printed for Andrew Crook, at the " Green Dragon " in St. Paul's Churchyard ; and Henry Brome at the " Gun " in Ivy Lane, 1658.

In cut 12 is seen a stained-glass window in All Saints Church, North Street, York, representing St. Anne teaching the Virgin to read. It will be noted that a fescue forms part of the subject (see p. 242). Another stained-glass window with the same subject, but differently treated, is in West Wickham Church.   Cut 13 shows full size a bone fescue, known in some parts as a fetty, belonging to the Rev. F. E. Warren of Bardwell Rectory, Bury St. Edmunds, which was found in the wall

25

History of the Horn-Book

behind a mantelpiece in an old cottage not long ago pulled down in Bardwell. Fescues or pointers will also be found in the pictured portions of other pages in this work.

So far as can be found, the horn-book figures but once in old brasses.

Cut 12.

An impression and counter-impression in the Print Department of the British Museum are endorsed in pencil, " Impression from a brass formerly in the Chapel, but at this time in the Bursary of Queen's College, Oxford." An engraving on a small scale of the brass is given in Jefferson's *History and Antiquities of Carlisle* (Whittaker, London, 1838). While everything on a copper-plate intended for producing prints must be engraved backwards or from right to left, which is reversed in the impression, a brass is, of course, engraved the way it is read, from left to right, and an impression taken from it by inking and rubbing will read backwards. Hence the necessity of taking a counter-impression, which the reader doubtless knows is produced by laying a piece of damp paper on the first impression before the ink has time to dry and passing both sheets together through a press. The subject engraved on the brass in question represents in the foreground a bishop in canonical robes kneeling. His right hand is raised in the act of benediction. Facing

Cut 13.

him is a mixed crowd, some bearing implements of labour, and amongst the crowd is a child with a horn-book (cut 14). In his left hand the

26

History of the Horn-Book

bishop holds a symbolical candle with the inscription in Greek, "It shineth to those in darkness." In the background are a church and a college flanked by sundry symbolical sheepfolds protected by dogs from a fox a wolf, and a lion. The whole is abundantly labelled with Scriptural texts in Latin and Greek, and from a Latin inscription at foot of the plate we learn that Henry Robinson of Carlisle was for eighteen years most provident Master of this College, and for the same number of years most vigilant Bishop of the Church of Carlisle, and that he died piously in the Lord, aged sixty-three, on the 13th day before the Kalends of July (*i.e.* June 19) 1616, and was buried in the Church of Carlisle.

Cut 14.

A sort of cousinship with the horn-book may be claimed for the Nuremberg counter, inasmuch as beyond serving the purpose of casting accounts after the manner of the Semitic abacus, it was used for teaching children arithmetic and the A B C. Counters, alluded to in *Julius Cæsar*, Act IV. sc. 3, as "rascal counters," or worthless coins, were made in enormous quantities. Of some half-dozen examples of Nuremberg tokens in the collection of Sir John Evans, K.C.B., and four belonging to the writer, of which two are figured in cut 15, there is but one duplicate ; variations occur in all the others, showing they were struck from different dies. An illustration similar to that on the reverse of the token, but on an enlarged and more clearly defined scale, appears in Reisch's *Margarita Philosophica* (Bale, 1508). The moneychanger is represented by "Pytagoras" in connection with the science of Mathematics, which is divided into the four branches of Arithmetic, Geometry, Music, and Astronomy. Pythagoras also figures in another cut as Music in the symbolical Temple of Philosophy.

Cut 15.

History of the Horn-Book

The prices of horn-books are referred to in a poem by William Hornbye which appeared in 1622, entitled Hornbye's *Horn-book* :—

> Even so the *Hornbooke* is the seede and graine
> Of skill, by which we learning first obtained :
> And though it be accounted small of many,
> And haply bought for twopence or a penny,
> Yet will the teaching somewhat costly be
> Ere they attain unto the full degree
> Of scholarship and art.

In Earl de la Warr's collection of MSS. is one dated 1623—a year later than Hornbye's *Horn-book*—relating to a commission for the rating and valuing of goods, horn-books being quoted at threepence per dozen, which would allow of a very handsome profit if sold for a halfpenny each. Mr. John Guest, F.S.A., in his *Historic Notices of Rotherham*, which appeared in 1879, says that in the accounts of the Rotherham Charity School from Lady Day 1709 to Midsummer 1710 is the following item :— "*Paid for Bookes.*—12 Hornbookes, 2 dozen and a half spelling bookes, 15 Testaments, 9 Bibles, 6 common prayer bookes, 19 catechisme books, 24 paper bookes, 12 accidences, and 1 of Dr. Tallbott's bookes, and carriges, £2 : 15 : 9½." Unfortunately the items are not separately priced. In the MS. accounts of the Archer family is an entry : "Jan. 3, 1715-16, one horn-book for Mr. Eyres, 00 : 0 : 2." "One horn-book, gilt," the price being twopence, is an item in a bill dated 1735, and the Huth horn-book of about the same period or more probably a little later (see p. 337) has its price, three-halfpence, marked in figures on the back (see cut 148).

Writing to the *Times* on the 28th August 1882, Mr. Edward Walford says that a couple of horn-books were sold on the 15th of that month at Puttick and Simpson's rooms in Leicester Square. They formed lot 164, which brought six shillings. Another *Times* correspondent, writing on the 30th of the same month, says that the horn-books then sold were of the last century and "only worth what they fetched." The writer recollects seeing these horn-books, which were of the ordinary late type, before the sale, but they then interested him so little that he did not leave a commission with the auctioneers.

Sir A. Wollaston Franks's horn-book, for which he gave half-a-crown (see p. 324), is perhaps the cheapest acquired in late years by private

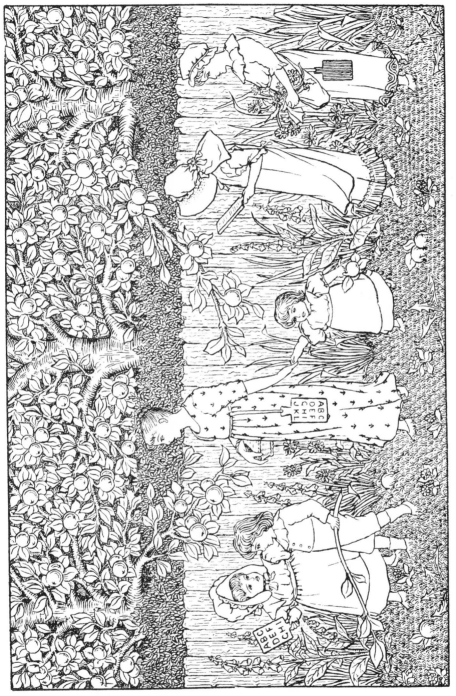

A PASTORAL.

G. Marion Jebb.

purchase. The writer's at five shillings, "picked up" at Oxford, may come next, and one in the South Kensington Museum at half a sovereign, third. At the other end of the scale is the Bateman horn-book which at auction fetched £65 (see p. 36).

The horn-book was elaborately but uninterestingly set to music as an exercise in the intricate time signatures of the day by Thomas Morley in 1608. It appears in an ingeniously written work entitled *A Plaine and easie Introduction to Practical Musicke, Set downe in forme of a diologue: Divided into three parts. The first teacheth to sing, with all things necessary for the knowledge of pricktsong. The second treateth of descante, and to sing two parts in one upon a plainsong or ground, with other things necessarie for a descanter. The third and last part entreateth of composition of three, foure, five, or more parts, with many profitable rules to this effect. With new songs of 2, 3, 4, and 5 parts. By Thomas Morley, Batcheler of Musicke, and one of the gent of her Maiesties Royall Chappell. Imprinted at London by Humfrey Lownes, dwelling on Breadstreet hill at the signe of the Star*, 1608. The opening is shown in cut 16.

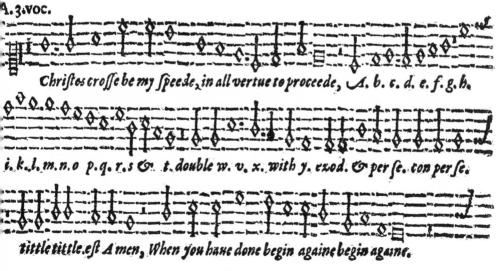

Cut 16.

History of the Horn-Book

Morley's horn-book seems never to have been scored in modern notation. Randall reprinted the volume in 1771 with most of the examples in modern score, but he shirked "Christes crosse" altogether. There is a later composition, in folio sheet form, dedicated to a City Knight, entitled "The First Part of the Horn Book set to Music in the key of D, etc. By a Country Organist"—probable date about 1794. This trifle is simply a travesty of the fashionable *scenas* of the latter half of the eighteenth century, and so far as it goes is not badly written.

CHAPTER III

A penny horn-book sold for £65—Description of the Bateman horn-book—A horn-book "the making of which employeth above thirty trades"—The Bateman horn-book and William Hone.

THE best-talked-of horn-book is that until lately in the Bateman Museum, Lomberdale House, Youlgrave, Derbyshire (cut 17). It is described in Mr. Bateman's own catalogue as follows :—" Horn-book, formerly used in teaching the elementary parts of education, found 10th March 1828 in the wall of an old house at Middleton ; each side is represented of the full size by the two accompanying plates. This excessively rare specimen consists of a thin board of oak with a short handle, covered at the back with leather stamped with an equestrian portrait of Charles I., above him a Celestial crown and cherub, indicating a period shortly after the King's execution in 1649. At the front is a paper with the alphabet, Lord's Prayer, etc., printed in black letter, which is protected by a piece of transparent horn secured by tacks—whence the name. When first discovered a narrow strip of thin brass surrounded the edge of the horn."

At the meeting of the British Archæological Association, held 12th

33

History of the Horn-Book

January 1853, when Mr. Thomas Bateman exhibited his treasure, Mr. Halliwell made the following observations :—" Horn-books are, perhaps,

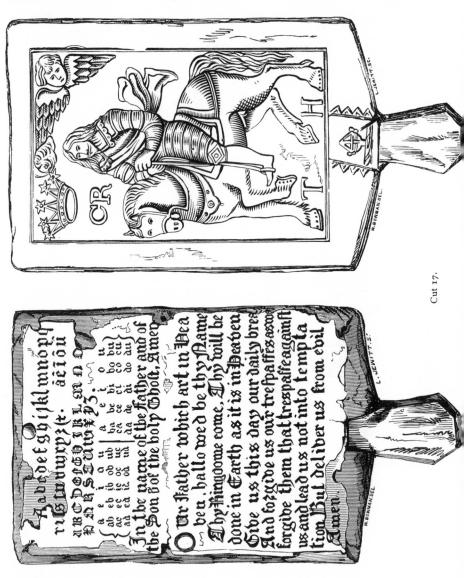

Cut 17.

the most curious relics of the educational system pursued by our ancestors that have been preserved to our times ; and yet we can scarcely say that,

History of the Horn-Book

absolutely obsolete as they now are, they belong exclusively to any early period, for they were in current use till the commencement of the present century. They are now, however, so little known, that few persons are aware of their exact character; and on that account, the very curious specimen in the possession of Mr. Bateman, here engraved, is extremely worthy of notice. They were called horn-books, because they were protected by thin sheets of transparent horn. There is generally, first, a large cross, the *criss-cross*, and then the alphabet, in large and small letters. The vowels follow next, and their combinations with the consonants; the whole being usually concluded by the Lord's Prayer and the Roman numerals. Sometimes, but not always, especially in ancient ones, we find Arabic numerals. Florio, 1598, mentions Centurola as ' a childes horne-booke hanginge at his girdle.' Horn-books of this early period are of the highest degree of rarity, and perhaps the specimen in Mr. Bateman's possession may be considered amongst the most curious known. It is a curious fact, that in after ages the rarity of a book or tract is almost invariably in inverse ratio to the extent of the impression. Thus, in tracts of the Elizabethan period, those which were circulated by thousands are now either lost, or exist in unique or very rare copies; while books of a serious nature, of which only small numbers were printed, may be easily met with. This bibliographical law is true in our own day, and it is said, on good authority, that it would be more difficult to form a collection of political satirical pamphlets of the reign of George III., than a similar collection belonging to the time of the Commonwealth. The subject is a curious one, and appears worthy of note."

The writer of an interesting paper entitled " The Horn-book of the Olden Day," in Willis's *Current Notes* for October 1855, says, in reference to the Bateman example, that the initials T. H. at the foot of the design stamped on back representing Charles I. on horseback were possibly placed there in compliment to Sir Thomas Herbert, a devoted servant of His Majesty. In a more prosaic spirit, I would suggest that they are likelier to be those of the engraver of the brass stamp. The cut illustrating a paper on the horn-book in Chambers's *Book of Days* (18) is a reduced copy of the Bateman horn-book.

The first portion of the Bateman heirlooms was sold by order of the Court of Chancery by Sotheby, Wilkinson, and Hodge, on the 14th April

History of the Horn-Book

Cut 18.

1893. Much curiosity was shown, and many guesses were hazarded, as to what amount the rare horn-book, described by a London daily paper as being stamped with the portrait of "a stout gentleman on a stumpy horse," would realise. Many well-known collectors attended the sale, and it was to the boldest, rather than to the richest to whom it fell. The bidding for the lot—No. 118 in the catalogue —began at ten pounds, reaching in a couple of minutes sixty-five, for which sum it was knocked down to Mr. Durlacher, who afterwards sold it to Dr. Figdor, a private collector of Vienna. That the rubbish of one generation becomes the treasure of another is a platitude, the use of which the indulgent reader may perhaps forgive on the understanding that it shall not be repeated. Under ordinary circumstances such a price would be simply ridiculous, but now thoughtless persons who own anything that can be dubbed a horn-book expect to get sixty-five sovereigns for it, and then come disappointment and wrath.

The Bateman horn-book is of a rare type, but unfortunately very imperfect. The faded brown morocco leather has gone from the handle, the back is much frayed, more especially at the right-hand edge ; the silver foil used in stamping the device of Charles I. is dulled to a leaden hue, the tacks are mostly oxidised out of existence, the brass edging to the horn has entirely disappeared, and the horn itself seems to have taken the fancy of predatory rats. It will be noted that the short "and" follows the alphabet of small letters, and appears also in the Invocation. Ever since

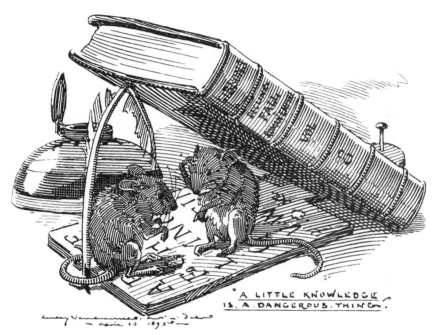

"A LITTLE KNOWLEDGE IS. A. DANGEROUS. THING."

Linley Sambourne.

History of the Horn-Book

it was found, the Bateman horn-book has been carefully preserved under double glass in a small mahogany case. Peacham (see p. 193), who lived in the time of Charles I., says in his *Worth of a Peny* that a horn-book, " the making of which employeth above thirty trades," can be bought for a penny. As it would be impossible to employ thirty trades unless the horn-book were covered, the example bearing the effigy of Charles I. in the Bateman collection was doubtless originally sold for a penny, which, allowing for the difference in purchasing power, would be a fair price. Another horn-book disposed of in the Bateman sale (lot 119) is mentioned on p. 337 ; a horn-book on card is noted on p. 351 ; and a couple of battledores on p. 414. The last three were sold together and formed lot 120.

Amongst Hone's unpublished notes is one relating to the Bateman horn-book :—" There is an old and curious horn-book in the possession of a gentleman of antiquarian taste and learning—William Bateman of Middleton, near Bakewell, Derbyshire—which he most obligingly forwarded to me for inspection. A written memorandum is on the handle : 'This horn-book was found on the 10th March 1828 ; measures three and three-quarter inches high by two inches and seven-eighths in width, exclusive of the handle, which is an inch long.' The alphabet is preceded by the Cross. The contents of the page are the same as mine but printed in 𝔟𝔩𝔞𝔠𝔨 𝔩𝔢𝔱𝔱𝔢𝔯. The wood, except the handle part, is wholly covered with roan or sheep leather, originally perhaps of a red colour, but now faded. The back is stamped with a figure of Charles I., bareheaded and in armour, on horseback, within a single line border ; at the top corner and facing the King there is a large celestial crown issuing from a cloud above his head ; and in the other corner, behind the cloud, an angel's face and wings ; under the crown are the letters C. R., below, between the feet of the horse T. H. This ornament was impressed upon the leather with a tool that indented into every line some metallic pigment, which has since oxidised to a dull leaden colour. That the page of a horn-book in the reign of Charles I. should be printed in black letter may seem remarkable to persons who do not know that black-letter contents type lingered in use for some editions of old school-books so late as the reign of ." The following letters, which have not before been printed, may fitly end this chapter :—

History of the Horn-Book

MIDDLETON, BAKEWELL, COUNTY DERBY,
February 11, 1831.

SIR—I think there is scarcely any notice nor any engraving in any of your preceding instructive and entertaining works of that curious little manual, the horn-book. Some years ago, one of them was discovered here on taking down an old farmhouse. It is of a date immediately after the *martyrdom* (!) of Charles I., as upon the back of it there is an equestrian portrait of that King stamped upon the leather, with a celestial crown above him. On the obverse there is simply the alphabets and the Lord's Prayer. If you think it might be a suitable decoration for your agreeable *Year Book*, with some observations of your own, I shall have great pleasure in giving you the loan of it for that purpose.—I am, sir, your most obedient servant, WILLIAM BATEMAN.

Mr. Hone, London.
(Address) Mr. William Hone,
13 Gracechurch Street, London.

MIDDLETON, BAKEWELL,
March 1831.

DEAR SIR—I am glad to find that the *royal martyr* Hornbook may be useful, and that you have some notes ready. I am sure nothing from me will be worthy to join with them ; in fact, until the receipt of your intelligent letter, I had not attempted anything by way of illustration, remaining satisfied with simply knowing that it was a "Hornbook." I take the liberty of enclosing with the Hornbook a Sovereign towards the expense of engraving it—if such expense in the "Year Book" falls upon you—if it does not then allow me to place it against the cost you were at in raising a monument to the fame of old tiger Ellenborough in Dec. 1817.

If you should make a northern tour I shall be extremely happy to see you here, and shew you some relics I have got together during some years in which we have been turning over and renovating the village—the access to us is now very easy, three Lond. and Manchester Coaches passing

40

History of the Horn-Book

daily within a short walk. If an engraving is made, may I beg 2 or 3 impressions upon separate paper. When you return the H.B. be so good as to send it by the Peveril Manchester Coach (from Laurence Lane, I think) and without paying carriage if you please—which I was really sorry you thought necessary to do for the letter.—I am, Dear Sir, your very obedient servant, WILLIAM BATEMAN.

CHAPTER IV

Horn-books with pedigrees—Pedigrees generally untrustworthy—A triplet of stories—
Lord Egerton of Tatton's Elizabethan silver horn-book—A horn-book from which
Frederick, Prince of Wales, son of George II., learned his A B C—Another horn-
book with a pedigree.

HOSE who have to do with pedigrees
of things if not of persons know how
little dependence is to be placed on
them. Fraud is not a factor so much
as forgetfulness or carelessness. A
relic, say a bit of china, is passed from
father to son. As it descends, the son
who has cared little about it, or may
have just waked up to its value, inno-
cently confuses one thing with another,
pastes a label on the wrong crock, and
the mischief is done. In dealing with pedigrees, one may keep in mind
the story of the club used in slaying Captain Cook, which, an American
humorist says, is in every reputable museum and collection of curiosities
in the four quarters of the globe.

Personal statements are often to be received with a heaped cellarful
of salt. Of this I am painfully aware, for after leaving my teens behind,
I once recalled to a merry-eyed aunt an accident which had befallen
me when a mite, and I recollect most uncommonly well enlarging on
the foolishness of a child being allowed to put a halfpenny in his mouth,

History of the Horn-Book

and the attendant danger of a lodgment in the throat. The choking agony suffered I was exactly and minutely describing, and I was proceeding to explain how I had been thumped, turned upside down, and drummed on the floor, when the merry-eyed, whose face had gradually assumed the colouring of a peony, suddenly exploded with boisterous merriment : " Why, Andrew," said she, " *it was your Uncle John !* " And so it was. But the story had been told so often when I was small that I had taken it unto myself.

An old gentleman who fondly believed he was speaking the truth, told me that when he was little the horn-book was made from horn run into an iron mould, with the A B C in sunk letters, and that the alphabet was filled in with molten lead. When it was gently suggested that horn could not be run into a mould, and that leaden letters therein or thereon had never been heard of, and, moreover, could have served no useful purpose, the conversation was abruptly turned into another channel. When that old gentleman was small, some wonder-exciting plumbing operations had no doubt distracted his attention from the horn-book.

There being nothing about the printed sheet to indicate accurately the time of its production, a horn-book with a pedigree fairly unimpeachable is of considerable interest. Amongst the most interesting horn-books with pedigrees is that lent to the Tudor Exhibition held at the New Gallery, London, in 1890 (cut 19). It is referred to in the catalogue as " No. 1038, Horn-book of Queen Elizabeth, lent by the Lord Egerton of Tatton," and it figures on a minute scale amongst the cuts in the illustrated edition. This beautiful filigree silver horn-book is stated to have been given by Queen Elizabeth to Lord Chancellor Egerton, the then owner of Tatton, and it has since been most carefully preserved in the family. The protective covering—slightly defective in one place—is of talc instead of the usual horn. The pretty open filigree silver-work at back, as that in other examples, is underlaid with red silk faced with talc. The silver handle has neither silk nor talc, and the overlapping silver tongue work, which forms a border and holds everything together, is perfect.

Though the owner is of opinion that there is no possible question as to the authenticity of this horn-book, doubts have been expressed about its age. Disbelievers have hinted that it is a changeling. They say that

43

the type looks later than Elizabeth,[1] and that the silver filigree is still more modern. The question arises as to whether it could have been printed in

Cut 19.

the time of Elizabeth. The evidence on this point is within easy reach, and we have only to refer to one or two[2] of the three hundred and fifty

[1] One might naturally expect to find black-letter (see p. 303).

[2] " A Report and Difcourfe written by Roger Afcham of the affaires and ftate of Germany and the Emperour Charles his court duryng certaine yeares while the fayd Roger was there. At London, Printed by John Daye dwelling ouer Alderfgate."

" Certain felect Prayers gathered out of S. Augustines Meditations, which he calleth his felfe Talke with God. At London, printed by John Day, dwelling ouer Alderfgate, 1573."

Both books, the first undated (about 1553), are in black letter, interfprinkled with Roman. The title-pages are set in Roman and Italic.

44

History of the Horn-Book

books known to have been printed by John Day, Daye, or Daie, whose numerous and beautiful founts of Roman and Italic type cut by himself and his workmen about 1567 gave the deathblow to black letter—founts of which he also produced—to find similar type. Further, it is almost certain that Day had founts in his possession in the time of Mary, from which the horn-book could have been printed. Type of the same face was used in Holinshed's *Chronicles* in 1587.

Allowance being made for careless workmanship and rough paper, the type used in the printing of this horn-book seems to have seen but little wear. The large lower-case u in the alphabet of capitals, which is repeated in " OUR " in the opening of the Lord's Prayer, points to a time when the u and v,[1] the uncial and capital forms of the same letter, were interchangeable, and the vowel was not distinguished from the consonant.[2] In the first Roman punches cut in 1465 by Scheynheym and Pannarts, the lower-case or small u only was given, the same letter as a capital appearing from French founders about the first half of the sixteenth century. Were it not that the letter u in both cases, where used as capitals, varies in the cutting and bears obvious signs of being alien—which is distinctly in favour of the early date assigned—one might reasonably assume that this horn-book was printed in France, or from French type imported into this country. The alien letter is either a u the right way up, or an n turned upside down, of a larger fount, the body of the type having been cut to make it range with the other letters. The small u as a capital letter will be found in cut 20, and others. In *P. Vergilii Maronis Opera, cum Annotationibus J. Min-Ellii* (Rotterdam : R. Leers, 1704) the u is extensively used in one fount of capitals, and in a smaller fount cast without this letter, the printer has used for a capital u a turned n, the face of which is larger than the capitals themselves. The strange letter is of course assertively prominent.

---

[1] For evolution of the forms of letters see Dr. Taylor's work on the Alphabet ; *Paléographie Universelle*, by M. J. B. Silvestre, etc. Those who prefer much in little may refer to Sir John Evans's paper *On the Alphabet and its Origin.*

[2] Johnson says in his Dictionary that as late as 1755 the two powers expressed in Modern English by the characters V consonant and U vowel ought to be considered as two letters ; but as they were long confounded while the two uses were annexed to one form, "the old custom still continues to be followed." In such words as *Duke* pronounced *dook*, 'Arry and 'Arriet retain the true primary sound of the letter U, the sound which it now represents in most European languages.

45

History of the Horn-Book

It is obviously unsafe to arrive at the age of type merely by the date of a book or document in which it is used.

The twisting of silver wire known as filigree work was practised by the early Celtic and Scandinavian tribes, and the ancient Greeks and

Cut 20.

Romans. There are, perhaps, few Egyptologists without specimens in their collections, and in India the manufacture is still largely followed. The elaborately-worked and beautiful enshrinement of Lord Egerton of Tatton's horn-book might be Maltese or Genoese, or from the hands of Continental workmen who found their way to this country. I acquainted the owner with the doubts expressed as to the genuineness of this heirloom,

Georgie Cave France (Mrs. Gaskin).

SPRING.

History of the Horn-Book

and said it had been suggested that the silver filigree might have been added at a later date, say in William III.'s time, when there was a revival in its manufacture. Here is the reply :—

"With regard to the horn-book, I am quite certain there has been no change in it since Charles the Second's time, when Lord Bridgewater's third son first came to Tatton. There was plenty of silver filigree work in the time of Queen Elizabeth, when no doubt this horn-book was made. There has never been any change in the horn-book, I think, since the time of Elizabeth. As it is extremely improbable that the gift of Queen Elizabeth to the Chancellor should have been altered in the revolutionary wars of the next century, and the first owner of Tatton, to whom the horn-book was given, died before the time of William the Third, I think you may conclude that the experts are mistaken as to the date of the case."

There would appear to be no sufficient reason to doubt that this is the original horn-book presented by Queen Elizabeth to one of Lord Egerton of Tatton's ancestors.

A valuable horn-book—valuable because it has a pedigree—of a late type is cut 21, presented by Mrs. Jeaffreson to her husband, Dr. Horace Jeaffreson of Wandsworth. It is covered with a brownish-red paper, faintly stamped on the back with an equestrian portrait of Charles II.

Cut 21.

The following is a letter from Mr. J. H. S. Thomson, the former owner, concerning its pedigree :—

49

History of the Horn-Book

" Referring to the horn-book you have obtained from me, I beg to state that it was given to my grandfather by an old friend, viz. Mrs. Gregson, to whom it was given by William IV., then Duke of Clarence, who told the said Mrs. Gregson that it was the book from which his grand-father learnt his letters. I may mention that Mrs. Gregson was staying at that time with Richard Sheridan, with whom the Duke of Clarence was on very intimate terms. The book has always been in our family.

"J. H. S. THOMSON."

(William IV.'s grandfather was Frederick, Prince of Wales, son of George II.)

There is obviously no reason why a child born to the purple should not have learnt its A B C from a brand-new horn-book, but hardly from a second-hand one. If the foregoing pedigree is accepted—and there appears to be no valid reason for its impeachment—we have proof of what is advanced elsewhere as merely conjectural : that makers of horn-books stamped on the backs of them, by way of ornamentation, designs which ought to have been discarded, including effigies of monarchs who had long been translated to a better land. Of course the maker could scarcely have been expected to destroy his stock, often large and valuable, of horn-books because of inappropriateness of ornamentation. This horn-book formed part of the exhibits of the Worshipful Company of Horners held in London in 1882.

A nice example in a tolerably perfect and bright condition, covered with brick-dust coloured paper, and stamped somewhat imperfectly on the back (cut 22) in black, with the device of a double-headed eagle,[1] is in the possession of Dr. T. G. Wright of Wakefield. This is one of the few horn-books with a pedigree, or rather with a bit of one. It belonged to Dr. Wright's mother, who received it from a friend with some doggerel verse, the original of which is still in existence. Here is a copy :—

Madam, a man of my acquaintance
Was lately talking of the entrance
Into all learning, and the rules
Now used in our modern schools ;

---

[1] The device of the double-headed eagle of the German Empire was used by a printer, William Vorsterman, 1500-1554.

History of the Horn-Book

Says he, " I think in future ages,
A Horn-book will be to the sages
A curious thing to look upon ;—
I wish that you could get me one."
I set about his will to do,
And fortunately I've got two,
The one of which I send to you.
Already obsolete they've grown ;
Then fifty years hence when they're shewn,
What will the learned in that day
About the Horn-books, Madam, say ?
When they're as rarely to be seen
As farthings coined by Anne our Queen ;
So Horn-books place in your Museum,
That those who're yet unborn may see 'em.
Yours indefatigably,   H. M.
Stockton-on-Tees, 10th August 1809.

Cut 22.

History of the Horn-Book

The two horn-books mentioned by " H. M." were sold in 1790 with the stock of a second-hand bookseller at Darlington. The companion is said to have found its way to Newcastle-on-Tyne, where it, or a similar one, was at a later date " picked up " by Mr. M'Cabe of Wakefield, then a bookseller in York. It was purchased from him for five pounds by Lord Morpeth, the literary Earl of Carlisle. " Hence," says Dr. Wright, " I conclude that this horn-book now rests at Castle Howard," but inquiry of the noble owner elicits that it has unfortunately gone amissing.

CHAPTER V

Horn-books in the form of a cross—The cruciform shape the scarcest—Memory h
of a "cross" horn-book—Balked by a dealer—Memory sketch of an ... ross"
horn-book—What Scoggin does *not* say about the "cross" horn-bo....

HE scarcest horn-book of all, a genuine example of which I have never seen, is undoubtedly that cruciform in shape. Were there no evidence whatever of the existence of the horn-book in this form, one would be justified in assuming from the habits of the times and the conditions of education that it must have taken it. The cross is found in many forms on the MSS. used in the monastic schools, and no doubt a religious turn was given to teaching by placing the alphabet, arranged in the form of a cross, in the hands of little children.

"The most ancient of these infant school-books," says Dr. Brewer, in his *Dictionary of Phrase and Fable*, "had the letters arranged in the form of a Latin cross, with A at the top and Z at the bottom, but afterwards the letters were arranged in lines, and a cross was placed at the beginning to remind the learner that 'The Fear of the Lord is the beginning of wisdom.'"

In the *Vocabulary of East Anglia*, by the Rev. R. Forby (vol. iii. by the Rev. W. T. Spurdens), 1840, London, 1858, we find " *Criss-Cross-Row, i.e.* Christ's Cross. The early horn-books for children had the alphabet arranged in, or on, the form of the cross. This horn-book, in the ages of Popery, was thus made conducive to the offices of their superstition. It was a small board, rather less than the size of this page (crown 8vo); on one side of which was the alphabet, as above mentioned, and on the other a crucifix, each on paper pasted to the board, and covered with a piece of clear horn as a defence. The top of the board had a projecting part, perforated, through which passed a string, by means of which it was worn, as a rosary is also suspended from neck or waist. CRISS-CROSS-ROW(*s*), the alphabet, as it stood in the horn-book in the shape of Christ's Cross; the consonants in the vertical, and the vowels in the horizontal part. Alas! a horn-book such as I learned my letters from would already be a thing for a museum."

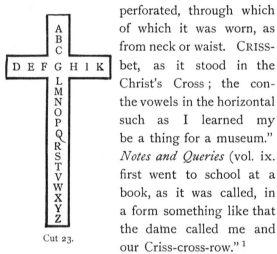

Cut 23.

A correspondent of *Notes and Queries* (vol. ix. p. 457, 1854) says: "I first went to school at a dame's and had a horn-book, as it was called, in which was the alphabet in a form something like that here given (cut 23), and the dame called me and other beginners to learn our Criss-cross-row." [1]

In connection with my inquiries on the subject, Mr. J. H. Slater wrote some time ago in the *Bazaar :* " There certainly is such a thing as a horn-book in the form of a cross, for we have seen one. The upper part of the cross contained the numbers from one to twenty, and the body extending the whole length of the horizontal arms had two different alphabets consisting of capitals and small letters." On asking Mr. Slater for further particulars, he tells me that the horn-book referred to—the horn imperfect—was a year or two ago in the possession of a Tottenham broker, but that now it cannot be traced. Mr. Slater recollects being struck with the curious and unusual shape of this horn-book, which, if so inclined, he might probably have purchased for sixpence or so. He has kindly provided a rough sketch from memory, which I have had turned into a presentable illustration (24).

[1] See chap. vi.

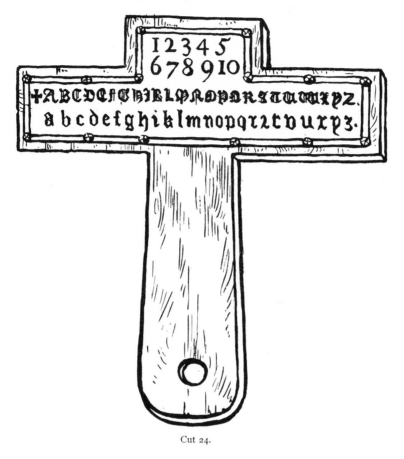

Cut 24.

The following letter, which appeared in the *Athenæum* of 12th May 1894, carries its own explanation :—

A HORN-BOOK IN FORM OF A CROSS

The Leadenhall Press, E.C.

Knowing that I am engaged in writing a work on the horn-book, a friend recently drew my attention to an example in the shop of one Signor Chanteri, a Folkestone dealer in curiosities. It was purchased by a Parisian dealer who happened to be visiting Folkestone. Before the deal was concluded, Signor Chanteri wrote me that another horn-book, in the form of a cross, had been placed in his hands for sale. Evidence of

History of the Horn-Book

a horn-book of this shape ever having existed is but slight, and my curiosity was strongly excited. I wrote at once for particulars, stating that I should like to buy it; but by next post I learned that the Parisian dealer had called and purchased both horn-books, taking them away with him.

I have since used every possible argument to induce Signor Chanteri to give me the name and address of the purchaser of the "cross" horn-book, and I have offered him two or three guineas if he will obtain a photograph of it, I paying all expenses in advance. In return for the promise of a copy of my work when ready, Signor Chanteri has sent me a sketch from memory, and this is all I can get. I believe that there is such a horn-book, and my motive for writing to the *Athenæum* is publicity —publicity here, in Paris, and in America, so that the dealer who purchased, or the collector who has acquired it, may courteously favour me with a full-sized photograph and description. In making countless inquiries about horn-books, this is the only instance in which I have been deliberately and senselessly balked.   ANDREW W. TUER.

Before the appearance of this letter, the dealer referred to wrote me that the "cross" horn-book was sold in a quarter where I could not hope to hear of it again. This may point to its having been disposed of in France. It is known that there are certain Parisian collectors who will not, if they can help it, allow their treasures to be described or pictured, a phase attending the accumulation of covetable curiosities and works of art happily but little known in England and America. Nothing came of the *Athenæum* letter but some amusingly scurrilous postcards from a chum of Chanteri's, who wrote under an assumed name and gave a false address, but when I let him know that I had his real name and address, a damp squib was choked in its own fizzle.

The rough sketch of the cross horn-book—for which hearty thanks, coupled with a heartier malediction, are due to Chanteri—is useful, as from it I am enabled to make a drawing (25) which may be taken to represent the original fairly well. After obtaining the promise of a sketch, I sent Chanteri a series of written questions with a blank space opposite each for reply, and from his notes I am enabled to give a few particulars of this interesting horn-book, no further tidings of which

Georgie Cave France (Mrs. Gaskin).

SUMMER.

have yet come to hand. The printed sheet cut to follow the shape of the cross has the alphabet, followed by 𝕬𝔪𝔢𝔫, all in black-letter capitals. The large crosses and scroll border seem to form part of the printed sheet. For securing the horn—which, by the way, can be almost as easily

Cut 25.

shaped with scissors as paper—whalebone takes the place of the usual strips of brass. The wood is oak blackened by age, a corner of the right branch has been broken off, and the foot of the handle is pierced. The back is uncovered and without ornamentation. I feel sure that Chanteri did his best to correctly sketch this horn-book, but being from memory, it is quite likely that some of the details are inaccurate. I know

History of the Horn-Book

not whether the horn covering is perfect, or, in fact, whether any of it is left. I do not lose sight of the fact that Chanteri may have been imposed upon, and that the "cross" horn-book he sold to a French dealer, and which now, perhaps, reposes in the cabinet of a Rothschild, may be spurious ; if the owner will come forward I shall be very pleased to settle the point for him.

Says Mr. Hazlitt :[1] "In the *Jests of Scogin*,[2] a popular work of the time of Henry VIII., and probably reliable as a faithful portraiture of the habits and notions of the latter half of the fifteenth and the opening decades of the following century, one of the sections relates 'How a Husbandman put his son to school with Scogin.' From the text it is plain that the lad was very backward in his studies, or had commenced them unusually late, considering that it was the farmer's ambition to procure his admission into holy orders. 'The slovenly boy,' we are told, would begin to learn his A B C. Scogin did give him a lesson of nine of the first letters of the A B C, and he was nine days in learning of them ; and when he had learned the nine Christ-cross-row letters the good scholar said, 'Am ich past the worst now ? ' "

The important feature in this passage is, says Mr. Hazlitt, "the reference to the Christ-cross-row, which contained the nine letters of the alphabet from A to I in the form of the cross. The time consumed in this particular instance in the acquisition of a portion of the rudiments is of course ascribable to a pleasant hyperbole on the scholar's phenomenal destiny."

It is a pity that Mr. Hazlitt should have gone out of his way to attach to these words a meaning they never possessed.[3] Scoggin does *not* say that the first nine letters of the alphabet formed the Christ-cross-row, neither does he say that they were arranged in the form of a cross. In

---

[1] "Schools, Schoolbooks, and Schoolmasters," a contribution to the *History of Educational Development in Great Britain*, by W. Carew Hazlitt. London : Jarvis and Son, 1888.

[2] Scoggin (not Scogin) appears to have been the Joe Miller of earlier days, on whose broad shoulders the witticisms of the time were heaped. The earliest complete edition known is in the British Museum, and it is entitled *The First and Best Part of Scoggin's Jests. Full of Witty Merthe and Pleasant Shifts done by him in France and other places ; being a Preservation against Melancholy. Gathered by Andrew Boord, Doctor of Physick. London*, 1626. Dr. Andrew Boord, physician to Henry VIII., and the original "Merry Andrew," died in 1549.

[3] In *The Child and His Book* (London : Wells, Gardner, Darton and Co., 1891), the best and most complete history of literature for children, its authoress, Mrs. E. M. Field, unfortunately accepts Mr. Hazlitt's statement.

History of the Horn-Book

monastic schools a cross arranged in such a way as to give the mystic 7 and 3, with the figures from one : to nine painted on the beads, may have been used as a counting · · · frame, but that there was ever a cross of any kind with the first : nine letters of the alphabet is most improbable.   Such a cross : would be equally valueless as an educational instrument or as a charm, and there is no record of it. Scoggin plainly says that the boy's master set him the definite task of learning the first nine letters of the A B C.   That it was the whole alphabet which was called the Christ-cross-row is not open to dispute.

CHAPTER VI

CHRIST'S cross, and its variants, Christs-cross, Christ-cross, Christ-crosse, Christe-cross, Christes cross, Crist-cross, Criss-cross, Cris-cross, Cris-crosse, Crisse-cross, 'Chris-cross, Chriss-crosse, Chrisse-crosse, and Christ's-cross row, equally elastic in its spelling, is applied to the ✛ preceding the alphabet, and to the alphabet itself, in horn-books and old primers.

The cross which the typefounder supplied with his type was the cross which the printer would naturally use. Another way of putting it would be to say that the printer had no choice in the matter. In Enschedé's (see pp. 99, 305) pattern-book of old types, a cross ✛ is placed at the end of the alphabet of capitals, and other alphabets are followed by signs, including the triplet of dots seen in the earlier horn-books. In cut 147, the printer, so far as the cross is concerned, was either " out of sorts "—that is, short of the proper sign— or he chose to assert his individuality by substituting a cut-down dagger belonging to a larger fount.

62

History of the Horn-Book

It will be noted on reference to cut and text numbered 26 that the "cross row" is mentioned in connection with a ready method of teaching children their A B C by means of dice. The book from which a portion of a page is facsimiled was written in 1653 by Sir Hugh Plat. Its title is *Jewel House of Art and Nature, London, Printed by Bernard Alsop, and are to be sold at his house in Grub Street near the Upper Pump.*

A ready way for children to learn their A.B.C.

CAufe 4 large dice of bone or wood to be made, and upon every fquare, one of the fmal letters of the crofs row to be graven, but in fome bigger fhape, and the child ufing to play much with them, 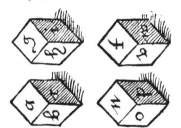 and being alwayes told what letter chanceth, will foon gain his Alphabet, as it were by the way of fport or paftime. I have heard of a pair of cards, whereon moft of the principall Grammer rules have been printed, and the School-Mafter hath found good fport thereat with his fchollers.

Cut 26.

The term Cross-row was sometimes used to indicate elementary knowledge of any kind. In early times the cross pledged the person making it by his faith as a Christian to the truth of what he signed, but its use by no means indicated illiteracy. In later days "*John Smith his mark* ×" was the common method of signing by high and low. Whence the byplay and word-juggling in the paradoxical puerility, *it followeth not that men of marke who make their marke make their marke.*

King James I., in his *King's Quair*, St. 13, p. 6, of Professor Skeat's edition (Scottish Text Society, No. 1), says that before he began to write he made a cross: "And maid a ×, and thus begouth my buke" (begouth = began).

History of the Horn-Book

" The round . . . J. O. makes with a Cris-cross in the middle of it," is from the *Rustick's Alarm*, written by Samuel Fisher, who, at the Restoration, was ejected from his living in Cheshire.

In this sense is a passage in Smollett's *Don Quixote* (*The History and Adventures of the renowned Don Quixote, Translated from the Spanish of Miguel de Cervantes Saavedra, By T. Smollett, M.D., London. Printed for A. Millar, over against Catherine Street in the Strand, MDCCLV.*) : " I am even ignorant of the a b c, but, provided I remember my Christ-cross, I shall be sufficiently qualified."

A Glossary of Provincial Words used in Teesdale in the County of Durham, London, J. R. Smith, 1849, gives : " Cris-cross. The mark of a person who cannot write his name "; and in Parish's *Dictionary of the Kentish Dialect and Provincialisms* (Trübner, 1887) we find : " Christ-cross (kris-kras) The Alphabet. The signature of a person who cannot write is also so called."

The usually accepted and probably correct explanation of the term Christ-cross-row for the alphabet is because the + usually preceded the alphabet in horn-books and primers. Webster gives as an alternative meaning that " it may be from a superstitious custom sometimes practised of writing it (the alphabet) in the form of a cross by way of a charm." Dr. Johnson says of the Cross-Row Alphabet that it is " so named because a cross is placed at the beginning, to shew that the end of learning is piety." " Christs-cross-row " is given by Cotgrave in his *French and English Dictionary* as *La Croix de par Dieu*. Quite recently a correspondent of *Notes and Queries* (8th S. III. June 3, 1893) mentions Canon Inchauspe, a learned and living Basque author, who says: " Dans mon enfance on apprenait l'alphabet sur un feuillet qui avait une Croix en commençant, avant l'A, et on disait croix à la Croix, puis A, B, etc."

" Cris-cross-row, *Christ-cross-row*, Cross-row, a provincial term for the alphabet, so called because a cross was placed at its beginning, + A B C," is given by Brocket in his *Glossary of North Country Words* (Charnley, Newcastle-upon-Tyne, 1846, vol. i. p. 113). Still later, Bartlett, in his *American Dictionary*, gives " Criss-cross, a game played on slates by children at school ; hence Criss-cross-row."

In his *Dictionary of Phrase and Fable*, Dr. Brewer gives *Criss-cross-row* as " the A B C horn-book, containing the alphabet and nine digits,"

64

a definition, repeated in the latest edition, which must not be accepted too literally. Perhaps Nares goes too far in saying that "Christ-cross-row" is probably derived from the practice of the Bishop, at the dedication of a church and altar, inscribing with his staff the Greek and Latin alphabets (cut 27) in the form of a cross (*crux decussata*) upon ashes strewn upon the floor. The scurrilous Thomas Becon, who on two separate

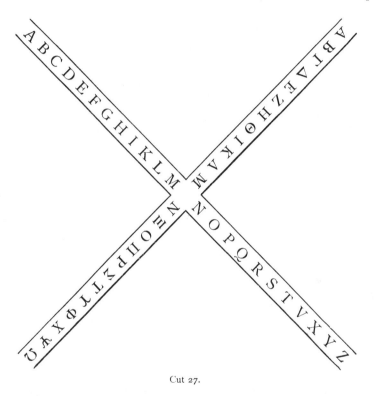

Cut 27.

occasions (1541 and 1543) had to recant at Paul's Cross, has something to say of "the order of halowing (consecrating) Churches" in his *Reliques of Rome* (1553). He gives a portion of the ceremony as follows :—" These things don, ther must be made in the pavement of the Church a crosse of ashes and sand, wherein ye whole alphabete or Christes crosse shal be writte in Greke and latin letters."

In Bernard Picart's *Ceremonies and Religious Customs of the various Nations of the known World* (1733), p. 374, the custom—one of great

History of the Horn-Book

antiquity, still observed in the Roman Church, and not obsolete as the author says—is thus described: " The Bishop advancing towards the Middle of the Church kneels down, and begins the *Veni Creator*, with his head uncovered and his Face towards the high Altar ; then one of the Sub-Deacons takes some ashes, and scatters them on the pavement, in Form of a Cross, as prescribed in the Pontifical. . . . These ceremonies are followed by some *Oremus's*, an Anthem, and the Song of *Zachariah*, and the Bishop, whilst some of his Officers are singing in Chorus, puts on his Mitre,[1] and with his Crozier draws upon the Ashes a double Alphabet in Capitals." Dedication or consecration crosses found painted inside churches are fully explained in a paper by J. H. Middleton, F.S.A., in the *Archæologia*, vol. xlviii. 1884, pp. 456-464.

In Chaucer's *Treatise on the Astrolabe*, A.D. 1391 (edited by Professor Walter W. Skeat for the Early English Text Society in 1872), the print of an astrolabe is divided⁓as to its rim into twenty-four parts, opening with a cross directly under the handle, followed by twenty-three letters of the alphabet. Three letters are omitted—the J, V, and W—and, but that there must be twenty-four divisions only (the cross forming one), the absence of the W would seem unaccountable. The Middle-English name for the alphabet was A B C. Thus when Chaucer describes the back of the astrolabe, he says, " Than folwen the names of the Halidayes in the Kalender, and next hem the lettres of the A B C, on which they fallen " (Part I. p. 11). In a work of so grave and interesting a character, it verges on the ludicrous to find that dreadful compositor—weak in his spelling, this one—at his pranks. The first line of the preface reads, " We find the existing MSS. of the Astrolabe are still humerous."

In Jennings's *Observations on Dialects in West of England* (London, 1825) we get " Criss-cross-lain. The alphabet ; so called in consequence of its being formerly preceded in the *horn-book* by a + which was no doubt devised by some of the sons of the church to remind us of the cross of Christ ; hence the term *Christ-Cross-line*, ultimately came to mean nothing more than the alphabet."

By Somersetshire folk the alphabet is still called the criss-cross-lane.

Crisscrosse as a surname appears in Cussan's *History of Herts*, vol. ii.

---

[1] This Alphabet represents the first Principles of the Christian Religion. The Cross informs us that the first thing a Christian should learn is Christ crucified—vide *Casalius, de Ritibus*, etc.

Georgie Cave France (Mrs. Gaskin).

AUTUMN.

History of the Horn-Book

p. 43 (temp. 1546): "A messuage and tenement with garden now or lately held by William Crisscrosse."

There is a dateless poem entitled *The Mayden's Crosse Rowe*, printed by Robert Wyer.

Shakespeare, in *Richard III.* (1597), Act I. sc. 1, has

> Hearkens after prophecies and dreams ;
> And from the cross-row plucks the letter G,
> And says a wizard told him that by G
> His issue disinherited should be.

Quite recently there was a discussion in *Notes and Queries* as to the meaning of the word " pluck "—" plucks the letter G." If one reads " picks out " or " points out " for " plucks," the sense becomes clear. Holinshed says : " Some have reported that the cause of this nobleman's [1] death rose of a foolish prophecie, which was, that, after King Edward should reign one whose first letter of his name should be a G wherewith the king and the queene were sore troubled, and began to conceive a grievous grudge against this duke, and could not be in quiet till they had brought him to his end."

In Grose's *Olio*, 1798, p. 195, is an entry : " An Irishman explaining the reason why the alphabet is called the Criss-Cross-Rowe, said, it was because Christ's cross was prefixed at the beginning and end of it."

The Old Egyptian Fortune Teller's Last Legacy, a scarce chapbook in the British Museum, which is reproduced in Mr. John Ashton's interesting *Chap-Books of the Eighteenth Century* (Chatto and Windus, 1882), contains on the title-page the intricate interlaced ribbon shown in cut 28. It carries the following text :—

> A + begins Love's Cris + Row,
> Love's not without A + or two.
> A double + begins this knot.
> Without + es Merit is not.
> This Knot and Love are both alike,
> Whose first and last are both to seek
> No + can stay true Love's intent
> It still goes on to What is ment

---

[1] George, Duke of Clarence.

And though it Meats with many A one
True Love makes a + seem none.
He that loves must Learn to know
A + begins Love's Cris + Row.

Cut 28.

"The black crosse before the row of letters" occurs in Cranley's *Amanda*, 1635, p. 44.

The references which follow to the cross, the cross-row, Christ-cross, Christ-cross-row, etc., are by no means exhaustive.

In a fifteenth-century book on manners, entitled *Book of Curtesye*, which appeared about 1477-78, is a suggestive verse :—

> In the morenynge whan ye vp rise
> To worshipe gode haue in memorie,
> Wyth crystes crosse loke ye blesse you Christ,
> Your pater noster saye in deuoute wyse,
> Aue maria with the holy crede,
> Thenne alle the day the better shal ye spede.

History of the Horn-Book

> To learn the baby's A B C
> Is fit for children, not for me.
> I know the letters all so well,
> I need not learn the way to spell ;
> And for the cross before the row
> I learn'd it all too long ago,

is from Breton's *Melancholike Humors*, 1600.

" The cross-row ; *alphabetum* " is given in *Phraseologia Generalis*, by William Robertson, A.M., Cambridge. Printed by John Hayes, Printer to the University, 1681. And are to be sold by George Sawbridge at the " Bible," on Ludgate Hill, London.

Tindale has " A man can by no means reade, except he be taught the letters of the crosserowe.".—*The exposition of the fyrste Epistle of Seynt Ihon with a Prologge before it, by W. T.*, 1531.

> *Alphabetum primum Beardii.*
>
> Cammels Crosse Rowe,
> Doth playnely showe
> Without lyes or gyle :
> His foolyshe feattes
> Which raging freattes
> The truthe for to revyle.

This broadside poem, ornamented on each side with very elaborate woodcuts, and printed by William Copland, 1552, contains fifty-six lines in couplets, each beginning like Psalm 119, with the letters of the alphabet in their due order. Who the Mr. Cammel was who lent his name to it is not known.—*Catalogue of a Collection of Printed Broadsides in the possession of the Society of Antiquaries of London. Compiled by Robert Lemon. London*, 1866, p. 10.

> Nay if you turne and wind and press,
> And in the *cross-row* have such skill,
> I am put down, I must confess,

occurs on p. 192 in *A Spell for Ione, A Collection of Seventy-nine Black Letter Ballads and Broadsides, printed in the reign of Queen Elizabeth between the years 1559 and 1597, accompanied with an introduction and Illustrative notes. London, James Lilly*, 1867.

History of the Horn-Book

" H is worst among letters in the Crosse-row " (Heywood, *Six Hundred of Epigrammes,* 1562).

" A is the name of the first letter in the crosrewe among the Hebrues, Greekes and Latines. But whether this common usuall order in our Alphabet or crosrewe, was so placed and appointed by counsell and learning from the beginning, etc.," is from *An Alvearie or Triple Dictionarie, in English, Latin, and French : Very profitable for all such as be desirous of any of those three Languages.* This *Alvearie* was published in 1573, and was the work of John Baret, who studied at Cambridge and took his B.A. degree in 1554-55, afterwards becoming M.A. and M.D., although there is no mention of his ever having practised as a physician. He was a Fellow of Trinity College, Cambridge, and is said to have died in 1580.

In *Actes and Monuments of matters most speciall and memorable, happening in the Church, with an Vniuersall history of the same. wherein is set forth at large the whole race and course of the Church, from the primitive age to these latter tymes of ours. with the bloudy times, horrible troubles, and great persecutions agaynst the true Martyrs of Christ, sought and wrought as well by Heathen Emperours, as nowe lately practised by Romish Prelates, especially in this Realme of England and Scotland,* . . . (1583), vol. ii. p. 831, is an account of " Persecution in the Dioces of Lincoln." The author, John Foxe, speaking of " Benet Ward of Bekennesfield and his father, and of Edmund Dounes," says, " To Ward this was layd, that the foursayde Pope had receaued a Booke of the Ten Commaundementes. He had also the Gospels of Mathewe and Marke. Of the same Warde he learned hys Christe Crosse rowe : Five partes of the eight beatitudes."

" Shee that knowes where Christes crosse standes will neuer forget where great A dwels," is quoted as an old saying in *Tell-Trothes New yeares Gift, Being Robin Good-fellowes newes out of those Countries, where inhabitas neither Charity nor honesty : London, imprinted by Robart Bourne* 1593.

Amour XI.

Thine eyes taught mee the Alphabet of love,
To con my cros-rowe ere I learn'd to spell ;
For I was apt, a scholler like to prove,
Gave mee sweet lookes when as I learned well,

History of the Horn-Book

is from Michael Drayton's *Ideas Mirrour, Amours in Quatorzains, che serve é tace assai dormanda. At London, Printed by Iames Roberts for Nicholas Linge. Anno* 1594.

An historical commonplace-book in the possession of Mr. R. H. Warwick, of Burgage Manor House, Southwell, written in the time of James I. and Charles I. by William Davenport, of Bromhall, near Stockport, in Cheshire, contains a series of satirical poems inveighing bitterly against the Duke of Buckingham. One has the following lines :—

> Our cross-row's turn'd, a signe off monstrous luck,
> When D. ledd the English cross over St. George's brooke.

" Hee learned to frame his cases from putting Riddles and imitating MERLINS PROPHESIES, and so set all the Crosse rowe together by the eares," is from one of the " Characters " headed "A meere Common Lawyer " in *New and Choife Characters, of feuerall Authors, Together with that exquifite and vnmatcht Poeme, The Wife, Written by Syr Thomas Ouerburie. London : London. Printed by Thomas Creede, for Laurence Lifle at the Tygershead in Pauls Churchyard,* 1615.

" For his knowledge, he is merely a Horne-booke, without a Christcrosse afore it," occurs in *A Button-maker of Amfterdam,* in the same work (see p. 193).

> *Plato* and *Aristotle* were at a losse
> And wheel'd about again to spell *Christ-Crosse,*

is in *The Temple, Sacred Poems and Private Ejaculations. By Mr. George Herbert, Cambridge, Printed by Thom. Buck, and Roger Daniel, printers to the Univerfitie,* 1633.

Speaking of chronograms, and of the year 1578 in particular, the author of *Speculum Mundi* says : " Unto which they adde the number of the letters (a, e, n, t, s) in *adventus,* which were not numerall before, yet by their naturall position in the alphabet, or crosse row, they give 56."— *Speculum Mundi, or A Glasse representing the Face of the World. Whereunto is added a Discourse of the Creation, together with a consideration of such things as are pertinent to each dayes worke. Written by John Swan, Mr. of Arts, Late Student of Trinitie Colledge, Camb. Pri. in Cambridge by T. Buck and R. Daniel,* 1635, Chap. i. sec. 3, p. 23.

History of the Horn-Book

The very children, ere they scarce can say
Their Pater Noster, or their Christ-crosse A,
Will to their Parents prattle, and desire
To taste that Drinke which Gods doe so admire,

is from Tatham's *Fancies Theater*, a poem in praise of sack which appeared in 1640.

"The beginning of learning is the letters, and the beginning of letters is . . . that most profane, superstitious and Antichristian Letter which they call Chriss-crosse."—*New Sermon, Newest Fashion* (1640?).

In a poem (p. 322) called *Christ Church Windows*, the author, John Cleveland, the Cavalier poet of Cambridge, remonstrates with those who would have them removed—

Shall every Saint have a *John Baptist's* doom?
No limb of *Mary* stand? Must we forget
Christ's Cross, as soon as part the Alphabet?

The Works of Mr. John Cleveland, containing his Poems, Orations, Epistles, collected into One Volume, with the Life of the Author. London: Obadiah Blagrove, at the Bear and Star, over against the little North Door in St. Paul's Church Yard, 1687.

"Christ Cross," in the sense of the beginning, is used in Philip Quarles's *Emblems*, p. 124, ed. 1812—

Christ's Cross is the chriscros of all our happiness.

Thomas Colwell was licensed by the Stationers' Company in 1559 to print a *Newe Yeres Gyfte, or a New Christe-crosse Roo, called Purge the old Lavyn that yt may be Newe doo.*

G(*erarde*). "I could say something of semi de crosses, but bicause they have bin counted prodigious, I will for this time passe it ouer.

L(*egh*). "I pray you leave of, and shew me some other lesson. For you vse me lyke a dull scoller, to kepe me at the Christe cross rowe a hole wyke together: werefore as it hath pleased you to enterlace the blason of Armes with the knowledge of other things: So would I likewise desire at this time to knowe howe officers of Armes were first made,"

is from Gerard Legh's *Accedens of Armory*, 1576.

74

History of the Horn-Book

In *The Tragicall Raigne of Selimus* (1594) we find, " I was faine to runne through a whole alphabet of faces : now, at the last, seeing she was so cramuk with me, I began to sweare all the crisse-crosse-row over, beginning at great A, little a, till I cam to W X Y."

> Of letters and syllabs to way the quantitie
> Old knowing naught without masters auctoritie :
> Who teach us how to read, and put into our pawes
> Some little Chriscrossrow instead of civill lawes,

appears on p. 23 in *Babilon, a Part of the Seconde Weeke of Guilliavme de Saluste Signevr Dr. Bartas, London*, 1596.

> 'Tis I ! who I ?   I, quoth the dog, or what ?
> A Christ cross row I ?—Act III. sc. 2.
>
> Why, you may find it, sir, in th' Christ cross row.
>
> Act V. sc. 1.

Both are excerpts from *The Pleasant Historie of the two angrie women of Abington as played by the Right Honourable the Earl of Nottingham, Lord High Admiral, his servants.   By Henry Porter*, 1599.

In Act III. sc. 1 of *A Pleasant conceited Comedie Wherein is shewed how a man may chuse a good Wife from a bad.   As it hath bene sundry times Acted by the Earle of Worcesters Seruants.   London : Printed for Mathew Lawe, and are to be solde at his shop in Paules Church-yard, neare vnto S. Augustines gate, at the Signe of the Foxe*, 1602, Mistress Arthur is speaking to her man-servant Pipkin, and says : " When that is done, get you to schoole againe."

Pipkin. " I had rather plaie the trewant at home, than goe seeke my M. at schoole : let me see what age am I, some foure and twentie, and how haue I profited ?   I was fiue yeare learning to crish Crosse from great A, and fiue yeare longer comming to F.   I there stucke some three yeare before I could come to Q, and so in processe of time I came to e perce e, and comperce, and tittle, then I got to a, e, i, o, u, after to our Father, and in the sixteenth yeare of my age, and the fifteenth of my going to Schoole, I am in good time gotten to a Nowne."

Of John Cooke, the author of *A Pleasant conceited Comedie*, nothing is known.   He seems to have been the author of *Fyftie Epigrams*,

75

History of the Horn-Book

1604, and of a comedy entitled, Green's *Tu Quoque, or the Cittie Gallant,* 1614.

In Hornbye's *Horn-Book,* 1622 (see p. 213), are several allusions :—

> And from Christ's Cradle, to his bloody Crosse,
> In *Christ-crosse-row* is Character'd each losse.
>
> .   .   .   .   .   .
>
> He that hath *Patience* is a perfect man,
> And well is skild the *Christ-Crosse-row* to skan :
>
> .   .   .   .   .   .
>
> Then to conclude, these *vertues* first doe flow
> From the *Originall,* the *Christ-crosse-row.*
> The little infant that receives his birth,
> To passe his *pilgrimage* vpon the earth,
> Takes first a respite, and a time to grow,
> Before he comes vnto the *Christ-crosse-row ;*
> And at his *Baptisme,* euen from the *Font,*
> Receiues the Crosse of *Christ* vpon his front,
> In signe that he should neuer shame nor feare,
> The Crosse of *Christ* and *Christian* life to beare.
>
> .   .   .   .   .   .
>
> The *Horn*-booke and the happy *Christ*-crosse-row.
>
> .   .   .   .   .   .

" I sweare . . . by the crisse-crosse-row, by the whole Alphabet."— *Celestina,* xviii. 180 (1633).

Christ-cross-row, as expressing the rudiments, is used in Act III. sc. 1, p. 31, of a play by one who preferred writing to Law : " God sa' me, she is not come to the Criss-cross-row of her profession yet."—*The Disappointment, or The Mother in Fashion ; A Play, as it was acted at The Theatre Royal. Written by Thomas Southerne, London. Printed for Jo. Hindmarsh, Bookseller to His Royal highness at the Black Bull in Cornhil,* 1684.

> Wilt thou yet learn ? then cast thine eye below
> See his great Name is in thy Christ-Cross-Row,

occurs in *A Divine Horn-Book : or the First Form in the true Theosophic School, wherein is taught the knowledge of God's Great Name Jeova in the House of Letters, etc., by H. L., London : printed for the Author,* 1688 (see p. 220).

76

Georgie Cave France (Mrs. Gaskin).

WINTER

History of the Horn-Book

And if you know
The Christ-Cross-Row,
You soon may Spell and read :
In this smooth Way
From Day to Day
You will run on with Speed,

is from William Ronksley's primer, *Child's Weeke-work*, which appeared in 1712.

In one of his anonymous and undated works, which appeared in 1725, John Dunton, a prolific author and a noted London bookseller, alludes to the Christ-cross-row on p. 59, vol. i. of *A Voyage Round the World :* "The names of my *School-Masters* were Mr. A B C D, and almost all the *Christ-cross-row* over."

for Mortals ne'er shall know
More than contain'd of old the Christ-cross-Row,

is from Tickell's *Poem in Praise of the Horn-Book* (see p. 223).

"Four years in travelling from Christ-cross-row to Malachi," is from Sterne's *Tristram Shandy*, v. xlii. 1762 ; the explanation being, according to the *New English Dictionary*, that the Old Testament was the reading-book of the highest class.

Wordsworth speaks of "Infant-conning of Christ-cross-row" in his *Excursion* (viii. 419, 1814).

Now Sal, ya see, had been to school,
She went to old aunt Kite :
An so she was 'en quite a fool,
But could read pretty right.

She larnt her A B C, ya know,
Wid D for Dunce and Dame,
An all dat's in de Criss-Crass-row,
An how to spell her name.

These are the 56th and 57th verses of *Dick and Sal ; or Jack and Joan's Fair ; A Doggerel Poem. The Reader is requested to be sparing of his criticisms, and to look for nothing more in this Poem than the title expresses, viz. doggerel.* Dover, Rigden, *circa* 1845.

Kingsley's *Water Babies* (1863): "Twelve or fourteen neat, rosy, chubby little children, learning their Chris-cross-row."

79

History of the Horn-Book

The complete alphabet was at times cast on English church bells, some examples being preceded by the ✠.

"Christ's cross me speed" has a religious origin relating to the Atonement. It is explained in the *New English Dictionary* as "a formula said before repeating the Alphabet ; hence used allusively."

> Crosse was made all of red
> In the begynning of my boke,
> That is callyd god me sped
> In the fyrste lesson that j toke
> Thenne j lerned, a, and b,
> And other letters by her names
> But always God spede me.
> Thought me nedefull in all games
> Yf j played in feldes other medes
> Stylle other wythe noys,
> I prayed helpe in all my dedes
> Of hym that deyed upon the cross.

This is from an undated book printed by Wynkyn de Worde, *Bartholomaeus de Proprietatibus Rerum ;* a general history of Nature, written in Latin by Bartholomew Glanville, a Franciscan monk, who lived about 1360. It was translated into many languages, and into English by John Trevisa, Vicar of Berkeley, in Gloucestershire, in 1398.

> And where ye sey ye wol be wrothe also,
> Withouten cause, hardily it shal not nede,
> Ye shal have cause y-nouke whereso ye go,
> In thoute and worke ye shal not faile indede !
> How long agoo lerned ye, Crist crosse me spede !
> Have ye no more lernyd of youre a b c
> Whan that ye list ye shal have cause plenté,

is from a poem by John Lydgate, a Benedictine monk at Bury (born c. 1375, died c. 1461), called *The Prohemy of a Marriage betwix an olde man and a yonge Wife, and the counsail, etc.*, and is taken from MS. Harl. 372, fol. 45-51, said to be the only copy in existence.

The poem of *Piers the Plowman's Crede* (fourteenth century), edited by Professor Skeat for the Early English Text Society, begins : " Cros and curteis Crist, this begynnynge spede ! " = May the cross, and may courteous Christ, speed this beginning.

History of the Horn-Book

An early school lesson preserved in MS. Rawl., 1032, commences :
" Christe me spede in alle my worke."
Skelton (*Against Venemous Tongues*, 1528) says—

> For before on your brest, and behind on your back
> In Romaine letters I never founde lack ;
> In your *crosse row* nor Christ crosse you spede,
> Your Pater Noster, your Ave, nor your Crede.

In Morley's *Introduction to Music* (1597) we have—

> Christe's crosse be my spede,
> In all vertue to proceed.

Nicholas Breton, who was connected by marriage with the soldier poet, George Gascoigne, says : " Now we in the country beginne and goe forward with our reading in this manner Christs Crosse be my Speed, and the Holy Ghost : for feare the Divell should be in the letters of the Alphabet, as hee is too often when he teacheth od fellowes to play tricks with their creditors, who instead of payments, write I O V, and so scoffe many an honest man out of his goods."—*The Court and Country, or a Brief Discourse between the Courtier and Country-man ; of the Manner, Nature and Condition of their liues, etc. Written by N. B., Gent., London. Printed by G. Eld for John Wright, and are to be sold at his Shoppe at the Signe of the Bible without Newgate,* 1618.

> In my beginning, God be my good speed,
> In grace and vertue that I may proceed,

is from Hornbye's *Horn-Book,* 1622 (see p. 213).

Two modern five-verse Canticles, with strong points of resemblance, and evidently built upon ancient versions, appear in Willis's *Current Notes,* No. 59, for November 1855, and No. 61 for January 1856. Portions only of each are given.

> Christ his Cross shall be my speed !
> Teach me Father John, to read ;
> That in Church on holy-day,
> I may chant the psalm and pray.
>
> .   .   .   .
>
> Teach me letters A B C.
>
> .   .   .   .

History of the Horn-Book

Teach me Father John to say
Vesper verse and matin-lay ;
So when I to God shall plead,
Christ his Cross shall be my speed !

Christ his Cross shall be my speed !
Teach me, dear Mamma, to read ;
That I may in Scripture see
What his love hath done for me.

. . . . .

Teach me letters A B C.

. . . . .

Teach me, dear Mamma, to pray,
Bible verses day by day ;
So when I to God shall plead,
Christ his Cross shall be my speed !

In one of his notes in the Henry Irving *Shakespeare*, Mr. Frank A. Marshall says : " I have been told that in dames' schools in the North of England it used not long ago to be a custom for children to say their letters thus—Christë's cross be my speed ! A B C, etc."

In the tellers' cash-books of the Bank of Scotland, established some two hundred years ago, religious inscriptions on the leaves are commonly found. One has—

In my beginning God me speed,
In grace and virtue to proceed.

CHAPTER VII

How a horn-book was made—Horn-books badly made and horn-books well made—
How a leather or paper covered horn-book was decorated—Brass blocks used in
decorating—St. George and the Dragon gilt horn-books—The brass rimming or
"latten" on horn-books—Peculiar tacks used in fixing—How the tacks were made
—Letter from Professor W. Flinders Petrie—The horn facing, or "lantern leaf,"
used on a horn-book—The Horners' Company—Impossible statements about the
horn-book—Horn-covered labels on old books—A horn washing-tally—A horn-
book cover.

ORN-BOOKS made in immense quantities at a low price were at times turned out in an unworkmanlike and slovenly manner. The oak, roughly split, might be nearly a quarter of an inch thick at one end and fine down to a sixteenth at the other. On the same horn-book the brass rimming would be of different widths ; it might begin at one end an eighth of an inch wide and slope off to almost nothing, the "vanishing point" being tucked in under the next piece. The horn was roughly cut and projected beyond the edges of the brass. More frequently, however, we find the oak uniform in substance, planed smooth and the horn-book in its details properly finished.

History of the Horn-Book

How a horn-book was made and put together is arrived at by working backwards. After being cut to a proper size, the printed sheet received a dab of glue or paste to keep it in position on the oaken base ; the horn was laid on the top, and over it one of the pieces of thin narrow brass, through the central part of which an iron tack, known as a " rose head," was driven half-way home. The strip of brass is so thin that a slight blow with a hammer on the tack head would drive the point through brass, horn, and paper, into the wood. The horn seldom split under the treatment. Then, without much regard to sequence, followed the other pieces of brass, each being secured by a tack in the middle. The four metal slips being in position and free to work from their centres, the overlapping ends were adjusted, trimmed with shears or scissors,—thin brass is almost as easily cut as paper—and a tack driven home in each corner, making eight in all. Finally the central tacks were also driven home.

In making a leather-covered horn-book, the oaken base of which is usually a little thinner than in those uncovered, the leather was fixed with hot glue on the back of the oak slab, the previously-pared edges being brought over on to the front margins. The handle required a separate piece of triangular-shaped leather ; two sides lapped over, the third form-ing a tongue, the outline of which, after it had been glued down in its place on the handle, could still be seen.

The ornamental device was impressed on the leather back from a heated brass block. The handle was also decorated in the same manner from another block or tool usually bearing some simple floral device. Silver or gold foil, and in paper-covered examples Dutch metal, was some-times laid on before the stamping. In paper-covered horn-books we find impressions printed in black ink or sunk impressions without ink ; these latter sometimes so faint that the device can only be made out by allow-ing the light to fall at a particular angle.

Cut 29 is an impression from a heavy old brass block formerly used for stamping leather and paper backs of horn-books, on which is deeply engraved a conventionally-treated device of St. George and the Dragon. From the trappings and armour it must have been engraved not later than the first half of the sixteenth century. This interesting block is in the collection of Mr. H. Syer Cuming, F.S.A., who, when a boy, rescued it at the outlay of a few pence from a rag and bone shop. It is much worn,

History of the Horn-Book

and has evidently been used in the decoration of many thousands of horn-books, and probably the covers of catechisms also. Cut 30 is the same device carefully restored to its original condition. The name at foot—Hartry—is probably that of the blockcutter. It would be a matter for wonderment if St. George the patron Saint and military protector of

Cut 29. Cut 30.

England, who for centuries has typified all that is noble and courageous, and whose name as a battle-cry incited British soldiers to deeds of daring, did not appear on the backs of horn-books.

Boileau opens " The Argument" in his *Heroick Poem* [1]—

> . . . . *what needs a* Proëme,
> *To Vamp a Three-half-penny* poëme ?
> *No*, Reader, *No ; 'twas never writt*
> *For thy sake, but for little* Chitt.

---

[1] *Le Lutrin: an Heroick Poem*, written originally in French by Monsieur Boileau, made English by N. O., London, printed by J. A. for Benjamin Alsop at the "Angel and Bible" in the Poultry, 1682.

85

History of the Horn-Book

St. George *oth' back-side of the* Horn-book,
The Dragon kills, to Humour Scorn-book.
And thus to wheddle in young Fops,
The gilded Sign hangs o're the Shops.

And fifty years later Thomas Tickell imaginatively describes the blood of the Dragon dying the scarlet cover of the horn-book—

Behind thy Patron Saint in Armour shines,
With Sword and Lance, to guard thy sacred Lines :
Beneath his Courser's Feet the Dragon lies
Transfix'd ; his blood thy scarlet cover dies.

Allusions to gilt horn-books occasionally occur. In a paper read by Mr. W. Harry Rylands, F.S.A., in February 1885, before the Historic Society of Lancashire and Cheshire, is given a transcript of " A true and p(er)fect Inventory of all the goods and Chattels of ROBT. BOOTH, late of WARRINGTON in the COUNTY OF LANC. STATION[R] deceased. Prized by us THOMAS BULLING THOMAS GEE JOHN PENINGTON and RAPHE GOULBORNE, the ffifte of ffebruary Año doɱ 1647.

(1) Impr. 16 dozin and two plaine horne-bookes at
1od. doz. . . . . o 10 9
5 doz. halfe guilt[1] horne-books at 18d. doz. . o 8 3 "

Halliwell says that in a bill dated 1735 mention is made of " one horn-book gilt," the price being twopence. A gilt horn-book is alluded to in *Sir Courtly Nice*, 1685, p. 14.

Mrs. Alice Morse Earle, the author of *Customs and Fashions in Old New England*, tells me that in the early lists and advertisements of American stationers, gilt horn-books and plain horn-books frequently occur, and that "gilt horns" and "plain horns" (horn-books) are mentioned in the *Pennsylvania Gazette*, 4th December 1760.

Nor, in one hand, fit emblem of thy trade,
A *Rod*, in t'other, gaudily array'd
A *Horn-Book* gilt and letter'd, call I Thee
Who dost, in form preside o'er A B C,

---

[1] Presumably gilt on one (the ornamental) side only. But as horn-books, so far as we know, were never, and could not have been, gilt on both sides, the use of the word "halfe" seems an unnecessary straining after exactness of description. It may be, however, that "halfe-gilt" referred to a patch of gold foil dabbed on to the ornamentation in the same manner as the gingerbread horn-books mentioned on p. 442.

HARDER THAN PULLING.

Henry S. Tuke.

History of the Horn-Book

is from poems by C. Churchill, from the *Poem of Gotham, an Invocation to Study*, p. 17, 1763.

In writing to Willis's *Current Notes* in November 1855 about horn-books, Professor Westwood says—presumably in reference to one of those now in the Bodleian Library (see pp. 17, 322)—that it has the figure of the reigning monarch, with his initials printed in gold on the back from a rude wood-block. All trace of gold has now disappeared which, unless some other horn-book is referred to, is puzzling. As to the "rude wood block," the reader knows that the stamping of horn-books was done from brass, wood being incapable of standing rough usage and the necessary pressure.

The brass,[1] known as latten, sometimes inaccurately described as copper, protective edging to the horn, varied in substance. The thinnest I have met with on horn-books measures .003 = 333 sheets to the inch, but the more usual substance was .004 = 250 to the inch, and occasionally .005 = 200. "Latten brass" or latten, the metal being hammered—in later days rolled—into thin sheets, has been extensively used in the manufacture of church utensils—

> . He had a cross of *latoun* full of stones.—CHAUCER.

> My bell candlesticks of latten, a chafing-dish of latten.
> Will of Dame Elizabeth Hill, 6th March 1500.

Tickell speaks of the brass rimming on a horn-book—

> In comely Wainscot bound,
> And golden verge enclosing thee around.

The few fortunate possessors of early horn-books may not all have noticed that the heads of the iron tacks used for fixing the thin strips of latten over the horn were forged or hand-hammered into four facets somewhat in the shape of a rose diamond, converging to a boss at the top, hence the term "rose head" by which they were known. The boss served a good purpose in keeping the horn from being scratched when the horn-book was laid on its face. The rose head was to a large extent superseded by the flat-headed and cheaper machine-made tack about 1820. The rose head, however, still continued to be made, but in always diminishing quantities, until at last orders entirely ceased.

[1] Tin as a rimming I have seen but once (see p. 295).

History of the Horn-Book

Diligent inquiry brought to light a parcel of old tacks with forged heads, of which I was glad to become the possessor. As it will be known to the reader, passing mention only need be made of the fact that as late or later than the middle of the last century, hand-made tacks and nails passed as currency in many of the northern villages of this country.

A rose head, known also as a Flemish tack—in cut 31 depicted full size, and also enlarged to show the facets more distinctly—was made from a long piece of iron termed a slit nail-rod, which was heated in the nailer's hearth; the shank and point were formed roughly with the hammer on a miniature anvil, or "steady" (cut 32). The shank was then all but cut off, and the rough

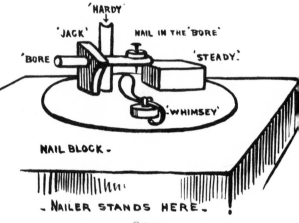

Cut 31.

Cut 32.

tack dropped into a drilled hole or "bore." While in the bore the head was made with four separate blows with a hammer, one blow forming each facet. During the operation, the finished tack became separated from the nail-rod and was jerked out of the bore by a contrivance underneath called a "whimsey."

We can now leave the tacks and say something about the horn which covered the alphabet, and from which the horn-book derives its name. Professor W. Flinders Petrie, the learned Egyptologist and explorer, writes me: "The principle of covering over a design with transparent material is very old. Among Schliemann's finds at Mykenæ is a knob of rock-crystal hollowed out and painted inside with an imitation of veined agate. At Gurob I found a hollowed crystal case, cut like an oval watch-glass, painted inside with a figure of the *berona* or phœnix. At Tanis I found a sheet of glass painted with figures of the signs of the zodiac in a

History of the Horn-Book

circle. This is not painted glass in the usual sense of transparency ; but a design on the back of the glass in opaque colours and gilding, intended to be seen through the glass which protected it. I do not recollect any similar example of a design protected by glass, at Pompeii, or in other Roman remains. Next there is the general usage in Saxon jewellery of plates of crystal or garnet to cover over the delicate gold work and so preserve its texture. These forms of protection descend to our modern glazed brooches and miniatures, and painted glass paper-weights. But they are the forerunners also of the use of horn for covering writing. It is possible that horn might have been used for covering public notices in mediæval times, or notices might be put up inside horn windows."

Primitive man used horn, and it was in early days that those who followed him turned its translucence to account in window panes, which invited the ingress of light, and for lanterns which permitted its egress. The Romans had horn window-panes, and for the same purpose the Chinese do not now disdain its use. The old-fashioned horn lantern (sometimes, says Skeat, spelt *lanthorn*, by a singular popular etymology which took account of the horn used for the sides of lanterns) is still made to illumine badly-lighted warehouses and cellars, and the thin veneers of ox-horn used for covering horn-books, which are cut in spirals and afterwards flattened by means of heat and pressure, are to this day known in the trade as " lantern leaves." At the Horners' Exhibition held in London in 1882 were shown "Three specimens of Clear Horn Leaves for Lanthorns, as now used by farmers in Yorkshire." The Worshipful Company of Horners, of which an interesting history was written by Mr. Charles Henry Compton in 1891, is one of the most ancient of the corporate bodies. Horn Fair was held at least as early as the time of Henry III., and was continued annually until abolished in 1872. "All sorts of winding horns and cups and other vessels of horn were bought and sold," and although we are not directly told so, it is fair to assume that horn-books formed a regular part of the itinerants' stock-in-trade. The charter of the Company was granted by Charles I., and although its control over the trade has never been actually abandoned, it has ceased to be exercised. The last occasion on which the Company enforced its rights against persons infringing its monopoly was in 1745. The court was informed that persons not freed of the Company had bought rough horns which they

History of the Horn-Book

manufactured into lantern leaves and disposed of them within the city of London and twenty-four miles distance. Proceedings were ordered to be taken against the persons so offending.

John Timbs, in his *Things not Generally Known*, says : "The horn-book was not always mounted on a board. Many were printed on the horn only, or pasted on its back, like one used five-and-forty years ago by a friend when a boy at Bristol." Mr. Timbs, whose irresponsible statement has been many times repeated, is wrong, and his Bristol friend of "five-and-forty years ago" had a treacherous memory. A moment's reflection would have shown that if the wording were printed on the under side of the horn, it would read backwards, and if printed on the upper or outside, it would rub or wear off. Horn-books could never have been printed on horn. A thin sheet of horn softened in hot water will take a type impression badly, but on laying it on a piece of oak the printed matter becomes almost illegible. In regard to the statement that the printed sheet was pasted on the under side of a piece of horn through which the letters were read, an anonymous magazine writer supposes that "the greater number were made this way." A leaf of horn thus treated would twist, split, and break up, and through a slab thick enough to retain its form, the letters could hardly be read. Horn-books such as these are purely imaginary.

Cleaveland, Cleavland, or Cleveland (*Works*, ed. 1687, p. 326), says that other material than horn was used for facing the horn-book. He speaks of two persons who followed a threadbare scholar who had mended his doublet with a poem, and who, "like boys in horn-books, read it through the cloth." Halliwell takes Cleaveland literally, but, if allowance be made for carelessness of expression, the correct reading would appear to be *as in the horn-book boys read through the horn, so the scholar read through the cloth.*

When horn was first used as a protective material for writing can only be surmised. In most of the large public libraries at home and on the Continent are manuscripts with labels covered by horn on the outside front cover. The position is sometimes in the centre, but perhaps oftener towards the top left-hand corner. The title (and occasionally the name of the donor) is written on parchment or vellum, covered with a thin plate of horn, firmly secured with brass tacks or nails which penetrate the leather

92

History of the Horn-Book

or vellum cover and underlying oak boards. As a protection against dust, the horn is sometimes edged with narrow leather strips. In York Minster Fabric Account, 1421-22, is an entry that Thomas Hornar de Petergate was paid two and sixpence for "hornyng et naillyng superscriptorum librorum" (*Surtees Soc.* xxxv. 46). In the accounts of Eton College for 1521 it is recorded that a craftsman, one Andrew Lisley, was employed some months binding and repairing books, his pay being fourpence per day, with an allowance of one shilling per week in commons. Amongst materials purchased for his use were one hundred plates of horn. Entries of a similar nature are to be found in the Cambridge University Records.

"Some years ago," writes Mr. Hone in an unpublished note, "I saw a manuscript volume which was certainly written early in the thirteenth century, perhaps in the twelfth. It was in fine condition and retained its original binding of stout oak-boards, cased with goat-skin leather, and having upon the outside of the upper a pane of horn, and bordered by projecting gems, interspersed with golden studs, and at each corner a large bold boss or knob of gold, to protect the jewelled border and the horn, which shewed beneath it a written inscription denoting the subject of the work. This early mode and purpose of horning upon book covers was likely to have suggested the thought of covering the alphabet, etc., for children upon a piece of board, and hence may have originated that implement of instruction emphatically called the Horn-book."

Amongst the relics of Haddon Hall is the horn-covered washing-tally, shown, slightly reduced, in cut 33. In regard to mounting, it is like a horn-book, the brass rimming and horn being kept together by a number of ornamental nails. The period may be Charles I., but the lettering looks even earlier. The base is of beechwood, quarter of an inch thick, covered with linen on back and sides. The names of the different articles of clothing "sent to the wash" being printed from copperplate, argues that the tally was in common use. The face is divided into squares, each with a revolving brass dial pierced with a round hole, through which only one number at a time is visible. The dials are outside the horn, and there is a pin at the side for turning them round until the proper figures appear. To show the method of working, one of the indicators is omitted in the cut. The list looks quaint enough to modern eyes :—" Ruffes,

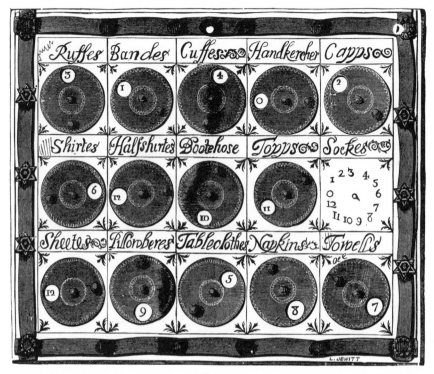

Cut 33.

Bandes, Cuffes, Handkerchers, Capps, Shirtes, Half Shirtes, Bootehose (stout stockings worn inside long boots), Topps, Sockes, Sheetes, Pillowberes (pillow cases), Table-clothes, Napkins, and Towells." A somewhat similar washing-board or tally is described in *Ten Thousand Wonderful Things* (Routledge).

Mr. Zaehnsdorf, the bookbinder, has lately patented an ingeniously constructed case made of horn for the protection of fine specimens of binding. It is made of a single sheet of horn bent completely over and open at one side only where the fore-edge of the book comes. At top and bottom is a piece of tough leather covered with millboard. When the case slides over the book, the whole of the binding can be distinctly seen through the translucent horn.

CHAPTER VIII

ONE may attempt to form a rough idea of the date of a horn-book from the shape of the type, the manner of the printing, and the appearance of the mounting. But it is the easiest thing in the world to be out by a century or more. Mr. Henry Bradshaw and Mr. William Blades have both left valuable hints for arriving at the dates of undated books, the tricks, mannerisms, and methods of the typesetters providing the key. Unfortunately these " peculiars " of the printer are not apparent on a bit of paper containing little beyond the alphabet and Lord's Prayer. The owners of horn-books are averse from allowing their treasures to be taken to pieces in the hope of finding a watermarked date in the paper, especially as in such a scrap the chances are all against its being there at all. In the absence of other evidence, there is nothing but the thing itself and the intuition born of observation, to guide us in arriving at the age. Broadly speaking, the age of a horn-book is so difficult to determine, that experts usually decline to advance an opinion.

In dealing with things covetable and old, there is a tendency to put

95

back dates as far as possible.   There was obviously nothing to hinder type formes for printing horn-books, and blocks for stamping their backs, passing from hand to hand until worn out.   It is therefore quite probable that a horn-book which came into existence during the reign say of George I. may have been printed from type set up in Charles II.'s time and backed with a block representing Charles I.   In the absence of evidence to the contrary, the owner of a horn-book bearing the effigy of Charles I. will of course believe that it was made in the time of Charles I. It obviously could not be earlier, but it certainly might be later.

As a further illustration we may refer to cut 34 representing a black-letter horn-book printed to-day, but the type, or rather the matrices, from

Aabcdefghiklmnop
qrꝛſstvuwxyzꝫ.:.
ABCDEFGHIKLMNOP
QRSTUWXYZ:-

{ ab eb ib ob ub } { ba be bi bo bu }
{ ac ec ic oc uc } { ca ke ki co cu }
{ ad ed id od ud } { da de di do du }

In the Name of GOD the
Father, the Sonne, and
of the holy Ghost. Amen.

Our Father, which art in Heaven, Halowed be thy Name: Thy kingdome come: Thy Will be done on Earth, as it is in Heaven: Giue vs this day our daylie Bread: And forgiue vs our trespasses, as wee forgiue them that trespasse against vs: And leade vs not into temptation, But deliuer vs from evill: For thine is the kingdome, the Power, and the Glorie, for euer, and euer, Amen.

Cut 34.

Aabcdefgh
klmnopqrꝛ
stvuwxyz.
ABCDEFGHIKLMNO
QRSTUWXYZ

In the Name of GOD th
Father, the Sonne, &
the Holie Ghost: Amen

Our Father, which art in Heaven, Halowed be thy Nam Thy kingdom come: Thy wil done in Earth, as it is in heaven Giue vs this day our daily bre And forgiue vs our trespasses, wee forgiue them that trespa against vs: And leade vs not in temptation, But deliuer vs fro evill. For thine is the kingdom power, and glorie, for euer, Am

Cut 35.

PUZZLED SPRITES.

97

History of the Horn-Book

which the type was cast, are said to have come into existence 1680-90. They belonged to Robert Andrews the type-founder, who, in 1683, succeeded the celebrated Joseph Moxon. But if we are to believe Mores—whose authority is hardly open to dispute—the matrices formed part of the plant of Moxon himself, and are therefore considerably earlier than the date ascribed.[1] These venerable relics are in the possession of Sir Charles Reed and Sons of the Fann Street Letter Foundry, London.

Another black-letter horn-book printed to-day (cut 35) is from beautifully cut type, still in use, cast by the first Caslon. It need hardly be pointed out that in both these illustrations (34 and 35) the type has been purposely set in a faulty manner; it is also printed from in a manner to accord as nearly as may be with the roughly-pulled impressions usually found on horn-books.

In trying to arrive, even approximately, at the age of the numerous horn-books figured in these pages, I have badgered and worried many experts, including Mr. Theodore L. de Vinne, the well-known American expert on matters typographical, who writes :—

"I have compared the letters in your numerous cuts of horn-books with those of a great many books in my collection, in the hope that I might find some positive indications of their origin. I find none whatever. The Roman letter of the XVIIth century used by English printers came largely from Holland. The punches and matrices used by English founders were more Dutch than English. It would be hazardous to assume that the types of any book were cast or set either in Holland or England. They could have been done in either country. The same difficulty is met with in tracing the black letter. The English printers of the XVIth century bought these black letters in Rouen or Paris. Many English books were there printed. The early English type-founding printers were French, and French styles soon prevailed over the Flemish style introduced by Caxton." In another letter Mr. de Vinne says : "I do not feel warranted in specifying the age of any one of these horn-books."

I sent a number of cuts to Messrs. J. Enschedé and Sons,[2] the old-

---

[1] *Vide* Reed's *History of the Old English Letter Foundries*, London, Elliot Stock, 1887, pp. 194, 312.

[2] Jean Enschedé, of the celebrated firm of Jean Enschedé et Fils of Haarlem, became a type-founder in 1743 by purchasing the foundry of H. F. Wetstein, whose punches had been cut by

History of the Horn-Book

established type-founders of Haarlem, with a view to an opinion as to the age of the horn-books represented. They replied that as printers used the same material and type "centuries after each other," and as founts used in the sixteenth still appear in the eighteenth century, it was quite impossible to express any opinion whatever.

Herr Theodor Goebel of Stuttgart, who has made a lifelong study of typography and has written much of great value on the subject, writes me that in his opinion we can arrive at the period when a horn-book *may* have been printed, but not when it *was.*

In reference to a cut of a horn-book I sent to him, Professor Skeat says : " It is just one of those things which may be of almost any date from 1550 to 1800."

Mr. William Morris, who had a sound knowledge of typography both practical and theoretical, declined to commit himself as to the age of any of the horn-books of which I showed him representations.

J. M. Fleischman. Enschedé not only introduced new types but increased his founts with old matrices and punches from old-established foundries. In 1743 there were in Holland a number of second-rate foundries, which were gradually acquired either by Enschedé, or by the brothers Ploos van Amstel, whose foundries also were finally acquired by Enschedé. Of the numerous punches and matrices few remain. The foundries acquired either by the brothers Ploos van Amstel, or J. Enschedé et Fils, include those of Blaen, a celebrated printer of Amsterdam ; Antonie and Hendrik de Bruyn (later the Elix foundry), Amsterdam ; J. van de Velde, Amsterdam ; Jan Smid and Johannes Dann ; Brouwer and Weyer ; J. L. Pfeiffer ; C. Nozeman, Haarlem ; and finally the Elzeviers, whose foundry, then in the hands of Jan Roman et Cie., was put up for sale in 1767 and bought for 2165 florins by Jean Enschedé and the brothers Ploos van Amstel, who shared it between them. Later on the foundry of Ploos van Amstel became in turn the property of the Enschedé firm.

CHAPTER IX

Silver horn-books—Silver horn-books broken up for old metal—Silver horn-books used as menu-holders—Silver horn-books described and pictured—Iron horn-books in the form of spelling lessons—Leaden horn-books—Their antiquity—Leaden horn-book moulds—A leaden horn-book, probably the oldest in existence—Leaden images—A German leaden horn-book—Bone and ivory horn-books—Their use by the well-to-do—Examples described and pictured.

AT one time there must have been many horn-books mounted in silver, but nearly all have been broken up for the sake of the metal. The result is that silver horn-books are exceedingly scarce. The reader will have noted the fine example with a pedigree described in chapter iv. It is obvious that as days passed the silver case would sometimes be turned to other uses ; the printed sheet and wooden backing would be removed, and perhaps a mirror substituted, or with very little trouble the case could be so altered as to admit of a card being thrust in from the top. Lieut.-Colonel Lambert, who has made of old silver a lifelong study, tells me he has seen what once must have been silver horn-books used as menu-holders, and a friend of the writer has a couple of such cases sold to him many years ago for this purpose. The silversmith could not have suspected that, had he left these horn-books as they were, they would have been worth many times their present value.

Dr. Mackenzie (see p. 269) speaks of some one living near Bristol, probably a collector with more enthusiasm than discretion, who removed the wooden back and had his horn-book mounted on a silver plate. This would seem to have disappeared, or it may, perhaps, have been restored by the repentant owner to its original form.

The silver horn-book, probably Dutch, belonging to the Rev. Sir George Croxton Shiffner, Bart., of Coombe Place, near Lewes, is a fine example, and but for the disappearance of a small portion of the scalloped border at the top, and a little fogginess in the last line of the printed matter, is absolutely perfect. The illustration (36) gives this horn-book full size. The base is a thin slab of oak bevelled at the edges, the

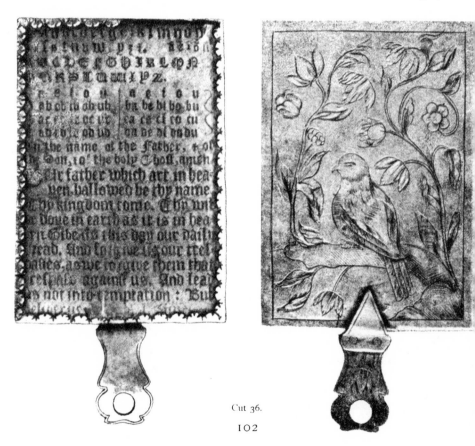

Cut 36.

History of the Horn-Book

effect being as if the horn-book had been padded towards the centre. The back is elaborately engraved with the burin, the design representing a bird perched on a branch surrounded by conventionally-treated foliage and flowers. The horn protecting the lettering is held by the scalloped edging. The handle, riveted on, has engraved on the front a single border line following its shape, and on the back an inverted tulip. The condensed type used in printing the sheet is of French origin, and as the horn-book is most probably Dutch, it may be assumed that the Dutch printer was possessed of French founts, which, like founts of other nationalities, were sold to all comers. We find the same type in Holinshed's *Chronicles*, printed in 1587.

A well-preserved silver horn-book (cut 37), owned by Mrs. Sophia Harford Adlam of Chew Magna, Somerset, has for generations been an

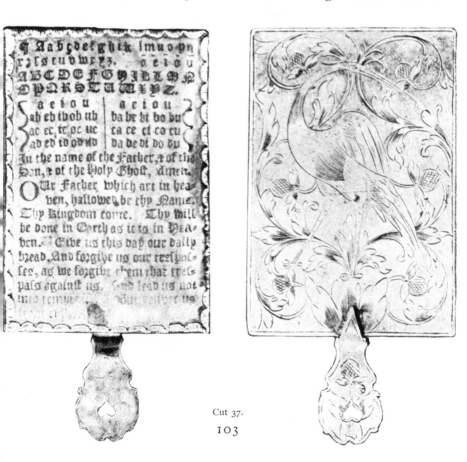

Cut 37.

103

Cut 38.

heirloom in the Harford family. This also is evidently of foreign manufacture, and with the exception of a piece chipped out towards the end of
the Lord's Prayer, which exposes the oaken base, is perfect. It will be
seen that the incising on back is of a different design from that previously
noted. In the handle is a heart-shaped hole. The printer seems not to
have possessed a cross of proper size, and evidently thinking it of no particular significance, he got out of the difficulty by substituting an ordinary
paragraph mark. It will be noticed that the types used in this horn-book
and that previously described—evidently from the hands of different
printers—are not of the same size.

History of the Horn-Book

An example—to which unfortunately no history is attached—of a horn-book ornamented with filigree silver (cut 38) was presented some years ago to the City of Birmingham Museum and Art Gallery by Mr. Sam Jevons. In the case where the horn-book reposes is a printed label—

"HORN-BOOK, in silver filigree case, early eighteenth century. These so-called horn-books are now rarely met with. They were usually made of the commonest materials, and so have been nearly all destroyed. They formed the child's first lesson book or A B C of former days. This one appeared to have been made for the scion of some princely or noble family."

The capital "U" is omitted from the alphabet, and in the opening word of the Lord's Prayer the "U," evidently an alien letter, is of lower-

Cut 39.

case shape. A curious misprint is the word "hollowed" for "hallowed.' The construction of this horn-book, which is in almost perfect preservation, is precisely the same as that of other examples noted (cuts 39, 19, etc.). Of the encasing silver filigree something is said on pp. 43 and 46, where mention is made of the fine example similarly enshrined, owned by Lord Egerton of Tatton, which is said to have been given to one of his ancestors by Queen Elizabeth.

The design in filigree silver of Canon Nevile's horn-book (39) is the same as cuts 38 and 19, the differences being due to the manipulation of the craftsman ; it is made and put together in the same manner. The printed page, which age and damp have done their best to stain and destroy, has the lower-case or small "u" in the alphabet of capitals, which is repeated in the word OUR (OUR Father). Both these letters, whether makeshifts or not, belong to the same fount. There is a curious misprint. In place of the word "them" in "as we forgive them," the printer has put "us our," which occurs immediately above in "and forgive us our." It seems strange that so bad a misprint should appear in so fine a horn-book, and it is one indication that horn-books encased in silver were not uncommon. It will be noted that the examples engraved of silver-encased horn-books vary considerably in the printing, and it would seem certain that they were the work of different hands.

Canon Nevile writes : "I am sorry to say that I can tell you nothing about the horn-book I sent you. It belonged to my mother, whose maiden name was Swainston. Her father, Dr. Swainston of York, married an heiress of the Strangwayes family, and I feel sure that it came through that family. It has never, to my knowledge, been exhibited, except a year ago at the Church House, Lincoln, at a little Exhibition got up in aid of the funds."

The filigree silver horn-book (cut 40) is owned by Miss Moultrie of Farnham, Surrey. Her father, who if now alive would be one hundred and seven years of age, learned his letters from it. The letter "U" in the alphabet of capitals is of the ordinary or modern shape. Both sides are faced with talc, and underneath the talc at back is the red silk foundation usual in horn-books of this class. It will be seen that the silver tonguing, which in other examples noted laps over on the front or printed side of the horn-book, is here at the back. The lopsidedness of the pair of illustrations

John Leighton.

results from an attempt to show the silver edging between back and front. The owner states that, when she was a child, the "horn" at front got broken away and was replaced with talc. This, I think, must be an error due to forgetfulness. The broken "horn" was most probably talc and was

Cut 40.

replaced by the same substance. The old talc is still at the back, and all known horn-books of this class are both faced and backed with talc. It might be suggested that in replacing the broken talc the silversmith reversed the rimming, but this has not been done.

Whether horn-books with a base of iron instead of wood were used in

History of the Horn-Book

early days is extremely problematical. There is no record of them. The few known examples are all late. Cuts 7 and 8 represent full size a couple of iron horn-books in the collection of Mr. J. Eliot Hodgkin, F.S.A. They form part of a series of printed spelling lessons, and were exhibited by a former owner at the Exhibition of the Horners' Company in 1882. The base is of thin sheet-iron, the edges overlapping the horn. An example of a late iron horn-book for teaching children to write is shown in cut 6.

Inscribed leaden tablets have been very largely used. In recent years one with a Latin inscription was dug up at Bath, which dates back to the Roman occupation. Another, rescued from a Dalmatian grave, has inscribed in cursive writing of the sixth century a charm in Latin against evil spirits. Recording or writing on soft plates of lead, a metal which readily lends itself to incising with a point, is mentioned by Pliny and dates back to very early times.[1] It is natural to suppose that a material so easily manipulated should have been used for horn-books.

On 27th November 1851 (vide *Archæologia*, vol. l. 34) Sir George Musgrave, F.S.A., exhibited by the hands of Captain W. H. Smythe, V.P. and Director, a leathern case, with a brass clasp, in which were two engraved pieces of hone-stone, with evident marks of having been used in casting metal horn-books for children. They are figured [2] in cut 41, and are thus described in a letter dated Eden Hall, 18th November 1851 :—

"Seven years ago a labourer digging among the ruined walls of Hartley Castle, the habitation of my family from Edward the Second's time till 1700, when it was partly pulled down, found a cannon-ball ; and a few days afterwards at the same place he discovered a mouldering leathern case, with a brass clasp, in which were engraved pieces of hone-stone, which I now forward for your inspection. They look to me like moulds for casting leaden horn-books for little children, with rude figures of birds and crosses on the other side ; and they are certainly very curious. I have mentioned lead because there are old mines of that substance in the manor, and the stones are blackened a good deal as if from the pouring in of molten metal. I have cut out wooden models of them and made some sealing-wax impressions ; and if you deem them of sufficient importance, pray present them to the Society of Antiquaries. I would

---

[1] " That they were graven with an iron pen and lead in the rock for ever ! "—Job xix. 24.
[2] The symbolic decorations were probably added to induce children to use these horn-books as toys.

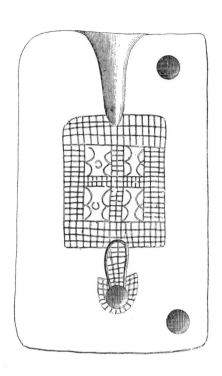
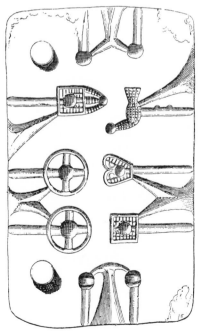
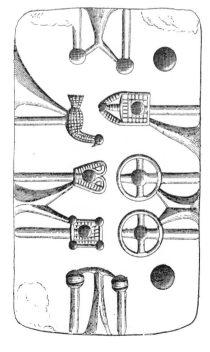

Cut 41.

III

History of the Horn-Book

very gladly give the moulds themselves to the Society, only being found in the ruins of an old family mansion, I wish to deposit them with the Luck of Eden Hall.[1]   GEORGE MUSGRAVE."

Mr. J. H. Macmichael mentions this discovery in a paper on " The Horn-book and its Cognates," read before the British Archæological Association in 1891. After saying that the Society of Antiquaries is now in possession of " casts " of these moulds he proceeds : " In these illustrations the eye should, I think, be gratified to find some account of the hitherto missing link connecting the horn-book with the runic or Danish calendar [2] in respect of the devices apparent on the moulds, which are so strikingly similar to those on the runic or clog almanack that their origin and import cannot be doubted.

"First appears the cock, emblem of St. Peter. In the almanack engraved in Dr. Plot's *Natural History of Staffordshire*, however, St. Peter is represented as the Janitor of Heaven, by two keys endorsed, and *not* crossed ; but the other four devices will all be found to correspond very closely with those on the almanack. Next in order is the heart of the Virgin Mary,—a symbol which in the almanack, published in Camden's *Britannia* (Gough), is placed against each of the six days appropriated to her calendar-feasts. Thirdly, the square device is in all probability that of St. Gregory, the patron Saint of children,[3] whilst the triple formation at the end of another square device perhaps represents the Three Passion-nails, in allusion to the legend of the Saviour having descended upon the altar surrounded by the instruments of His crucifixion, at the intercession of St. Gregory on behalf of one of his congregation who doubted the Real Presence at the Mass.[4]

[1] In Sam Jefferson's *History and Antiquities of Cumberland, etc.* (Carlisle, 1840), p. 407, we are told that " The curious ancient glass vessel called the ' Luck of Eden Hall,' on the preservation of which, according to popular superstition, the prosperity of the ancient family of Musgrave depends, is of green coloured glass, ornamented with foliage, and enamelled in different colours. The case of leather, in which it is carefully preserved, is ornamented with scrolls of vine leaves, and on the top are the letters I.h.c., from which it appears probable that this vessel was originally designed for sacred purposes. From the style of the ornaments, it appears to be of as early a date as the commencement of the fifteenth century or probably earlier."

[2] Brady, in his *Clavis Calendaria*, says that the Runic almanacks bore the characters of pagan superstition until about the fourth century, when they partook of both heathen and Christian emblematical devices, so as to be more generally saleable. After the seventh century they were wholly Christian.

[3] See Calendar of the Anglican Church, Parker, 1851, Brit. Mus. Lib. 4826A.

[4] In the legend depicted in the Calendar of the Anglican Church, and copied from an old MS. in the Bodleian Library, the nails, three in number, are conspicuously figured.

" Finally, *i.e.* in the absence of any knowledge as to what the linear formation and roundels at the top and base of the mould may signify, the circular device, no doubt, stands for the wheel of St. Catherine,—a symbol of the patroness of learning and education which is also seen upon the clog almanack. We thus have the symbols of four of the most popular of the Saints of mediæval ecclesiology."

The notched wooden clog, log or block, almanack or portable calendar, described by the Swedish historian Olaus Magnus and others, and illustrated in cut 42, is not uncommon. Examples are in the British Museum, the Bodleian Library, Oxford, and in libraries and museums both here and on the Continent.

The Dr. Plot (who wrote in 1686) quoted by Mr. Macmichael supposes that the clog almanack was brought to this country in early times by our Danish invaders. " It seems," says a writer in Chambers's *Book of Days*, " to bear the same relation to a printed almanack as the old wooden Exchequer tallies bore to a set of modern account books." The clog almanack was of hard wood, about eight inches long, fitted with a loop at one end for hanging. Primitive though it was, it served the purpose

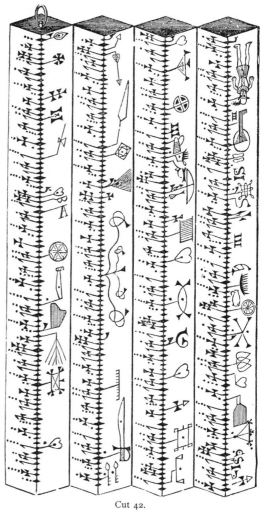

Cut 42.

of a perpetual almanack. Each day is shown by a separate notch, that marking the first day of the month being turned up. The notches denoting Sundays are somewhat broader than the others, and with a little trouble the golden number and the cycle of the moon can be found. The doctor separately describes the hieroglyphically indicated feasts.

To return to the horn-book. The central and principal portion of a leaden horn-book, engraved in cut 43, has been very kindly given to

Cut 43.

me by an antiquarian correspondent, Mr. William E. A. Axon of Manchester. It has evidently been cast at an early period from a pair of moulds closely resembling those found at Hartley Castle. This horn-book was formerly in the collection of Mr. Charles Bradbury, a well-known collector of archæological curiosities, and has never been exhibited or before described or engraved. The cut shows the exact size ; the thickness of the body is three thirty-seconds of an inch, and double that on the four corners on the alphabet side, where there are projecting bosses for the protection of the lettering. The weight is fractionally over half an ounce.

In assuming this little plaque—probably the oldest horn-book in existence—to be unique, the great counterfeiting of antiques cast in lead, christened by the makers " Pilgrims' Signs," naturally comes to mind. The aggressively assertive pretension of brand-new age on the face of these bastard leaden vases, images, medals, and plaques, due to the hell-broth of the chemist-mechanic, is branded into the very soul of collectors. The chief episode connected with the ensnaring, befooling, and undoing of the counterfeiters is distinctly savoury to the palate. It will be remembered that inquiry was made by one of the suspicious for the effigy of a supposed bishop. A sketch was supplied with the name of the defunct pencilled thereon, and in a very short time a leaden image turned up, mitred complete and lettered at foot FABRICATUS ! Though useful as a warning, rubbish such as this is hardly likely to receive the honour accorded to the false denarius, the principal coin of the Romans, which Pliny tells us was so well done as to be worth a small fistful of genuine denarii.

A DAME'S SCHOOL.   *Ambrose Dudley.*

History of the Horn-Book

An engraved mould of hard stone, probably sixteenth century, for casting leaden German horn-books or tablets is figured, together with an impression, full size, in cuts 44 and 44a.   Of its former history nothing

Cut 44.

Cut 44a.

is known.   It was recently purchased from a dealer at Nuremberg by Herr Oscar Roesger of Bautzen, in whose collection it now is.

Horn-books or tablets made of thin slabs of ivory or bone, with engraved lettering, were fairly plentiful during the latter half of the last and the early years of this century.   None of those depicted in cuts 46, 46a, 47, and 48 can be much earlier.   They were necessarily expensive, and their use must have been confined to the well-to-do. Some of these tablets for teaching children seem to have been of considerable size.   The writer has a portion of an ivory one, a mere slip measuring eight inches in length.   The width of the complete tablet was probably about five and a half inches.   The illustration (45), showing both sides, is reduced to one-fourth of the length.   There is room for ingenuity in deciphering the matter.

Cut 45.

The ivory horn-book (reproduced full size in cut 46), belonging to Mr. Roger S. Draper, was some years ago fished up during Thames dredging operations. The ivory is stained a rich sienna brown by the action of the mud, which causes it to look older than it probably is. The thickness is three thirty-seconds of an inch. The front bears the alphabet in sunk capitals, and on the back is incised a buzzard, or it may be intended for

Cut 46.

the falcon, which forms part of the arms of the Scriveners' Company. The handle is ornamented on both sides with a double device, the upper representing rays of light, and the lower a star, the two divided by a border.

It will be noted that while the bone horn-book engraved in cut 46*a* is a little larger than cut 48, the alphabets are not on so bold a scale.

History of the Horn-Book

The small letters are differently set forth, and, to make room for the vowels, are more crowded. The conventional ornamentation on the handle also differs. This horn-book, the antecedents of which are not known, belongs to the writer, and was bought of a dealer.

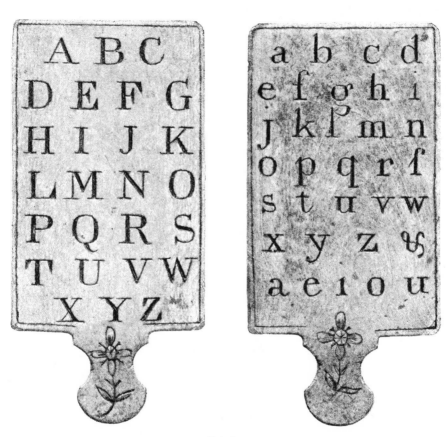

Cut 46a.

The handsome ivory horn-book, belonging to Dr. Fraser of Dublin, was purchased from a dealer. It is unfortunately not quite perfect. Back and front are shown full size in cut 47. This is the only ivory horn-book I have seen which was made for suspending. A ribbon or string was run through the holes in the two top corners, the horn-book being carried handle downwards. Report says that this horn-book came with some trinkets from a

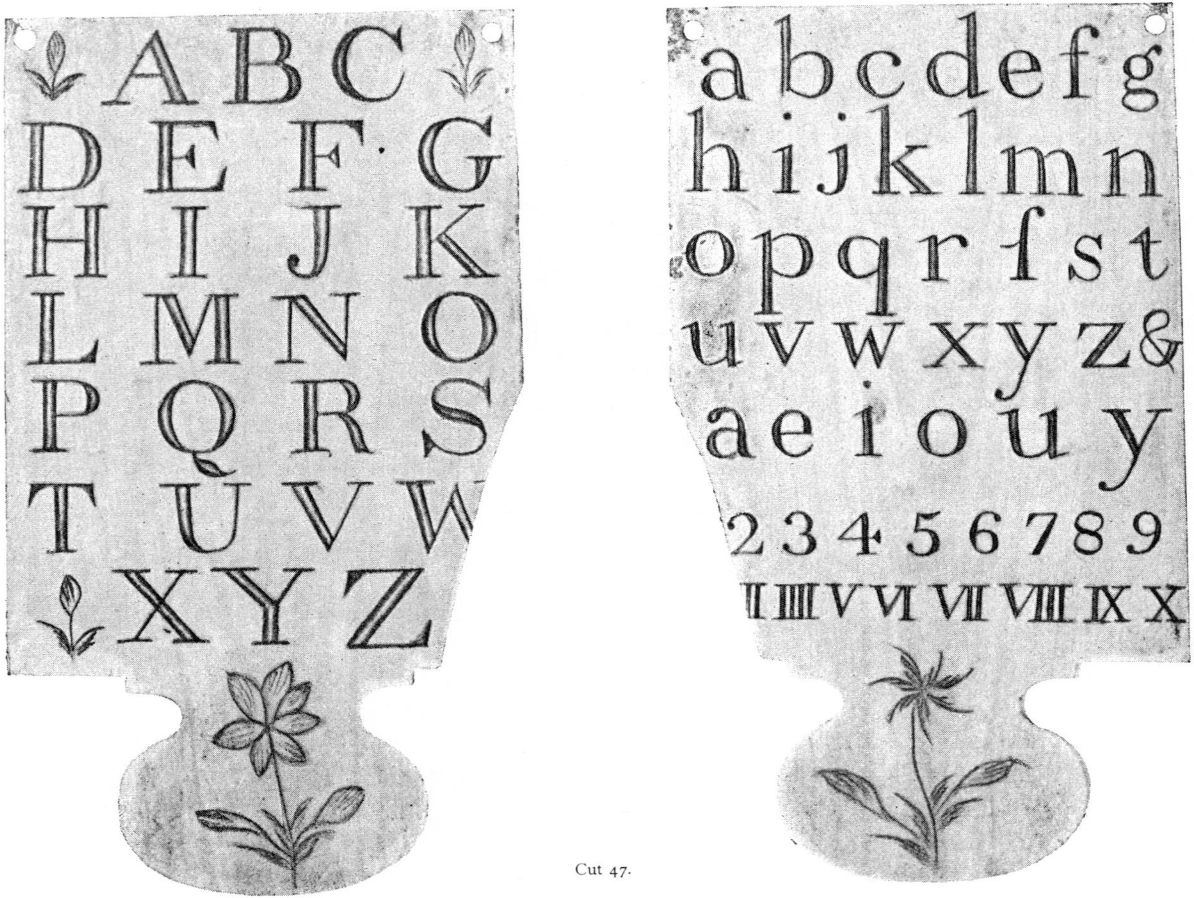

abcdefg
hijklmn
opqrfst
uvwxyz&
ae io u y
2 3 4 5 6 7 8 9
I II III IIII V VI VII VIII IX X

ABC
DE FG
HIJ KO
LMN RS
PQ
TU VW
XYZ

Cut 47.

nobleman's family, but this may be dealers' embroidery.   The ivory is one-sixteenth of an inch in thickness.

The ivory horn-book, cut 48,—a bare sixteenth of an inch in thickness —belonging to the Rev. Fred. E. Warren, B.D., of Bury St. Edmunds, is reproduced full size.   The sunk letters have evidently been filled with

Cut 48.

black pigment, much of which has now disappeared, especially towards the centres.   On the back is the complete alphabet in small letters, finishing with the ampersand.   It will be noticed that the letter "s" is twice repeated, the first being long.   On both sides of the handle are roughly engraved devices, in which there is no trace of the pigment.   This tablet was found walled up in a neighbouring and now demolished cottage built a century ago.   Another ivory horn-book corresponding with Mr. Warren's, except that the ornamentation on the handle is not quite the same, is in the collection of Mr. Robert Drane of Cardiff.

The alphabet engraved on ivory or bone cut up into squares, a letter on each, formed an instructive toy, and is in use in our own day. Cowper has (*Convers.* p. 11, 1781)—

> As alphabets in ivory employ
> Hour after hour the yet unlettered boy.

An Edinburgh correspondent has written an interesting letter :—

" My eldest brother and I learned our letters from an A B C horn-book sixty years ago in Nova Scotia. And the venerable relic—for it was old even then—was used as a plaything by us for many a day. But I am sorry to say that I do not know what has become of it. Although called a horn-book, it was made of ivory, and had the capital letters and the vowels in small letters on one side ; but I cannot now recollect whether the small letters were on the other side or not. My impression is that they were. And it was shaped something like enclosed bit of paper, the little hole being intended for a ribbon to pass round the neck. If this note is of any use, you are welcome to it, only I do not wish my name to be mentioned." The " bit of paper " is somewhat larger than cut 46*a*.

CHAPTER X

The horn-book in Scotland—Hone's thirty years' unsuccessful hunt for a Scotch horn-book—Unpublished letters to William Hone (1832)—Examples of Scotch horn-books in the Mackenzie collection and in the University Library, Glasgow—The Aberdeen horn-book belonging to the Earl of Crawford and Balcarres—The example in the British Museum, and that in the collection of Mr. N. Q. Pope of Brooklyn (N.Y.).

COTCH horn-books are exceedingly scarce. The following interesting and hitherto unpublished correspondence bears on William Hone's thirty years' unsuccessful hunt for one:—

EDINBURGH, 67 GT. KING STREET,
10th *October* 1838.

To William Hone, Esq.

MY DEAR SIR—Eureka! Eureka! I have found it! The Horn-book *did* exist in Scotland. So far to unburden my mind of the delightful intelligence, but let me proceed in due order, and record faithfully the result of my enquiries. I called upon Dr. Jamieson on Saturday last, and laid your queries before him : strange to say, he had *never heard* of the Horn-book, and begged of me to inform him " what like it was." Upon my describing it he said that he was pretty certain it had *never* been

123

History of the Horn-Book

used in Scotland. I reminded him that Burns had introduced *Death and Dr. Hornbook*, and asked whether he thought that alluded to a Scottish custom, or whether Burns had merely heard the term from intercourse with the English Borderers? He replied, "The *latter* was most probable." This confirmed my opinion previously expressed to you ; but luckily, as the sequel will testify, we were all "*in the wrong box.*" As regards the prefix of the Cross he seemed to think it was merely placed there as a *charm* or as a remnant of the Old Popish Superstitions. He knew of no particular value attached to the letter A, but suggested that in conjunction with the Cross it might refer to the expression in the Apocalypse : "I am Alpha and Omega"—"the first and the last." Such is the sum and substance of my conversation with Dr. Jamieson on these points. Upon the following (*last*) Monday, having occasion to be in our Library, I happened in course of conversation with Mr. David Haig—one of the sub-librarians—to notice the "*Horn-book,*" when, after I had in accordance with his request described to him what it is, he surprised me by exclaiming : "*Odd, Man, I* was taught from one of *these things!!*" You may conceive my delight and astonishment, and my immediate and close interrogations on the subject. The following is the result. He informed me that he was taught by an old woman in Kelso, whose name was *Janet Turnbull.* She was a very rigid Presbyterian, which he thinks accounts for his being placed under her care, as his Father was a very strict Calvinist. She had an only son, who was drowned ; from which period she regularly kept the Anniversary, not certainly as a *red* but a *black* letter day, and spent it in prayer and solitude. When irritated by the children's inattention or non-preparation of task, she *thumped their pates* with the Horn-book. This must have been *thirty-two* years ago complete, as Haig is now *thirty-six*, and was sent very early to school. The Horn-book was termed the "*A B Broad*" (pronounced in our Bœotian dialect "*aw bay Broad*"), *i.e.* the "*A B Board.*" Haig does not think there can be any existing now, but he has promised to write to Kelso (his native town) and endeavour if possible to find one for me, but he fears the search will be vain. I am not to be discouraged however, and my hopes are buoyed up by other circumstances whereof you shall presently learn, as I purpose at my earliest leisure to make a *Paul Pry Avatar* upon all the cottages in the country. Haig talks with great regard of the old girl and her piety. He says that one day she came to his father's house, when he was more advanced in youth and at another school, and asked him whether he "still read his Bible." Upon his saying, "Na, na, bibles are out o' the fashion now" (meaning that the reading of the bible did not form part of the system of tuition at the school where he was), she replied (understanding him in a literal sense), "Deed aye, ye say richt, Bibles *are* out o' the fashion." Here endeth my confab with Haig. On returning home I found a letter from Dr. Jamieson lying on my table, which I now transcribe for your edification : " Hone, friend, and Antiquary, lend me your eyes ! "

W. B. D. D. Turnbull, Esq., Fife.

DEAR SIR—Since I had the pleasure of seeing you, I made enquiry at Mrs. J., who is a native of the County of Angus, and well acquainted with its customs, in regard to the *Horn-book*. She recollects distinctly, that nearly sixty years ago, in the writing-school of Dundee, which she attended, all the copies were framed, with a cover of *horn* above them, to serve as glass, but more adapted to a school, as being of less brittle materials. She thinks it probable, although she does not recollect the fact, that in former times the Alphabet, used in schools, might be guarded in a similar manner. If you have any ancient friend in Dundee, or in the same county, you might obtain some further intelligence.

My good wife also recollects the phrase, applied to those who had not begun their education : " Ye have na got the length of your *horn-book* yet."

This information is so meagre that I fear it is scarcely worth communicating to Mr. Hone. But it is all that I have met with. If anything else occur, you shall have it.—I am, my dear sir, yours truly,

JOHN JAMIESON.

4 George Square, 8th October 1832.

The above is "the tottle of the whole" of the worthy doctor's communication.

I was rather doubtful as to the exact resemblance between the Scotch and English Horn-book, having been informed by several persons whom I reminded of the "*a b broad*" that it merely consisted of the Capital Alphabet without Cross or Lord's Prayer, but the elder Haig (James)

History of the Horn-Book

informs me that it was exactly similar (from my description) to the English containing both these. Those with the Capitals are of latest date, some twenty-five or thirty years back, for example.—Believe me ever yours most sincerely,   W. B. D. D. TURNBULL.

The rare Scotch horn-book printed at Glasgow in 1784, and figured cut 49, is labelled "probably unique," and forms part of the Mackenzie collection in the South Kensington Museum. It is remarkable as to its mounting, the printed sheet (left unvarnished) being cut close, and stuck on to a piece of round-edged amber-tinted horn nearly an eighth of an inch thick. The horn, here obviously out of place, is modern, and although the printed sheet is genuine, from this particular horn-book it is pretty certain that no child ever learned its letters. Fortunately it is on record that so strange a mounting is due to the freak of a late owner (see p. 267).

Another example of this horn-book, the impression being exactly the same and in perfect condition—which, through the courtesy of the librarian, Mr. James Lymburn, I have had an opportunity of examining,—is in the University Library, Glasgow. The paper sheet is mounted on an oaken slab stained very dark brown and polished at the back, the shape following the border and handle, but the oak projecting therefrom three-sixteenths of an inch all round. The thickness of the slab is also three-sixteenths of an inch.

It has been asserted that in the Scotch horn-book the cross preceding the alphabet was always omitted. In illustration 49 it will be noted that while the opening cross is absent, there is one under the imprint: "Glasgow: Printed and Sold by J. & M. Robertson, MDCCLXXXIV," and that there are miniature crosses in the breaks in the border. In the example just described, in place of the cross at foot is a carefully-drilled hole measuring nearly a quarter of an inch in diameter, which is unnecessarily large for a string or ribbon for suspension. It looks as if some one had quarrelled with the cross and had bored it to death.

The Earl of Crawford and Balcarres's fine horn-books, which, by the courtesy of the owner, I have had an opportunity of carefully examining, consist of four impressions in black letter of as many different horn-books printed on one sheet of fine wire-laid paper with the watermark of a pot.

IN SCHOOL.   *Wm. Luker, jr.*

A b c d e f g h i k l m n o p q r ſ s t u w x y z

A B C D E F G H I K L M N O P Q
R S T V W X Y Z

In the Name of GOD the
Father, the Sonne, & of
the Holie Ghoſt: Amen.

Our Father, which art in Heaven, Halowed be thy Name:
Thy kingdom come: Thy wil be
done in Earth, as it is in Heaven:
Give us this day our daily bread
And forgive us our trespaſſes, as
wee forgive them that trespaſſe
against us: And leade us not into
temptation, But deliver us from
evill: For thine is the kingdome,
power, and glorie, for ever, Amen.

A a b c d e f g h i k l m n o p
q r ſ s t u w x y z, :.

A B C D E F G H I K L M N A
O P Q R S T V W X Y Z

ab eb ib ob ub an en in on un
ac ec ic oc uc ap ep ip op up
ad ed id od ud ar er ir or ur

In the Name of GOD the
Father, the Son, and of
the Holy Ghoſt: So be it.

Our Father, which art in Heaven, Halowed be thy Name:
Thy kingdome come: Thy Will
be done in Earth, as it is in Heaven: Give us this day our Daylie
Bread: And forgive us our trespaſſes, as wee forgive them that
trespaſſe against us: And leade us
not into temptation. But deliver
us from Evill: For thyne is the
kingdome, Power, and Glorie
for ever, and ever. So be it.

Aabcdefghiklmnop
qrstubwxyz3ᵗ,:.
A B C D E F G H I K L M N O P
Q R S T U W X Y Z ; -! ( )

ab eb ib ob ub ba be bi bo bu
ac ec ic oc uc ca ce ci co cu
ad ed id od ud da de di do du

In the Name of GOD the
Father, the Sonne, and
of the holy Ghost, Amen.

Our Father, which art in Heaven, Halowed be thy Name:
Thy kingdome come: Thy Will
be done on Earth, as it is in Heaven: Give vs this day our daylie
Bread: And forgive vs our trespasses, as wee forgive them that
trespasse against vs: And leade vs
not into temptation, But deliver
vs from evill: For thyne is the
kingdome, the Power, and the
Glorie, for ever, and ever, Amen.

Cut 50.

Aabcdefghiklmnop
qrstubwxyz3ᵗ,:.
A B C D E F G H I K L M N O P
Q R S T U W X Y Z ; -! ?

In the Name of GOD the Father, the Sonne, and of the
holie Ghost, So be it.

Our Father, which art
in Heaven, halowed be
thy Name: Thy kingdome
come: Thy will be done on
Earth, as it is in Heaven:
Give vs this day our dayly
Bread: And forgive vs our
Trespasses, as wee forgive
them that trespasse against
vs: And leade vs not into
temptation, but deliver vs
from Evill: For Thyne is the
kingdome, power, and glorie, for
ever, Amen.

Printed at Aberdeen, by G. Raban.

To face p. 129.

History of the Horn-Book

The original, enshrined by Zaehnsdorf, has been laid down on cardboard, and was purchased from Messrs. Pearson and Co.   It will be noticed in the

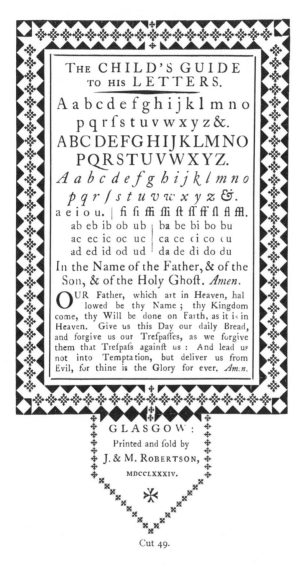

The CHILD'S GUIDE
to his LETTERS.

A a b c d e f g h i j k l m n o
p q r ſ s t u v w x y z &.
ABCDEFGHIJKLMNO
PQRSTUVWXYZ.
*A a b c d e f g h i j k l m n o
p q r ſ s t u v w x y z &.*
a e i o u. | fi fi ffi ffi ft ff ff fl fl ffl.
ab eb ib ob ub ┃ ba be bi bo bu
ac ec ic oc uc ┃ ca ce ci co cu
ad ed id od ud ┃ da de di do du
In the Name of the Father, & of the
Son, & of the Holy Ghoſt. *Amen.*
OUR Father, which art in Heaven, hal
lowed be thy Name ; thy Kingdom
come, thy Will be done on Faith, as it is in
Heaven.   Give us this Day our daily Bread,
and forgive us our Trefpaffes, as we forgive
them that Trefpafs againſt us : And lead us
not into Temptation, but deliver us from
Evil, for thine is the Glory for ever. *Am.n.*

GLASGOW :
Printed and fold by
J. & M. ROBERTSON,
MDCCLXXXIV.

Cut 49.

facsimile illustration (cut 50) that the impressions are laid head to head, as if they formed part of a sheet of a book, which proves, if proof were needed, that at the time this horn-book, or to be more exact, these horn-

129

books were printed, they were very extensively used, in this case four varieties being produced at each pull of the press. At foot of one of this interesting quartette is an imprint : " Printed in Aberdene, by E. Raban."

In his *Aberdeen Printers*, Edward Raban to James Nichol, 1620-1736 (Aberdeen : Edmond and Spark, 1886), Mr. J. P. Edmond puts the date of Raban's horn-books at 1622, which is probably as near as it

Cut 51.

can be fixed. From that it is an uncontro-first printing-press in lished in 1622, and was the first printer nothing of him until in Edinburgh at the Cowgate Port. In the to St. Andrews, pointed printer to the wards went to Aber-known to have printed Thesis, which was to July 1622.

Returning to the quartette sheet by Raban, another im-fresh, is in the British Museum, book, containing the alphabet, four times repeated. E. Raban, scription is incorrect, for it has single sheet contains the text books. The authorities pur-

Mr. Edmond we learn verted fact that the Aberdeen was estab-that Edward Raban there, but we know 1620,when he printed sign of the A B C in same year he removed where he was ap-University, and after-deen, where he is the King's College be disputed on 22nd

of horn-books printed on one pression, beautifully clean and and is thus catalogued : " Horn-syllabarium, and Lord's Prayer, Aberdene, 1620 ? " This de-already been noted that the of four widely-differing horn-chased it in December 1879 for

fifteen pounds, through Messrs. Ellis and White, of New Bond Street, in the first portion of the sale at Sotheby's (lot 1540) of the library of Dr. David Laing of Edinburgh. This horn-book, or rather horn-book sheet, is said to have been taken out of a copy of Boëthius, to which it had formed a fly-leaf. Dr. Laing secured it at the sale of the Jervise Library, 1878, for three shillings ! A third example was sold in Messrs. Sotheby's rooms on 4th December 1890, and was bought for a collector by Mr. James Bain, the Haymarket bookseller, for £26 : 10s. A fourth impression is in the

History of the Horn-Book

collection of Mr. N. Q. Pope of Brooklyn (N.Y.), to whom it was sold by Mr. B. F. Stevens, the American bookseller of Trafalgar Square, who purchased it privately.

In a paper read by Mr. Alex. Mackay before the Sutherland Association at Edinburgh, in May 1894, is a reference to a Scotch horn-book :—

"In the Summer of 1834 the Swordly (parish of Farr, Sutherlandshire) fathers got a young lad from Annadale to teach the young idea how to shoot in the matter of education, but to the best of my recollection he was not very successful, as he was there only for four months. All I remember is each scholar had a spālag, that was, a thin piece of board (wood), part of which formed a handle, like a hand-looking-glass. On the board a leaf with the alphabet was pasted (shown quarter size in cut 51), for a book would have been worn out long before the pupil was expected to learn the letters. This was similar to what Burns gave the term Horn-book to, and applied to the Schoolmaster of Tarbolton in his famous satire."

In one of the character sketches entitled "Boanerges Simpson's Encumbrance" in *The Stickit Minister* (p. 165), by S. R. Crockett, (London : Fisher Unwin, 1895), we get ". . . like Henny-penny in the horn-buik wi' your finger in your mooth," which a footnote describes as "A picture in the old-fashioned child's primer." Mr. Crockett writes me on this passage : "Curiously enough in Galloway, or at least by my grandmother and the old people, our ' penny-book ' or primer was called a horn-book. It was the common name for it indeed, and I used it as a boy, though I was ' man muckle ' before I ever saw a real ' horn-buik ' or knew what it meant. ' Henny-penny in the horn-buik ' referred to an old print of a woman feeding chickens which was in our primer : it had some connexion with a rhyme about the disappointment which Henny-penny suffered. But alas! I have forgotten what. I am much interested in your horn-buik ploy."

CHAPTER XI

NTIL quite recently the most diligent search failed to bring to light a single horn-book in America. The honour of discovering the first—the only one known when these sheets went to press —belongs to a distinguished American authoress. Long before Mrs. Earle's work was published every learned society, the principal libraries, and the best-known collectors, had been persistently badgered without result. The Pilgrim Fathers knew their horn-book, and when they left these shores in the *Mayflower* and settled in New England, they must certainly have taken it with them. There can be no doubt whatever that the horn-book has been extensively used in America.

Funk and Wagnalls's *Standard Dictionary* (London and Toronto: Funk and Wagnalls Co.) gives " Horn-Book, a child's primer, as formerly made, consisting of a thin board of oak and a slip of paper with the nine digits, the alphabet and Lord's Prayer printed on it, covered with a thin layer of transparent horn and framed ; hence any primer or handbook ; also rudi-

History of the Horn-Book

mentary knowledge." In Mackellar's *American Printer* is a cut of a horn-book borrowed from Chambers's *Book of Days*. Underneath is printed, " Horn-Book of the Seventeenth Century," but not another word in all his three hundred and eighty odd pages has Mr. Mackellar to say about it. We find in *Collections of the Massachusetts Historical Society*, vol. v., fifth series (Boston : published by the Society, 1878), on p. 344 an entry (under date 27th April 1691) from the Diary of Samuel Sewall (1674-1729, vol. i. 1674-1700): " This afternoon had Joseph to school to Capt. Townsend's Mother's, his cousin Jane accompanying him, carried his Horn-book." Joseph was Sewall's eighth child (out of fourteen which his wife bore him), and was born 15th August 1688. His cousin Jane Tappan or Toppan was born 28th September 1674.

One would think that Benjamin Franklin must certainly have printed horn-books, but in the ten-volume edition of his works by Sparks they are not even mentioned. In J. R. Lowell's Biglow Papers (*Works*, 1879, p. 179) we find, " Thrift was the first lesson in their horn-book "; and in an article on " Poetry in America," in *Scribner's Monthly* for August 1881, is : " The poor books of one generation are often the horn-books for the people, the promise and cause of better work in the next."

In American literature mention of the horn-book is not uncommon, and instances need hardly be multiplied. But I will add a passage from Mrs. Alice Morse Earle's *Customs and Fashions of Old New England* (David Nutt, 1893):—

" Their horn-books, those framed and behandled sheets of semi-transparent horn, which were worn hanging at the side and were studied as late certainly as the year 1715 by children of the Pilgrims, also managed to instil with the alphabet some religious words or principles. Usually the Lord's Prayer formed part of the printed text. Though horn-books are referred to in the letters of Wait Still Winthrop, and appear on stationers' and booksellers' lists at the beginning of the eighteenth century, I do not know of the preservation of a single specimen to our own day. I often fancy I should have enjoyed living in the good old times, but I am glad I never was a child in colonial New England—to have been baptized in ice water, fed on brown bread and warm beer, to have had to learn the Assembly's Catechism and 'explain all the Questions with conferring Texts,' to have been constantly threatened with fear of death and terror of God, to have been forced to commit Wigglesworth's ' Day of Doom ' to memory, and after all to have been whipped with a tattling stick."

As to what a tattling stick is, Mrs. Earle confesses ignorance, but children, then as now, were given to tattling, or idle talk, and the meaning seems sufficiently evident.

A special inquiry addressed to Mrs. Earle, in which I pointed out that a careful search would probably lead to the discovery of horn-books in America, bore fruit. But Mrs. Earle's letter is so full of interest that it may well be printed in full.

242 HENRY ST., BROOKLYN, N.Y.,
17th June 1894.

DEAR SIR—I have received from you a letter dated February 13, with enclosures and newspaper, all relating to horn-books. I wrote in answer a short note saying I would make every effort to discover a horn-book in America for you. This note you cannot have received, for in a letter to Messrs. Scribner's you so state. I think in my haste I must have mis-directed it. I now enclose to you a print of a horn-book which I have unearthed. And I have had my account of it type-written, as there are stupid or perverse editors who persist that they cannot decipher my hand-writing. This of course I indignantly resent, believing that my writing is as clear as print.[1] But I have just had a hard blow to my pride in a letter from the editor of the *Journal of American Folk Lore.* He wrote to me requesting a paper. I answered him that I had none suitable for his magazine except one on Lord's Day Tokens. He wrote back that he could not imagine how a paper on Long Stockings could relate to Folk Lore, but was willing to believe that I would make it all right, and to please send it. Thus did he interpret my writing. And by the way, these same Communion tokens would form a very interesting subject for your pen and press. I had already planned a magazine article on Horn-books and Primers. I hope the delay in answering you will not make my information too late to be of service to you.—I am, very sincerely yours,

ALICE MORSE EARLE.

Mrs. Earle type-writes :—

" In my book entitled *Customs and Fashions in Old New England* I

---

[1] Mrs. Earle's handwriting is clearer than print.

History of the Horn-Book

state that I do not know of the preservation in America of a horn-book until our own day. The publication of that statement has brought to me a large amount of correspondence on the subject of horn-books, which I have supplemented by careful inquiries of my own in many directions. There certainly is not a single horn-book in any of our large public libraries or historical collections in America, nor in any of our large private libraries or collections of antiques and curios ; but I have found one horn-book—salvage from a New England farmhouse—and I take pleasure in sending to you its counterfeit presentment. It is rather dilapidated, both horn and paper being torn. On the back is a picture of Charles II., which might reasonably be said to afford a probable date of manufacture. The absolute annihilation of horn-books in America is most surprising. They were certainly in constant use in early colonial days. I find in the Winthrop letters, as late as 1716, the Winthrops of

Cut 52.

Boston town sending gifts of horn-books to their country nephews and nieces in outlying settlements. In 1708, in the account book of the Old South Church of Boston, one item of expense was £1 : 10s. for ' Hornes for Catechizing.' In old stationers' lists I see gilt horn-books and plain horn-books frequently advertised. As late as December 4, 1760, in the *Pennsylvania Gazette*, with Bibles and primers appear 'gilt horns and plain horns,' which were certainly horn-books. This sole and lonely little horn-book survivor is now owned by Mrs. Elizabeth Robinson Minturn.

135

History of the Horn-Book

She was a Robinson of old Narragansett stock, and her ancestors owned, and used this horn-book. The Narragansett planters were among our most opulent colonists, and were the only Church of England settlers in New England. Many curious and interesting relics are now owned by their descendants. Each summer I go to Homogansett Farm, the country home of my husband's ancestors, and still owned in the family. It has about a mile and a half of water-front on Narragansett Bay, and is a most romantic and historic spot. I shall make careful search throughout the summer, and may find some stranded wreck to add to your list."

The American horn-book (cut 52) discovered by Mrs. Earle accords with others pictured in these pages and was probably imported from the mother country. Whether horn-books were made in America there is at present no evidence to determine. Now that one has turned up, which wherever made, has lived its life in America, others will probably be found. The quest is worth pursuing, and the collector whom luck favours will be envied by his fellows.

CHAPTER XII

Flemish horn-books—The ballbret or ballboard—The horn-book in Flemish prints and pictures—Albert Dürer's monogram—German horn-books—Hopfer's horn-book—Tablets—The German horn-book in prints and pictures—French horn-books—The "Croix de par Dieu"—An old primer "La Croix + Depardiev"—The French horn-book in prints and pictures—Italian horn-books—A missing print—The Italian horn-book in prints and pictures—Notes on Norwegian, Swedish, Kurdish, Mexican, Finnish, Polish, and Hebrew horn-books.

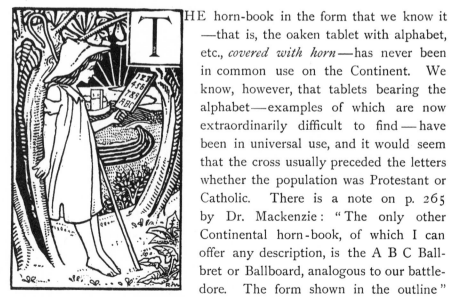

THE horn-book in the form that we know it —that is, the oaken tablet with alphabet, etc., *covered with horn*—has never been in common use on the Continent. We know, however, that tablets bearing the alphabet—examples of which are now extraordinarily difficult to find — have been in universal use, and it would seem that the cross usually preceded the letters whether the population was Protestant or Catholic. There is a note on p. 265 by Dr. Mackenzie: "The only other Continental horn-book, of which I can offer any description, is the A B C Ballbret or Ballboard, analogous to our battledore. The form shown in the outline" (much reduced in cut 53) "is common to Germany, Bohemia, Sweden, Norway, and Denmark." This information, and the description from

137

which the doctor was enabled to pen the outline, came from M. Octave Delepierre, a learned French antiquary, who died in 1879.

For the purposes of this volume, I have applied for examples of these tablets to all the second-hand booksellers in the countries named, sending an impression of cuts 53 and 54, the Flemish horn-book as sketched by M. Delepierre and exhibited by Dr. Mackenzie, with the

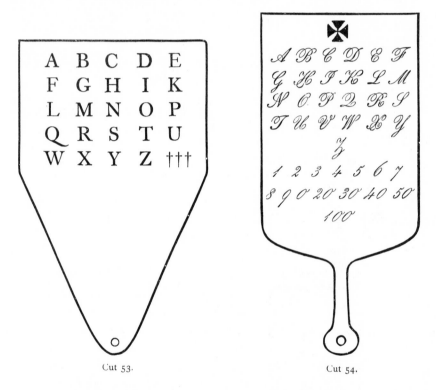

Cut 53.   Cut 54.

result that I have been unable to secure or hear of one.   Beyond some half-hundred courteous acknowledgments, letters to Continental museums and public libraries asking for information have proved equally fruitless.

The undated—probably seventeenth century—Flemish horn-book (cut 55) in the Steine Museum at Antwerp is of peculiar interest, inasmuch as it is the only example of a Continental horn-book—that is, a true horn-book protected with horn, and not a mere abecedarium—that I can hear of. It will be noted that the second alphabet is mixed up in such a way that

AT PLAY.   Wm. Luker, jr.

a child having mastered the capitals would be unable, from their position only, to name the small letters. One gathers from the imprint that this specimen was made at Dordrecht, Netherlands, by H. Walpot, abiding in front of the Town Hall. The firm dates back to the sixteenth century.

Cut 55.

There may of course be other examples of Flemish or Dutch true horn-books in private hands, but, notwithstanding that in early days Holland largely supplied the English market, the horn-book does not appear to have ever taken root as a Dutch institution. The cut is the exact size of the original, which would appear to be simply an experimental imitation of those made for use in this country. The base is of uncovered oak, and the alphabet is printed from type on paper.

In a print in line—probably De Valk's work—containing numerous

History of the Horn-Book

figures entitled "A Flemish Feast," without painter's or engraver's name, is a child (cut 56) with a horn-book suspended from her girdle. A friend of the writer possesses a marginless mezzotint from a Flemish picture (scraped probably by an English engraver), representing a bearded man in a Rembrandtish hat teaching a boy from a horn-book, or rather from an unmounted bordered sheet of paper, with the alphabet in bold capitals divided into three lines. Underneath is the *Laudate Dominum* abbreviated to "Laud^e Domin^m," and following the Pater Noster, on which the boy has his finger.

Cut 56.

In Rembrandt's group, now in the National Gallery, "Christ Blessing little Children," a child is depicted with a horn-book or tablet (cut 57) suspended from the girdle. In "A Family at Dinner Table," engraved by Claes Jansz Visscher in 1609, is a figure of a boy (cut 58), with a horn-book similarly suspended. Cut 59 shows a portion of a picture, "The Village School," by Jan Steen (born 1626, died 1679). It is interesting, as showing the method of carrying the horn-book suspended from the girdle. The large box immediately under the horn-book was commonly

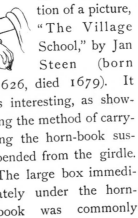

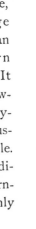

Cut 57.

Cut 58.

142

History of the Horn-Book

used for holding school-books. The second group shown in cut 60, where a mischievous boy has hung his horn-book on the parrot's perch, forms part of the same picture. The two children with horn-books in cut 61 form part of a picture by Adriaen Janzoon van Ostade (born 1610, died 1685) representing a Dutch village school.

There can be little

Cut 59.

doubt that the tablet (cut 62) used by Albert Dürer (1471-1528), Aldegrever, Altdorfer, and other Continental engravers for enclosing their monogram was suggested by the horn-book tablet, which, on the Continent, seems generally to have had the handle at the top, or side (*vide* cuts 63, 87, etc.).

Cut 63 represents a late Dutch A B C board or tablet unprotected by horn, which forms a portion of the frontispiece to the Catalogue of a Scholastic Exhibition held at Amsterdam in 1860.   It was lent by Mr. Menlevelt, of Amsterdam, but is now unfortunately lost.

The *A B boordje* is said to have been largely used in Holland during the seventeenth century, when it was considered a good method "for teaching children in a very short time."   Its use was continued until recent days.

Cut 60.

143

History of the Horn-Book

We know that the Germans were not behind the Dutch in the manufacture of school-books for the English market, but the Germans, like the Dutch, declined to adopt the horn-book. There is no equivalent in the German, Dutch, or Flemish languages—in all of which we should

Cut 61.

expect to find it—for " horn-book." The Dutch have *a b boordje* (a little board with A B), which is simply an abecedarium or tablet such as has been universally used in some form or other since the necessity was felt for pestering bairns with lessons.

A stone mould for a leaden German horn-book is referred to on p. 117, and is illustrated in cuts 44 and 44*a*.

Hopfer's horn-book facsimiled in cut 64 is adverted to on p. 265, in Dr. Mackenzie's paper, and therefore little more need be said. In his hitherto unpublished notes, Hone says of it : " D. Hopfer, a German artist of the 16th century, engraved a plate which seems to have been intended for the page of a horn-book. The print is $3\frac{1}{2}$ inches high by $5\frac{1}{2}$ inches wide, and of Roman capitals in three lines, but without the cross and without ' &,' the ' little and,' after the last letter. The alphabet runs in three long lines, the wide way of the plate, within a scroll of ornaments : at the bottom, in the part immediately about where the wood would come, there is an arch of cherubs over a Triune head, symbolical of the threefold character of

Cut 62.

Cut 63.

144

Cut 64.

God. I know not whether in the horn-books of Catholic countries on the Continent the cross preceded the alphabet, as in the English horn-books. Hopfer, I have the strongest reason to believe, was a Protestant, and a zealous adherent to Luther. In engravings from various old paintings, the alphabet or horn-book is introduced in connexion with the subject, and it is always displayed in the form of Hopfer's alphabet, namely, in long lines the wide way of the wood."

The illustration 65 is one of a group of four children, and is taken from a *Künstbuch*[1] of Jost Amman's, published at Franckfurt in 1580. The boy sketched is engaged in pointing out the letters with a fescue to another child who is not shown in the cut.

The print, numbered 66, of a wolf teaching geese from an alphabet

---

[1] "Der Ander Theil dess newwen Kunstbuchs, in welchem Reissen unnd Mahlen zu lehrnen; Allen Kunstliebhabenden zu nutz an tag geben; Durch die Kunstreichen und weitberühmten Jost Amman & Tobias Stimmer." Gedruckt zu Franckfurt am Mayn, in Verlegung S. Feverabendts, 1580.

History of the Horn-Book

tablet or horn-book is from p. 182 of *Researches into the History of Playing Cards, with Illustrations of the Origin of Printing and Engraving on Wood*. By Samuel Weller Singer. London: printed by T. Bensley and Son, for Robert Triphook, No. 23 Old Bond Street, 1816. The original, also by Jost Amman, the famous painter and engraver of Nuremberg (1539-91), forms one of a pack of cards afterwards republished in book form (Iodoci Ammani, civis Noribergensis, Charta Lusoria, Tetrastichis illustrata per Ianum Heinricum Scroterum de Gustron, Megapolitanum, Equitem a P. L. Caesareum . . . 1588), with Latin verse, by J. H. S. de Gustron, at the top, and a free rendering in German underneath, inculcating the advantages of Industry and Learning over Idleness and Drunkenness. The four suits are Books, Ink Balls used by printers, Wine Pots, and Drinking Cups.

Cut 65.

In a small plate, "Aurora," part of which is shown in cut 67, engraved by Hendrik Goltzius at the beginning of the seventeenth century, a child is represented with what appears to be a horn-book suspended over the

Cut 66.

Cut 67.

146

right arm.   The horn-book, however, may be a satchel with the leathern

Cut 68.

pocket turned next to, instead of away from, the child's body, more
especially as another child in the same print is depicted with a satchel of

somewhat similar shape in which a pocket, open at the top and nailed down at the sides, is indicated.

In Dr. Albert Figdor's fine collection of antiquities in Vienna is a fourteenth-century tablet used for teaching children, probably in a convent school. In cut 68 it is reproduced quarter size. The numerals in Roman characters from one to a thousand are painted on both sides.

A B C tablets are mentioned by Franz Anton Specht in his *History of Education in Germany, from the Earliest Times to the Middle of the Thirteenth Century,* published at Stuttgart in 1885. It may be noted here that the Saint Walaricus (Valery) referred to founded the monastery of Leuconaus at the mouth of the Somme, and died in the first quarter of the seventh century ; while Bishop Samsen, Welsh saint and bishop of Dol, flourished in the fifth century.

Cut 69.

" To instruct little boys in the art of reading, small tablets or leaves were chiefly used, inscribed with the letters of the alphabet in regular order. Such an A B C tablet received Saint Walarich when he was guarding sheep near a school, and filled with the desire of intellectual instruction, he begged the master to write down the A B C and to tell him the meaning of it. Perhaps upon such tablets there were also a few syllables and words serving for the first spelling exercises. Of the Bishop Samsen it is recorded that through Heavenly direction he was able to learn all the letters of the alphabet in a single day, and what is more wonderful still, within a week he was able to distinguish words."

If German horn-books, or rather alphabet tablets, should turn up, one might reasonably expect to find them

History of the Horn-Book

decorated with the double-headed eagle of the German Empire, or the emblem of wakefulness, as in cuts 69, 70 from a German A B C of 1703. In those of an earlier date we should look for the Roman character.[1]

It is apparently hopeless to expect to find German horn-books, or rather alphabet tablets, such as that depicted in cut 71, which represents

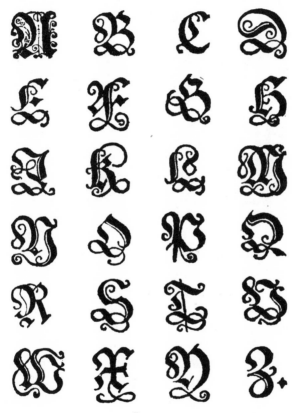

Cut 70.

a portion only of a large wood engraving in Gregory Reisch's interesting compendium of moral, rational, and natural philosophy entitled *Margarita Philosophica*, of which the earliest edition was printed at Heidelberg in

---

[1] The reader will have noticed in some parts of German Switzerland that the outside of the house is often adorned with Scriptural and moral texts carved or burnt into the wood. The custom is a very old one, and the earlier examples are in Latin in Roman letters, but in the middle of the seventeenth century we find the German vernacular in black letter.

History of the Horn-Book

Cut 71.

1486. Therein is represented a symbolical figure of Grammar in the guise of an uncomfortably gowned wooden - faced lady of severe aspect, who with one hand unlocks the Temple of Knowledge, and with the other presents a horn-book to an ungracefully clad and equally wooden-faced schoolboy. The Temple of Knowledge is represented in several stages, each symbolising a department of science, and worthies with whom each department is traditionally connected gaze stolidly from windows or holes in the wall. The youth who is receiving the horn-book—its formidable size will be noticed—is apparently about to be introduced to Priscianus on the ground-floor. But a small portion of the cut is here shown (71). In the elaborately-designed symbolical title-page, Grammar is typified by a little girl holding a horn-book (cut 72). The horn-book (cut 73) is from a woodcut representing the

Cut 72.

Cut 73.

Institution of Languages in *Margarita Philosophica Nova*, Argentoratum, J. Gruninger, 1512. The upper central portion of this engraving typifies God giving the tables of the ten commandments to Moses, and the remainder the different literary nations of the civilised world—Hebrews, Greeks, Latins, etc. In *The Science and Literature of the Middle Ages and the Renaissance*, Paul Lacroix makes use of some of the cuts.

NEVER TOO LATE.   *Ambrose Dudley.*

History of the Horn-Book

The allegorical figures—quite uninteresting but for the introduction of the horn-book—in cuts 74 and 75 are taken from a work on Logic, written by Dr. Thomas Murner, and published at Strassburg on the feast of St. Thomas of Canterbury (29th Dec.), 1509.   The full title is: *Logica Memorativa.   Charti ludiũ logice, sive totius dialectice memoria : & novus Petri hyspani textus emendatus : Cum jucundo pictasmatis*

Cut 74.

Cut 75.

exerçitio : Eruditi viri. f. Thome Murner Argentini ordinis minorum : theologiæ doctoris eximii.

The fool teaching the ass Latin (cut 76) is taken from Dr. Thomas Murner's *Narrenbeschweerung* (Strassburg, 1518).   The schoolboy will tell us that the artist has attempted to point the satire by putting bad Latin on the horn-book, *Asinus* being masculine and *Stulta* feminine. Dr. Thomas Murner, a celebrated German satirical writer, was born at Strassburg 1475, and died probably at Heidelberg about 1536.   He was invited to England by Henry VIII., and came over here in 1523.

In his *French-English Dictionary* (1611) Cotgrave gives "*Horn-book —tablette, carte,* and *La Croix de par Dieu,*—the Christ's-cross-row, or, the

153

History of the Horn-Book

horn-book wherein a child learns it," and under *carte*, "a child's horn-book or abece." Abel Boyer, a native of Castres in Upper Languedoc, who,

Cut 76.

when he came to this country, was appointed French teacher to Queen Anne's little son, the Duke of Gloucester, defines in his *Dictionnaire Royal Français et Anglais* (1702): "A Horn-book, un Abécé pour un enfant qui apprend à lire."

Littré says : "Croix de par Dieu, Croix de par Jésus," alphabet for teaching children to read, thus called because the title is decorated with a cross known as the Croix de par Dieu—that is to say, Cross made in the name of God. "He is a man who knows medicine thoroughly, as I know my Croix de par Dieu" (Mol. *Pourc.* Act I. sc. 7). "That century (that of Louis XIV.) is pre-eminent to yours in everything, from astronomy to the Croix de par Dieu" (Paul Louis Courier, *Lettres*, ii. 210).

An old primer, *La Croix* ✠ *Depardiev*, with the Paternoster, Ave, Creed, etc., is described in the privately-printed *Bibliothèque Rothschild* (1884). The annotator tells us that the custom of preceding the alphabet with a cross has been continued to his own time, and that in some families children are still taught to read : ✠ (Croix de Dieu) A B C D, etc. The old Croix de par Dieu was also a catechism. When Molière, he continues, in *M. de Pourceaugnac* (Act I. sc. 7) makes the apothecary say, "He is a man who knows medicine thoroughly, as I know my Croix de par Dieu," it is meant "as I know my alphabet and catechism."

Larousse gives the same definition and quotation, but also adds another from La Fontaine :—

> . . . Eh, monsieur, can I read ?
> I've never learnt more than my Croix de par Dieu.

And as a by-meaning he says : "First rudiments of any art or science : in everything there is the Croix de par Dieu."

In Willis's *Current Notes* for October 1855 it is stated that in a

History of the Horn-Book

painting by Crespi, "known as the *Schoolmistress*, the matron has the horn-book placed before the child resting on her knee, and with her finger points to the letter she requires to be named." Crespi's picture, containing numerous figures, is in the Louvre, and so far as the schoolmistress pointing to the letter she requires to be named, is correctly described, but what the child is looking at is not a horn-book, neither is it so depicted in the large engraving by Lavalé, or the smaller one by Dambrun. It is simply a sheet of paper with the alphabet thereon.

A literary Parisian correspondent set my mouth a-watering by writing that he had seen in the *Bibliothèque Nationale* a magnificently-illuminated manuscript, in the borders of which an ape holding a horn-book is many times depicted. I was bound to get at that ape, and after a long and weary correspondence he and other members of his tricky tribe were unearthed under pressmark—"B B 8°. 50,—Pontificalis Liber incipit, etc., Pontifical de Guillaume Durand : Arranged for the Church of Bourges." The illuminations of this grand fourteenth-century manuscript are caricatures in which personages are represented by animals, especially apes, some of which carry books in their arms. But, alas ! they are ordinary volumes and ne'er a horn-book amongst them.

The horn-book shown in cut 77 forms part of a picture painted by the French artist Jean Raoux (born 1677, died 1734), entitled " L'Enfance," belonging to a set of the " Four Ages." The composition is one of children engaged in different sports, while the horn-book lies neglected on the floor.

Cut 77.

Giuseppe Baretti, who, while sojourning in this country, taught Italian, numbering among his pupils the family of Mr. Thrale, the brewer, to whom he was introduced by Dr. Johnson, published his *Dictionary of the English and Italian Languages* in Venice in 1795. Therein he gives : " A Horn-book, s. un abbici, un libretto pei ragazzi, in cui è l'alfabeto."

There is a small woodcut, copied in illustration 78, in a glass case in the corridor near to the Arts Library of the South Kensington Museum, described as taken from a Florentine school-book, to which the date of about 1490 is assigned. The label says that it shows " boys using horn-

155

History of the Horn-Book

books." The pedagogue and the pupils on his right and left, who seem well advanced in physique and years, are using ordinary books. The monitor in the foreground on the left seems to be catechising the younger boy who faces him, and who has evidently been learning from an alphabet tablet or horn-book, another being on the floor. This cut has evidently been removed from a copy of the *Epigrammata* of Joh. Bap. Cantalycius,

Cut 78.

printed at Venice in 1493, or from the *De Structura Compositionis* of Ferrettus, printed two years later at Forli, in both of which it occurs.

Cut 79, *Grammatica* (with a reference in the lettering to Hermippus, the Greek grammarian), in which the alphabet, minus the letters J, U, and W, is boldly figured on a horn-book tablet, is a reduction from the first of a series of seven prints emblematical of the Liberal Arts engraved by an Italian artist, whose style bears some affinity to that of Giulio Bonasone, and of whom nothing is known except that he signed some of his plates with the letter B. The illustration 80 is reduced from one of a set of seven prints by Beham (see p. 9).

The five cuts (81, 82, 83, 84, and 85) are reductions from caricatures

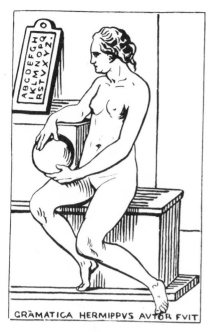

GRĀMATICA HERMIPPVS AVTOR FVIT

Cut 79.

Cut 80.

Cut 81.

BENCHE RAGAZZO IO SON VO FAR IL MASTRO

Cut 82.

Cut 83.

Cut 84.

Cut 85.

History of the Horn-Book

by an Italian painter and engraver, Giuseppe Maria Mitelli or Metalli (born 1634, died 1718). Some of them can hardly be deemed caricatures at all, but where the boy elects to play the schoolmaster the humour is sufficiently pronounced.

An unhandled alphabet tablet or horn-book forms part of a picture

Cut 86.

by Correggio. The subject is a child reciting his letters (86). When Schidone's (Bartolommeo Schidone (Schedone), 1560-1616) picture, " Le premier des Devoirs " (*vide* cut 87, reduced), was stippled in this country by Robert Cooper in 1816, it was re-christened " The Horn-book," and impressions from the copperplate formed part of the prizes in Tomkins's *Lottery of Pictures*. The subject, in which figures the Italian horn-book of the sixteenth and seventeenth centuries, was also engraved by Robert

159

Strange in an oval in reverse, and later was mezzotinted on a smaller scale (cut 88 is quarter size), under the title of " A Girl at School," by D. Allan,

Cut 87.

who, as a comparison will show, took considerable liberties, more especially in the treatment of the horn-book.

Hone, and also Kenneth Mackenzie, into whose hands Hone's notes

History of the Horn-Book

Cut 88.

fell, believed in the existence of a print representing the Virgin teaching the Infant Jesus from a horn-book. In *Notes and Queries*, Mackenzie inquired for it without avail. The Bridgewater Gallery has a picture by Schidone of the Virgin teaching Christ to read. The book, however, is an ordinary volume and not a horn-book, and it is just possible that here arose the confusion. The subject has of course been treated over and over again, but so far as I can find the book is always an ordinary volume.

A picture by Leonardo da Vinci, formerly owned by Mr. Beckford, was long known as " The Boy with a Horn-Book." The horn-book is a *tabella* held open by the child, and when the picture came to be catalogued in the Hamilton sale at Christie's, the title was altered to " A Laughing Boy."

The horn-book is introduced into one of twelve undated copperplate engravings by J. Clark, "humbly inscribed to Rich the Actor, Harlequin-General of Great Britain," forming a series entitled " The Characters of the Italian Stage," representing the birth, bringing up, and education of young Harlequin, published early in the last century by Robert Wilkinson, 58 Cornhill. Amongst the characters introduced are Harlequin, Pierrot, Punch, Columbine, Almanzor, and Mezzetin. In the twelfth plate, partly figured in cut 89, Harlequin is being taught from a horn-book. The following lines are printed at foot :—

Harlequin.	*Doctor.*
Come Sirrah ! on your letters look	There's a good Boy that's very brave
'Tis time you now should learn your book	What a Fine Pupil I shall have
Come, what's that Letter ? Can't you tell ?	Why if my Scholar thus goes on
That's a good Boy—'tis very well.	He will surpass his Father soon.

161

History of the Horn-Book

The Chief Librarian, Library of the University, Christiania, writes:
"Neither the Library nor the Museum of Antiquities is in the possession
of any examples of horn-books, neither can anything of the kind be heard
of as having existed in Norway." An English-Swedish Dictionary,

Cut 89.

printed by Hay and Stenbro, near Nyköping, in Sweden, 1757, gives: "A
horn-book, a b c bok."

Dr. Hans Hildebrand, of the Royal Historical Museum, Stockholm,
writes: "But what do you say to a horn-book, not a book, nor made of
horn, but really a horn-book of gold from Anglo-Saxon times but of
Swedish origin? I have in the Royal Historical Museum a golden bractea[1]
from that time with the whole Runic alphabet." I should say it is distinctly covetable and interesting, but hardly a horn-book.

[1] Thin plate of metal.

162

INDUSTRY.   *Francis D. Bedford.*

History of the Horn-Book

Professor Axel Erdmann, who doubtless refers to the horn-book *covered with horn*, writes from Upsala : " In regard to the use of horn-books in Sweden, all the authorities amongst whom I have enquired unite in denying the existence in our country of such abecedaria—at least if they have existed there is no single example left, nor can any reference be found to them either in literature or tradition."

Mr. C. M. Carlander of Stockholm, on the contrary, must mean the hornless alphabetical tablet when he says that the horn-book was at no time much used in Sweden, and that it has now entirely disappeared. Swedish reading-boards, which, says Mr. Carlander, have sometimes been confused with the horn-book, consist of wooden stands for supporting books, and on them are engraved not the alphabet but short sentences of a religious nature. The example from which he sends a rubbing measures fourteen inches in width and seven in height, and on it is engraved in Roman letters and repeated in Runic characters : " Salige ere de som höre Guds Ord og bevare det " (" Blessed are those who are hearing the word of God and keep it "). The lettering is interspersed with fantastical devices in which the cross in various forms predominates. The initials of the engraver, E. N. S., and the date 1782, are engraved at foot.

In the vicinity of *Nedra Ullerud's* Church in Wermland (a northern province of Sweden) there is a stone with a Runic alphabet, said to have been used by early Christian teachers for instructing the people. In the churchyard of Fohle, a parish in Gotland, is a tombstone on which is engraved an A B C brade (ballbret) and a birch rod. The church is said to have been built in 1096. Mr. Carlander tells me that gravestones with Runic alphabets—which he suggests might well be called Rune horn-books—are found in many different places in Sweden.

There is mention of a Kurdish horn-book amongst some duplicates from the Bodleian, sold at Sotheby's in May 1862. Lot 1081 is catalogued : " *Oratio Dominica XL Linguis expressa*, edidit H. Megiserus, *Francof.* 1593—Kurdish horn-book, presented to Mr. Wanley by H. W. Ludolf, *very rare*. Two tracts." As the two realised but a couple of shillings, both these tracts, the Lord's Prayer in Forty Languages and the child's book, must have been looked upon as unimportant. A similar A B C—it could not have been a horn-book—should be in the Bodleian Library, but search has failed to discover it.

165

History of the Horn-Book

Cut 90.

In the Bodleian Library is a bordered Hebrew alphabet, probably printed in Italy, which Dr. Neubauer puts as sixteenth century, evidently intended for teaching children their letters. It is a little imperfect at the bottom, or it would measure nine by eleven inches. It is probable that in use this alphabet would be mounted on a wooden tablet in horn-book fashion.

An early Mexican horn-book (reduced to quarter size in cut 90), painted on skin and mounted on a wooden base, is in the collection of Mr. George A. Plimpton of New York. The mystical representation of the Sacred Infant was originally in gold, some of which still remains. The cross and alphabet are in red, and the decorative edge is of a dirty yellow.

Mr. John H. Bohn, much of whose ripe experience has been gained as principal cataloguer for Messrs. Sotheby, Wilkinson, and Hodge, has a note of a

166

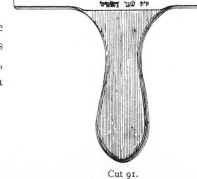

Cut 91.

History of the Horn-Book

horn-book he has seen which was printed in the Finnish dialect at Stockholm in 1744, and of a Polish one printed in 1754.

While it is not a horn-book which is represented, it may perhaps be permissible to note here that Mr. George Potter has in his collection a most interesting print engraved in line somewhat in Hogarth's style, entitled " Les Acaforth, ou les sept tours autour du cercueil," representing the old burial service of the Spanish and Portuguese Jews. The mourners, carrying horn-book-shaped wooden tablets (an example of one of these tablets is reproduced quarter size in cut 91), on which are the responses printed in Hebrew and English, walk in procession, making the seven circuits round the coffin and responding in monotone to the chanting of the rabbi. The officiating minister recites the seven lamentations, the last words of each being given by those present. On holidays and in the burial of females, the Circuits are not made, the 16th Psalm being sung in Hebrew instead.

" Tabléta—a little table or planke, a horne-booke such as children learne their A B C in," is from Percivale's (or Percyvall) *Spanish and English Dictionarie*, 1599. The " horn-book " would be an alphabetical horn-book without horn.

CHAPTER XIII

Miscellaneous horn-books—A horn-book of boxwood with the letters burnt in—A bone handle—A horn-book from an engraved plate of pewter—The remains of a horn-book—A beautifully-decorated back of a horn-book—An interesting nondescript.

HE horn-book shown in cut 92 (exact size) is a veritable curiosity. It is of boxwood, three-sixteenths of an inch thick, and the back is plain except that the name of its maker, Joseph Howell, is repeated. The wording, burnt in letter by letter, and the one ornamental device—probably a merchant's mark—repeated fourteen times, are from steel letters used for stamping metal. The side rules and dividing lines used as a guide for the lettering are much lighter in tint and appear to have been marked with an unheated metal bodkin. This horn-book is probably the handiwork of an ironworker's apprentice who has been thoughtful enough (for which we thank him) to put in the date. It was formerly in the collection of the Rev. Thomas Welton, LL.B., of Olney, Bucks ; the Rev. Edward S. Wilson of Winterton Vicarage, Doncaster, is now the happy owner.

Information about the interesting but somewhat meaningless cut (93) is unfortunately very meagre. It represents, full size, the bone handle

History of the Horn-Book

of a horn-book in the collection of Mr. H. Syer Cuming, F.S.A., who is
of opinion that it belongs to the early years of the seventeenth century.
This handle, with others, was dug up in Steel Yard, Upper Thames Street,

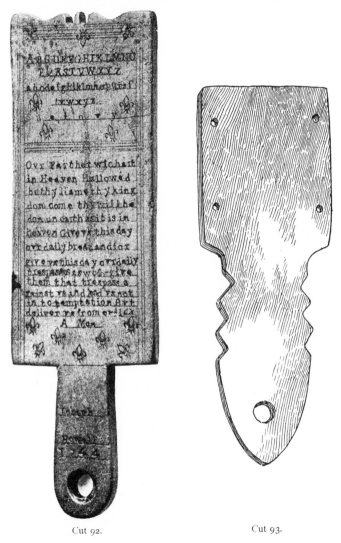

Cut 92. Cut 93.

in April 1865, together with the remains of several more or less perfect
horn-books, one of which still had the metal rim securing the horn to the
wooden base. The four punctures are nail-holes by which the handle was

169

secured to the base. Specimens of these excessively rare horn-books with bone handles are said to have found their way to the Guildhall Museum,

Cut 94.

but search has failed to bring them to light. There is reason to suppose that they have been stolen.

A very interesting horn-book, indeed, shown full size in cut 94, is from an engraved plate, probably pewter. Though titled *The British*

170

History of the Horn-Book

Battledore, it is not the less a horn-book because surrounded with a border of lettered cuts. It is evident that it has been made up from an earlier horn-book—note the bird initial O in "Our Father," further alluded to on p. 321. The date is approximately the third quarter of the last century. The owner of this scarce relic is the Rev. Christopher Wordsworth of Tyneham Rectory, Wareham, Dorset.

Mr. Burton, a Newcastle-on-Tyne antiquary, owns the remains of a horn-book found in pulling down an old house in his native city. It is a badly split, handleless oaken base, $2\frac{3}{4}$ by $3\frac{7}{8}$, on which everything except the tack holes has disappeared. If *they* go, there cannot be much horn-book left. Found in the same place, and belonging to the same owner, is the leather-covered decorated base of a horn-book, figured in cut 95. The front has been stripped and nothing is left but the bare oak. The conventionally treated, but very beautiful, design stamped on the leather springs from the centre at the foot in two trailing branches flowing in graceful curves over

Cut 95.

the panel, the rose, the thistle, and the acorn forming the centres of the convoluted stems, the panel being marked in "Vandyke" fashion on the outer line. There is in the general arrangement, and also in

171

History of the Horn-Book

certain portions of the foliated ornament, such as the pods of the acorn and the thistle, a treatment reminding one somewhat of Byzantine panel decoration. Both these horn-books were probably black letter.

A nondescript between the horn-book and battledore is *A new invented*

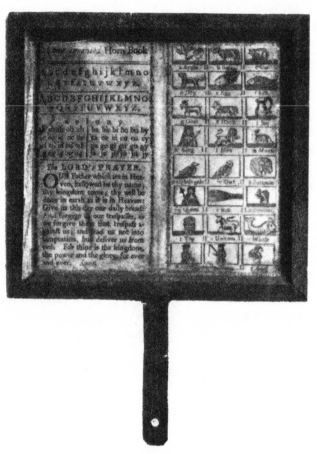

Cut 96.

Horn-Book, the property of the late Talbot Baines Reed, shown reduced to half the length and width in cut 96. The base is oak, and the printed sheet is protected with horn, the horn being framed under the rabbet. There were originally four brass triangular corner-pieces to hold the frame together, but one is missing. The name of the maker does not appear,

172

History of the Horn-Book

but it is the work of Thomas Saint, a noted Newcastle printer of children's toy-books, broadsides, and ballads, who succeeded John White of Pilgrim Street. The period is about 1775. An unmounted copy of the *New invented Horn-Book* is in the collection of Mr. Robert White of Worksop. Two copies were sold for a guinea each in the Hugo collection dispersed at Sotheby's rooms in 1877. Another copy is in the South Kensington Museum. The cuts are supposed by some to be by Bewick, but the most that can be accorded is that they may have been cut by one of his young apprentices. This horn-book was exhibited by Sir Charles Reed, its then owner, at the Caxton Celebration Exhibition held in 1877.

Cut 97.

A horn-book of some kind, which cannot now be traced, was exhibited at the Annual General Meeting of the Essex Archæological Society at Great Dunmow by a Mr. Thorne on 30th July 1867. The entry in the *Transactions* of the Society says that Mr. Thorne exhibited a horn-book, and said a few words as to its use by children, but of the example shown there is no description whatever.

The cut (97) is a *cliché* from a block which appeared in the *Illustrated London News*, 16th November 1850, with this note: "The specimen before us was lately found amongst the stock of a bookseller in Peterborough, Lincolnshire. It is about double the size here represented in facsimile." If the assertion as to size be correct, this horn-book, which is mentioned by Timbs in his *Things not Generally Known*, would appear to be the only one known of its class.

"A Horn-book, £5," was advertised in the Exchange column of the

History of the Horn-Book

Antiquary, November 1883. On inquiring later, it was found that the advertisement was from some one who called for replies, and who could not be traced.

The son of Mr. Bohn (Messrs. Sotheby's principal cataloguer) says that he once had a horn-book, which cannot now be traced, printed in 1712 "for the Running Stationers."

Mr. William Andrews says, in his *Bygone England*, that about thirty years since a horn-book was put up at Southgate's Auction Rooms, London, and "actually realised nearly twenty pounds." Further information would be welcome.

INCENTIVES TO WORK.   *Marion Thomson.*

Metz del.   Gaugi sculp.

SCHOOL.

Let Children that would fear the Lord   With rev'rence meet their parents word

Hear what their teachers say.   And with delight obey

                                                    Watts.

CHAPTER XIV

HORN-BOOKS are the easiest things in the world to imitate—badly. In the absence of the real thing many persons like to possess a copy. But when, for the sake of advantage, the copyist offers a curious spuriosity or a spurious curiosity, intending that one shall take it for what it is not and thereby be fooled, the ethicist seems justified in going for him and getting even with him if he can. Of spurious horn-books of this class there are very few, or if there are many, pains have been taken to keep them out of my way.

"The only black-letter horn-book," says Halliwell in notes in his folio *Shakespeare*, "that I have yet met with of indubitable authenticity was discovered some years ago in pulling down an old farm-house at Middleton, co. Derby, and it passed immediately into the valuable museum of Thomas Bateman[1] of Youlgrave." It need hardly be said that in thinking the majority of black-letter horn-books spurious Mr. Halliwell is wrong,

[1] See p 33.

History of the Horn-Book

the fact being that at the time of writing a spurious horn-book of any kind is a rarity indeed. What few spuriosities there are, or rather those I have been able to get hold of—and I cannot think that at present there are many more—are described herein. That the spuriosity maker has not been more industrious is accounted for by the difficulty in obtaining horn-books to copy from. The appearance of these pages will remove that difficulty, and a crop of spurious horn-books may be expected.

I have seen but one spurious horn-book of the late standard type, and for it nine pounds was given. Its extraordinarily fresh appearance at once struck me. It looked like a thing of yesterday. The owner says : " I am well assured that my horn-book has been in one family for genera- tions, and that it is a genuine old thing." Although I have pointed out that brass rimming and tell-tale modern tacks are fresh as paint, while the oak backing was probably shaped by an apprentice yet in his teens, he still thinks that he has got hold of something genuine and precious. More than afraid am I that this all too trusting retriever of trifles has been badly beguiled. Some people's geese remain swans to the end of the chapter.

The letter which follows appeared in the *Athenæum* of 6th October 1894 :—

SPURIOUS HORN-BOOKS

The Leadenhall Press.

The horn-book, from which our later ascendants learned their A B C,

is at last receiving attention from the "spuriosity" maker, and collectors must beware. A cleverly fabricated horn-book in the form of a cross, of which a sketch is enclosed, would be likely to deceive all but the elect. The size is about $4\frac{1}{2}$ in. by $2\frac{3}{4}$ in. ; the base is old worm-eaten oak, and the rimming confining the horn is iron, aged by a dip in the corroding hell-broth of the chemist.

How this spuriosity came into existence forms an amusing story, too long to tell here. From the same blunderer emanates another spurious horn-book on a larger scale, and of the

Cut 98.   178

History of the Horn-Book

usual octavo shape, with handle at foot. I shall be glad to hear from those who may have purchased either sort ; and as my illustrated work on the horn-book is nearly finished, I shall also be glad to hear from any readers who may have in their possession examples of genuine horn-books which I have not yet engraved or noted.   ANDREW W. TUER.

The amusing episode connected with this brace of spuriosities—who made them I do not know—will develop itself.

Cut 99, enlarged from that in the *Athenæum* letter, represents, full size, one of these spurious horn-books in the form of a cross, purchased by a lady correspondent for twenty-five or thirty shillings— she forgets which—from a country dealer. Some one or other victimised this worthy, who in turn inno-cently victimised my corre-spondent—at a profit. The horn, shaped to the form of the cross, is unpolished, and shows distinctly a series of fine and freshly-made diagonal lines left by the cutting tool, but there is not the slightest sign of the scratching and dulness caused by wear. The alpha-bet is lithographed on modern paper.

The second of this precious pair, shown quarter size in cut 101, belongs

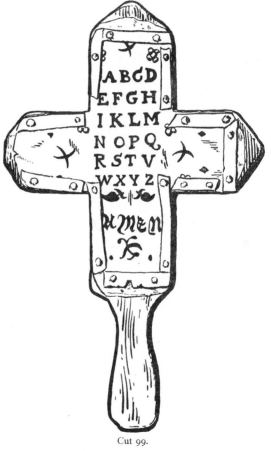

Cut 99.

to a curiosity dealer, Mr. W. H. Hills, of King Street, Ramsgate, who sent it to me on loan, explaining that he used it in connection with

179

History of the Horn-Book

a lecture he was fond of giving on antiquities relating to his own county. Mr. Hills said that he had been looking for a horn-book for many years, and had bought the one sent from some one in the town.

Both these spuriosities are based on illustration 100, which I extensively circulated when inquiring for horn-books to note in this work. The lettering was described to me by an elderly acquaintance, who made a memory sketch of it. The sketch, with a short description, I sent to my old friend Joseph Crawhall, who turned it into an illustration. Mr. Crawhall added the leaf and flower, which, being of a character seen in old primers, I retained. [I have, amongst others, an interesting A B C book in Flemish, oblong in shape, a page to each letter of the alphabet, printed at Antwerp by Jacob Mesens, "Rampart of the Lombards at the Signe of the Golden Bible," in 1645. Letters of the alphabet boldly displayed and cunningly formed, with much flourishing, occupy the pages in sequence, and in addition are other alphabets in various characters, several opening and closing with the leaf ornament referred to. Every page has also what are described on the title-page as "beautiful maxims" in verse.]

Cut 100.

It will be judged how unlikely—nay, impossible—it is that a horn-book with memory-lettering and Mr. Crawhall's ornamentation, *exactly* like the one depicted in cut 100, should ever have existed. The ostentatiously insistent *Amen* at foot is probably all that remained in the old gentleman's memory of the Lord's Prayer. He was quite positive about the alphabet and the cross. The corners of the oaken base may have been rounded as he remembered them, but the brass latten securing the horn would certainly have been in strips placed at right angles.

Both these spurious horn-books, the first in the form of a cross—genuine examples of which I had publicly inquired for and described as of the rarest form—and the second of the usual shape, are more or less slavishly copied from Mr. Crawhall's somewhat fanciful sketch. In Mr. Hills's horn-book an attempt has been made to round the edges of the brass latten, which is fixed with ten brass nails exactly in the positions assigned by the old gentleman in his memory sketch and

180

adhered to by Mr. Crawhall. A sheet of gelatine takes the place of horn. The base is of oak stained dark and rubbed over with sticky varnish. The dimensions, including handle—which as to length is unduly prolonged—are $11\frac{1}{2} \times 5\frac{1}{2}$ inches. When Mr. Hills was told that his treasure was unmistakably spurious, he replied that he had been doubtful about it for some time, but preferred keeping his opinion to himself until the horn-book had passed through the hands of one whom he was pleased to term an expert.

In August 1845 Mr. George Offor presented to the Trustees of the British Museum a horn-book magnificent to look upon. It is shown full size in cut 102. The base is of slightly polished oak, quarter of an inch thick, the edges rounded, and the brass latten, of unusual width and thickness, is secured by forty-four brass nails. The lettering is so obscured by the brownish-tinted horn that by mere inspection one cannot judge positively whether it is printed or

Cut 101.

written. On the back is pasted a label of old paper bearing a faded inscription in a modern and unknown hand :—

181

History of the Horn-Book

" What more could be wished for even by a literary gourmand under the Tudors than to be able to Read and Spell. To repeat that holy charm before which fled all unholy ghosts, goblins, or even the old Gentleman himself to the very bottom of the Red Sea, and to say that immortal prayer which secures Heaven to all who *ex animo* use it, and those mathematical powers by knowing units, from which spring countless myriads."

Dr. Mackenzie describes this horn-book in *Notes and Queries* (No. 69, 22nd February 1851) and asks, " Can any of your correspondents oblige me with the probable date of this *literally* literary treasure, or refer me to any source of information on the subject ? "

In a paper on the horn-book in the *British Bookmaker*, Mr. Frederick Rogers says, " This horn-book is not entirely genuine. Possibly Mr. Offor did not present it as a genuine specimen." Evidence that it was presented as spurious does not exist. The first catalogue entry is as follows :—

" A Horn-Book—The alphabet, syllabarium, Lord's Prayer, etc., written in black letter of the type and orthography employed in the first half of the sixteenth century. Pressmark 828 a 55."

In later years the entry was altered :—

" Horn-book, containing the alphabet, syllabarium, Lord's Prayer, etc. A fabrication in imitation of the black letter in use in the first half of the sixteenth century. London ? 1835 ? 4°. C. 45 a. 2."

A second example, in the library of Warwick Castle, is engraved two-thirds size by Mr. Halliwell-Phillipps—then James Orchard Halliwell—in his *Catalogue of Chap-Books, Garlands, and Popular Histories*, printed for private circulation in 1849. Of it he therein writes : " Horn-books are now so completely out of use that few persons are acquainted with their precise nature. The present one, which appears to be at least as ancient as 1570, is mounted on wood and protected with transparent horn." Under the cut are the words " Printed about 1570." Later, however, Mr. Halliwell appears to have become suspicious, for he pasted on the back of this horn-book a label with the following wording :—" A horn-book formerly used by children for learning their letters and alluded to by Shakespeare. Bought for me at Sotheby's by Bumstead, to whom I gave a commission of twenty guineas for it ; yet I am by no means sure that it is genuine and not an extraordinary forgery. Let experts judge. Old horn-books are exceedingly rare.—J. O. H." A little later still, Mr. Halliwell must

ABCDEFGHIKLMN
OPQRSTUWXYZ.
abcdefghiklmnopqrꝛsſtuvwxyz &c.

✠ a e i o u ✠ a e i o u ✠

ab	eb	ib	ob	ub	ba	be	bi	bo	bu
ac	ec	ic	oc	uc	ca	ce	ci	co	cu
ad	ed	id	od	ud	da	de	di	do	du

In the Name of the Father, and of the
Sonne, and of the holy Ghoſt. Amen.

Our Father which art in heauen,
hallowed bee thy Name.   Thy
Kingdome come. Thy will be
done in earth as it is in heauen. ✠
Giue vs this day our daily bꝛedd.
And foꝛgiue vs our trespaſſes, as
we foꝛgiue them that trespaſſe vs.
And let vs not bee ledd into temp=
tation : but deliuer vs from euill:
Amen. i.ii.iii.iiii.v.vi.vii.viii.ix.x.

Cut 102.

have become convinced that it was spurious, for in his scholarly collation of the early editions of Shakespeare he says : "Black-letter horn-books are exceedingly rare, and the greatest caution must be exercised in receiving any as genuine, several specimens having been fabricated of late years, and two,[1] both of which are believed to be spurious, have found their way into the British Museum." Mr. Halliwell goes on to say that the earliest known horn-book belongs to the seventeenth century, but there can be no doubt whatever that some of the horn-books noted in these pages came into existence in the century preceding.

What would appear to be a similar horn-book was exhibited at Iron-mongers' Hall in May 1861 by the late Rev. T. Hugo. It is stated—a statement to be accepted for what it is worth—to have been found behind the wainscot of an old house in Fenchurch Street in 1858. It is mentioned that the Lord's Prayer, instead of "lead us not," has "let us not be ledd," into temptation.

What immediately follows sounds a little like romancing, but is sober truth. While hunting about for matter bearing on horn-books, it one day struck me to look through my own scrap-books, in which for many years past I have been accustomed to store prints, papers, and odds and ends thought worthy of preservation. I found nothing relating to the horn-book, but in a mixed collection—also of my own gathering—of ex libris and typographical curiosities, I came across a printed horn-book sheet which I had absolutely forgotten ever having possessed. It is in appearance the same as the horn-books belonging to the British Museum and the Earl of Warwick.

There was no doubt whatever as to the means by which my sheet had been produced. It had been lithographed in a blackish-brown ink on paper certainly older than the invention of lithography, or, at any rate, than its practice in this country. There is a bold and well-defined water-mark of a lion rampant, with a seated figure of Liberty surrounded by palisading with gate in centre and legend in Roman capitals *Pro Patria.* Paper with this device, which is symbolical of the independence of Holland, and is sometimes seen on the Dutch stiver, was largely made by the well-known Van Gelder of Amsterdam, whose mills were established in 1782. The arms represented were first used by Count Willem the Third in the

[1] One only.

History of the Horn-Book

fourteenth century. The paper with this water-mark used for my spurious horn-book sheet was probably a blank taken from an old account book.

Much time I spent in trying to find out where my printed sheet came from, and the conclusion was arrived at that it had been purchased some years before at Sotheby's, when a quantity of manuscripts and papers was dispersed belonging to Sir Joseph and Lady Banks. As lithography was practised in this country some time before the death of Sir Joseph and Lady Banks, I was half inclined to lay the counterfeit—no doubt achieved without malicious intent—at the door of one or other of this remarkable couple. There seemed further reason because I purchased at Puttick and Simpson's salerooms on 28th June 1893 (lot 987) a volume containing manuscript notes in the handwriting of Sir Joseph, amongst which were a couple of sheets of foolscap bearing the same water-mark as that in my spurious horn-book sheet. Here seemed enough evidence to hang a man, but when I came to closely examine the water-marks one against the other, I found that, although apparently alike, they were not from the same wires, proving that the papers had been made at different mills and probably at different dates.

I importuned the late Earl of Warwick to allow me to take his horn-book to pieces, and he courteously gave his consent. In order that it should receive no damage, the British Museum authorities permitted me to employ the services of one of their experts, Mr. Robert Ready. In due time the Earl's horn-book was taken apart and the printed sheet damped off. It was found to be absolutely identical with my own, and had been lithographed from the same stone in ink of the same hue, and on the same paper, in which, however, the water-mark is absent. The oak, where covered with the printed sheet and the brass latten, is quite light in tint. The under surface of the brass, and where it has received protection by overlapping, is almost as clean as a new pin. The latten was fixed with what looked like old brass nails, but they proved to be three-quarter inch gimp pins made in modern days by a machine which cuts them in even lengths from a roll of brass wire, the head being automatically formed by a blow from a punch. The nails completely pierced the oak backing and had been nipped off and filed flush on the other side.

I was still not content, for there was the ghost of a chance that the example belonging to the British Museum might be the original from which

A NEGLECTED EDUCATION.

Ambrose Dudley.

History of the Horn-Book

the Earl of Warwick's and my own had been copied. I therefore begged permission, which was granted by the authorities, to have theirs also taken to pieces. This was carefully done by the same expert hand. But the British Museum horn-book turned out to be own brother to the Earl of Warwick's and my own. The triplet of spuriosities ran the gauntlet of smiling criticism from Sir A. W. Franks, Mr. Read, Dr. Garnett, Mr. Fletcher, Mr. Davenport, and other British Museum officials who were interested, not one of whom had a word to say in their defence.

The actual pulling to pieces I did not see, but if they had been new-born babes these horn-books could not have been more tenderly treated. A model of the face or front was prepared by Mr. Ready in some plastic material, into which the nails as they were carefully drawn were stuck upright, and at the conclusion of the examination each one was restored to its original position.

To look a gift horse in the mouth is supposed to argue a lack of wisdom and manners, but one cannot help wondering if the donor had any share in the inception and production of this horn-book ; whether, in fact, he presented it to the nation in a spirit of *diablerie.*

In the second of the only two chapters Dr. Mackenzie wrote of a projected work on the Horn-book (see p. 261), he refers to two of these spuriosities. He states that several copies are in existence, and that one is in the British Museum, and another in the collection of Mr. George Offor. In his paper on the Horn-book, read at the Society of Antiquaries, 7th May 1863, the spurious horn-book, believed by him to be genuine, is described by Dr. Mackenzie as being presented to the British Museum by Mr. Halliwell. Mr. Offor was really the donor. No horn-book was ever presented to the British Museum by Mr. Halliwell. When Dr. Mackenzie was engaged in horn-book researches (see p. 261) he received the following letter from Mr. Offor :—

GROVE STREET, SOUTH HACKNEY, N.E., CORNER OF VICTORIA PARK ROAD,
13th February 1860.

SIR—I have an old battledoor or Horn-book which it will give me pleasure to shew you, if you will make an appointment. Sixty or sixty-five years ago my father dealt in them. They were manufactured in Holland about 6-inch by 4—rough and cheap—they were horn-books, and as far as I can remember were sold at twopence or threepence each—at that time they were much used in small schools, but have mysteriously vanished like pins or pens. They are now very rarely found. You ought to search Nuremburg and the toy factories in Switzerland. Mine appears to be about the reign of Elizabeth the haughty or the meikle wise James. The Lord's Prayer has "Let us not be ledde into temptation."—I am yours truly,   GEORGE OFFOR.

P.S.—Cannot lend.   Hone gives an account of one.

It is a carelessly-written letter, and the horn-book which the writer "cannot lend," although the dimensions are wrong, and the bit from the Lord's Prayer is incorrectly quoted, is evidently the spuriosity.

George Offor, of Grove House, Hackney, was a dabbler in books, an exceedingly clever facsimilist and a very astute person. He sold his library at the rooms of Messrs. Sotheby, Wilkinson, and Hodge on the 27th June 1865. It is known that he possessed some horn-books, but only one appeared in this sale—"Lot 2024, A Horn-Book." On the night of the second day's sale (eleven days in all) a fire broke out at the auctioneers', destroying most of the books. The *débris* was purchased by the late William Stevens, the American bookseller, then in St. Martin's Lane, and was stowed away in bags unopened from 1865 to 1889, but when it came to be overhauled the horn-book was not there, so it must have perished in the fire.

Harking back to the sale, in the second day's was a 32mo copy of Cranmer's version of the *Psalmes with Annotacions* (1557), which was purchased by a Mr. Jackson. In later years it fell into the hands of Mr. Quaritch, who in 1883 sold it to the Bodleian Library for twenty-five shillings, including an impression like unto the spurious horn-book, but containing only the invocation and Lord's Prayer. Where Mr. Quaritch obtained this horn-book and printed sheet cannot now be traced, nor is it known whether they were sold together in the Offor collection. Hoping that the Bodleian might have acquired the original sheet from which the spurious horn-books had been copied, I looked it up, but alas! it proved to be a laid-down and imperfect lithograph exactly like my own—in fact, one of the same impression. My attention was kindly drawn to it by Mr. W. H. Allnutt.

History of the Horn-Book

The counterfeiter must have had a copy of some kind—the opening leaf of a primer or catechism, or even a horn-book itself—which one day may turn up. He would certainly not have omitted the word "against" in the Lord's Prayer, unless such omission occurred in the copy. The two small crosses at right and left are imperfect, but it would not therefore be absolutely safe to conclude that they point to a closely-cropped copy, and that the copyist had not the wit to make them perfect before he commenced his work. At the end of "*The newe testament in Englyshe,* translated after the texte of Master Erasmus : in anno M.D. XI. Prynted by Richard Grafton and Edwarde Whytchurche," is "A Table to fynde the Epistles and Gospels . . . whose begynnynge thou shalte fynde in the book marked with a crosse, ✠, and the end with halfe a crosse, ⊬ ." The use of the half-cross in this manner occurs both earlier and later, and in some examples a part of the missing limb appears.

The absence of water-mark in the British Museum and Warwick Castle examples of this spurious horn-book no doubt formed part of the scheme—that is, impressions on plain or unwatermarked portions of the paper were purposely selected for turning into complete horn-books.

The period aped is one when every man spelt as seemed to him best, but although the spelling of what some of our forebears might consider difficult words was governed by no hard-and-fast rules, there was some attempt at uniformity in simple words. Amongst other noticeable eccentricities one falls foul of "And let us not bee ledd into temptation "; " bee " and " ledd " against " temptation" point to the spuriosity maker, and a tinker at that ; whatever was the original form, it would seem to have been "improved." Out of twenty-six black-letter primers of the sixteenth century, consulted at the British Museum, there are but three variations from the usual text of the sixth petition of the Lord's Prayer— " And lead us not into temptation." One printed in 1539 (C. 35 b. 13) : *The Primer in English,* moste necessary for the educacyon of chyldren, extracted out of the Manuall of prayer, or Primer in English and late set forth by The last byshop of Rochester, at the comaundement of the ryght honorable Lord Thomas Crñwell, lord privie seale, Vice-regent to the Kynges hyghnes. Imprynted in Flete Strete by Jhon Waylande, at the sign of the blew garlande and be to sell in Pawles Church yarde, by Andrew Hester at the Whyt horse and also by Mychell Lobley at the

History of the Horn-Book

sygne of saynte Mychell. Cum privilegio ad imprimendum solum. This primer gives the text as " And let us not be led into temptation." The next in point of date (C. 35 b. 14): *The prymer both in Englyshe and Latin.* Anno M.D. XL. Printed in the late the graye freers by Richard grafton and Edward Whytchurche. Marke XI.—Whatsoever ye desyre in your prayer beleve ye shall receyve it and ye shall haue it. Cum privilegio ad imprimendum solum. Here we have : " And let us not be led into temptation."

Another variant is in (C. 25 c. 22) *The Primer in Englyshe and latin,* set forth by the Kynges maiestie and his Clergie to be taught, learned and read : and none other to be used through all his dominions. 1546. This copy gives, " And let us not bee led into temptacion." In the Bodleian Library : *The Prymer set forth by the Kinges highness, and his Cleargye to be taught unto chyldren throughout his dominions, all other set apart.* (1549, Gough Missal 44), The Lord's Prayer has, "And let us not be led into temptacoon." In *The Manuall of Prayer, or the Prymer in Englyshe* (Gough Missal 90), 1539, we get " And let us not be led into temptacion," and in *The Primer set forth by the kinges Maiestie etc.,* 1545 (Douce B. B. 123), " And let us not be led into temptation."

In July 1887 the Rev. Jerome J. Mercier had copies made of the interesting horn-book illustrated in cut 138 for sale at a bazaar, where they excited much curiosity and quickly changed hands at, it is to be hoped, bazaar prices. The copies are by no means facsimiles, and it was rough on the original that, for fixing the horn and printed sheet to the wood, the man who made them for Mr. Mercier used strips of tin instead of brass. Mr. Mercier attached to the handle of this quaint conceit a card bearing Shenstone's lines on the horn-book from *The Schoolmistress.*

Mr. F. Hockliffe, a Bedford bookseller of antiquarian tastes, has made some fairly good copies of an uncovered horn-book of the late standard type, one of which he has been good enough to send me. They would not deceive an expert, but they are not meant to deceive.

CHAPTER XV

EFERENCES in literature to the horn-book are fairly numerous, and if careful search were made the number of those given here might no doubt be largely increased.

In Shakespeare's *Love's Labour's Lost*, Act IV. sc. 1, p. 136, edition 1623, the youthful Moth, speaking of Holofernes, says—

> Yes, yes, he teaches boys the Horne-booke :
> What is Ab speld backward with the horn on
> its head.

In *Puritan Discipline Tracts*—Pappe with a Hatchet, being a reply to Martin Marprelate, 1589, reprinted, etc., London, 1844—is the following passage : —"Tuch, Ile bring in *Pueriles* and *Stans puer ad mensam*, for such vnmannerlie knaves as Martin, must bee set againe to their A B C and learne to spell Our Father in a Horne Booke."

In the *Collection of Old English Plays*, edited by A. H. Bullen in 1882, the horn-book is mentioned in " The Maydes Metamorphosis " (1600), Act III. sc. 1 :—" Now you go crying up and downe after your wench like a boy that had lost his *horne-book*."

191

History of the Horn-Book

Ben Jonson, in his *Volpone*, 1605, has—

Here
The letters may be read, through the horn,
That make the story perfect.—Act IV. sc. 2.

Thomas Dekker makes mention of the horn-book in a scarce tract, printed in 1607, entitled *A Knight's Conjuring: Done in Earnest:* "He resolved therefore to answere his humble orator; but being himselfe not brought up to learning (for the divell can neither write nor reade) yet he has been to all the vniversities in Christendom, and thrown damnable heresies (like bones for dogges to gnaw upon) amongst the doctors themselves; but hauing no skill but in his owne Horne-booke, it troubled his mind where he should get a pen-man fit for his tooth to scribbe for him."

In one of Nicholas Breton's rarest works (of which there is no copy in the British Museum) entitled *Cornucopiæ; Pasquil's Night Cap, Or an Antidot for the Headache. London, printed for Thomas Thorp*, 1612, we find—

Matters of Chiefe importance are in hast,
And for more speed dispatched by the horne,
Great light a Lanthorne, made of horne, doth cast,
Which with a candle in darke night is borne.
When little children first are brought to schoole
A Horne-booke is a necessarie toole.

Nicholas Breton also mentions the horn-book in his *Melancholike Humours in Verses of Diverse Natures* (there is no copy in the British Museum—the quotation is from a reprint with modernised text), (London, printed by Richarde Bradocke, 1600), wherein he sings of Love as "A Strange A B C"—

To learn the baby's A B C.
Is fit for children, not for me.
I know the letters all so well,
I need not learn the way to spell;
And for the Cross, before the row,
I learn'd it all too long ago.

Then let them go to school that list,
To hang the lip at—*Had I wist:*
I never lov'd a book of horn,
Nor leaves that have their letters worn;
Nor with a fescue to direct me,
Where every puny shall correct me.

History of the Horn-Book

"For his knowledge, he is merely a Horne-book," is from one of the characters, "A Button-maker of Amsterdame," described in "Wittie Descriptions of the properties of sundrie Persons," in *New and choife Characters of Severall Authors, Together with exquifite and vnmatched Poeme, The Wife, Written by Syr Thomas Ouerburie, London : Printed by Thomas Creefe, for Lawrence Lifle at the Tyger's head in Paul's Churchyard,* 1615 (see p. 73).

The following passage is taken from a rare tract in the Bodleian Library :—" Now for my learning, I hold it better to fpell and put together, than to fpoile and put afunder : but there are fome that in their childhood are fo long in their horne booke, that doe what they can, they will fmell of the Baby till they cannot fee to read " (*The Court and Country or a Brief difcourfe between the Courtier and Country-man : of the Manner, Nature and Condition of their lives, etc., written by N. B.*[1] *Gent. London. Printed by G. Eld for John Wright and are to be fold at his fhoppe at the Signe of the Bible without Newgate,* 1618).

"And may with fome impulfion no doubt be brought to paffe the A B C of war, and come unto the horne-booke."—*Thierry and Theodoret,* 1621.

Hornbye's *Horne-Booke,* a poem by William Hornbye, "Gent." (1622), containing numerous allusions to the horn-book, is quoted from on p. 213 *et seq.*

Peacham[2] has something to say about the horn-book in *The Worth of a Peny,* an amusing work which enjoyed great popularity.

"A Peny, beftowed in charity upon a poor body, fhall not want an heavenly reward. For a peny you may in the Low countries, in any market, buy eight feverall commodities, as nuts, vinegar, grapes, a little cake, onions, oatmeal and the like. A peny beftowed in a fmall quantity of Anifeed, *Aqua Vitae,* or the like ftrong water, may fave one's life in a fainting or fwound. For a peny you may hear a moft eloquent Oration upon our Englifh Kings and Queens, if keeping your hands off, you will ferioufly liften to David Owen who keeps the Monuments in Weft-minfter. Some for want of a peny have been conftrained to go from

---

[1] Nicholas Breton.

[2] *The Worth of a Peny: or, A Caution to keep Money.* With the causes of the scarcity and misery of the want thereof, in these hard and merciless times, etc. By Henry Peacham, Master of Arts, etc. London : S. Griffin, 1664.

O

History of the Horn-Book

Weſtminſter about by *London* Bridge to Lambeth, and truly ſaid *Defeſſi sumus ambulando.* You may have in Cheapſide your peny tripled in the ſame kind, for you ſhall have Peny-Geaſſe, Peny-Wort and Peny-royal. For a peny you may ſee any monſter, jack-a-napes, or thoſe roaring boyes, the Lyons. For a peny you may have all the newes in *England* and other Countries ; of Murders, Flouds, Witches, Fires, Tempeſts and what not in the weekly Newes-books. For a peny you may have your horſe rubbed and walked after a long journy, and being at graſſe, there are ſome that will breath him for nothing. For a peny an Hoſteſs, or an Hoſtler, may buy ſo much chalk, as will ſcore up thirty or forty pounds, but how to come by their mony that let them look to. For a peny you ſhall ſee what will happen a year hence (which the Devill himſelf cannot do) in ſome Almanack, or other rude Country. For a peny you might have been advanced to that height, that you ſhall be above the beſt in the City, yea the Lord Maior himſelf ; that is, to the top of Paul's. For a peny, a miſerable and covetous wretch, that never did or never will beſtow peny on a Doctor or Apothecary for their phyſick or advice, may provide a remedy for all diſeaſes, viz. a Halter. For a peny you may buy a diſh of Coffee to quicken your ſtomach and refreſh your Spirits. For a peny you may buy the hardeſt book in the world, and which at ſome time or other hath poſed the greateſt Clerks in the Land, viz. an Hornbook ; the making up of which Book imployeth above thirty trades. For a peny a Chamber-maid may buy as much red oaker as will ſerve ſeven years for the painting of her cheeks. For a peny the Monarch in a Free School may provide himſelf with as many Arms as will keep all his Rebellious ſubjects in awe. For a peny you may walke within one of the faireſt Gardens in the City, and have a Noſegay, or two, made you of what ſweet flowers you pleaſe, to ſatiſſie the ſenſe of ſmelling. For a peny you may buy as much wood of that tree which is green all the year, and beareth red berries, as will cure any ſhrew's tongue, if it be too long for her mouth, viz. A holly wand."

Peacham does not tell us what are the thirty trades employed in the making of a horn-book, but it is not difficult to put thirty together :—

Timber merchant.	Ink-ball maker.
Carpenter.	Tanner.
Horn merchant.	Skin merchant.

A B C MYSTERIES.   *Morley Fletcher.*

History of the Horn-Book

Horner.	Leather dresser.
Metal merchant.	Leather dyer.
Metal beater.	Paper-maker.
Smelter.	Paper-stainer.
Ironmaster.	Paper-embosser.
Tack-maker.	Colour-maker.
Punch-cutter.	Glue-maker.
Type-founder.	Stamp designer.
Type-setter.	Stamp engraver.
Press-maker.	Stamper.
Press-puller.	Gold-leaf maker.
Ink-maker.	Silver-foil maker.

Henry Peacham was born at North Mimms, Hertfordshire, and educated at Trinity College, Cambridge. He went to Italy, where he studied music and painting, and he also knew something of engraving and surveying. He died about 1640. Peacham published many books on most varied subjects, but the one best known is the *Compleat Gentleman*, the second edition of which appeared in 1634.

In a communication from Sir Robert Morey to the Earl of Lauderdale, dated Edinburgh, 14th September 1667 (vide *Lauderdale Papers*, printed for the Camden Society in 1885, vol. ii. No. 39, p. 57), we find :— "Amongst other things hee replyed that it was as easy to be understood as that A signified A, and B, B. So that hee that did not understand it might be put back to his Horn-book."

Says Buscon, one of the characters in *Don Pablo de Sagovia, by Don Francisco de Quevedo, a Spanish Cavalier: London, Printed for Henry Herringman, and are to be sold at his shop at the Blew Anchor in the Lower Walk of the New Exchange*, 1670, when sent to a school where fifteenpence a month was spent on his education and he became King of the Scholars, "they bought for me the first Rudiments of Art, vulgarly called the Horn-Book."

In that exceedingly scarce work, *A Book for Boys and Girls; or Country Rhimes for Children*, by J. B. (John Bunyan), London : printed for N. P., and sold by the Booksellers in London, 1686, the introductory verse closes with the following lines :—

History of the Horn-Book

Thus much for artificial Babes ; and now
To those who are in years but such, I bow
My Pen to teach them what the Letters be,
And how they may improve their A, B, C.
Nor let my pretty Children them despise ;
All needs must there begin, that would be wise
Nor let *them* fall under Discouragement,
Who at their Horn-book stick, and time hath spent
Upon that A, B, C, while others do
Into their Primer, or their Psalter go.
Some Boys with difficulty do begin,
Who i't the end, the Bays, and Lawrel win.—J. B.

Following the versification addressed to the Courteous Reader is an alphabet page (cut 103), in horn-book fashion, titled " An help to Chil-dren to learn to read Eng-lish."

The Benefice, a Comedy, by R. W. (Robert Wild), D.D., Author of *Iter Boreale*. Written in his younger Days : Now made Publick for promoting Innocent Mirth. Licensed and Entered, London : Printed to be sold by *R. Janeway* in Queen's Head Court, in Pater Noster Row, 1689, 4°. p. 30. (*Sir Homily*, an old curate, is asking from Marchurch, the patron of a living, the gift of it) :—

> *Marchurch.*—" In the *Living*? Why, how dare you think of such a thing ? With what Face canst thou ask it ? There's never a Scholar of you all deserves such a Living. (*Aside*) Ay, this Fellow hath been *Curate*, and taught School here this dozen years ; he may have Horn-book'd himself into some Money."

" First begin with the horn-book and then go on to the Primmer." —Wild's *Benefice*, 1689, p. 56.

The Pagan Prince : Or a Comical History of the Heroick Achievements of the Palatine of Eboracum. By the Author of *The Secret History of King Charles II. and King James II.*, Amsterdam (London), 1690. Speaking of the education of the Palatine it says (p. 2) : " Thereupon another Tutor was sought for, more proper for his years ; and, at last they found out an old *Sophister*, whose name was *Tubal Holofernes*, who first taught him his Horn-Book so exactly, that he could say it by heart backward. So that his Tutor seeing him run so prodigiously fast (for he had learnt both this and his Primmer in five

198

years and three months) began to read to him several other Authors of greater moment."

In advice as to what children should read (Æsop's *Fables* or *Reynard the Fox* being recommended), John Locke, in his *Thoughts on Education*, published in 1691, says : "What other books there are in

An help to Chil-dren to learn to read Eng-lifh.

In or-der to the at-tain-ing of which, they muft firft be taught the Let-ters, which be thefe that fol low

𝕬 𝕭 𝕮 𝕯 𝕰 𝕱 𝕲 𝕳 𝕴 𝕶 𝕷 𝕸 𝕹 𝕺 𝕻 𝕼 𝕽 𝕾 𝕿 𝖀 𝖁 𝖂.

a b c d e f g h i k l m n o p q r ſ t u w x y z.
A B C D E F G H I K L M N O P Q R S T V W
X Y Z.

a b c d e f g h i k l m n o p q r ſ t v u w x y z,
A B C D E F G H I K L M N O P Q R S T V W
X Y Z

a b c d e f g h i k l m n o p q r ſ t v u w x y z
The Vowels are thefe, a, e, i, o, u.

As there are vow-els, fo are there Con-fo-nants, and they are thefe.

b c d f g h k l m n p q r ſ t v w x y z.
There are alſo dou-ble Let-ters, and they are thefe.

ct ff fi ffi fl fi ffi ſt ſh.

Af-ter thefe are known, then fet your Child to fpel-ling, Thus T-o, to. T-h-e, the, O-r, or, I f, if L-n, in, M e, me,y-o-u, you ; f-i-n-d, find, S-i-n,fin : In C-h-ri-ſ-t,Chriſt,i-s,is,R-i-g h-t-e-o u-f- n-e-fs, Righ-te-ouf-nefs.

And ob-ferve that e-ve-ry word or fyl-la-ble (tho ne-ver fo fmall) muſt have one vow el or more right-ly pla ced in it.

For inftances, Thefe are no words nor Syl-la-bles, be-caufe they have no vow-els in them, name-ly, fl, gld, ftrnght, fpll, drll,fll.

Words made of two Letters are thefe, and fuch-like,If, it,is, fo, do, we, fee, he, is, in, my.

Words con-fift-ing of three Letters,
But; for, her, fhe, did, doe, all, his, way, you, may, fay, nay.

Cut 103.

English of the kind above-mentioned fit to engage the liking of children and tempt them to read, I do not know, but am apt to think, that children, being generally delivered over to the method of schools, where the fear of the rod is to inforce, and not any pleasure of the employment to invite them to learn, this sort of useful books, amongst the number of silly ones that are of all sorts, yet have had the fate to be neglected ;

History of the Horn-Book

and nothing that I know has been considered, of this kind, out of the ordinary road of the horn-book, primer, psalter, Testament and Bible."

Locke mentions Sir Hugh Plat's stratagem (cut 26) for teaching children the A B C.

Love's Last Shift, or the Fool in Fashion. A Comedy. As it is acted at the Theatre Royal by His Majesty's Servants. Written by C. Cibber, London : Printed for *H. Rhodes in Fleet Street ; R. Parker* at the *Royal Exchange*, and *S. Briscoe*, the Corner Shop of *Charles Street, Covent Garden*, 1696, p. 83, Act V. sc. 1. Sir William Wiseword is about to execute a Deed :—

> *Sir W.*—" Come, come, let's see, Man ! What's this ! Odd ! this Law is a plaguy troublesome thing ; for, now a days, it won't let a Man give away his own, without repeating the Particulars 500 times over : When in former times, a Man might have held his Title to Twenty Thousand pound a year, in compass of an Horn book."

The passage which follows occurs in a letter from Mrs. Susannah Wesley to her son, 24th July 1732, telling him how she brought up her family : " One day was allowed the child wherein to learn its letters ; and each of them did in that time know all its letters, great and small, except Molly and Nancy, who were a day and a half before they knew them perfectly, for which I thought them very dull, but since I have observed how long many children are learning the horn-book I have changed my opinion."—*The Works of the Rev. John Wesley, etc.* London, 1872, vol. i. p. 390.

William Shenstone, who learned his letters at a dame's school in Halesowen in Shropshire, refers to the horn-book in *The Schoolmistress*, that poem in imitation of Spenser being written at College in 1736 :—

> Lo ! now with State she utters the Command,
> Eftsoons the Urchins to their Tasks repair :
> Their Books of Stature small they take in Hand,
> Which with pellucid horn secured are,
> To save from Finger wet the Letters fair :
> The Work so quaint that on their Backs is seen,
> St. George's high Achievements does declare,
> On which thilk Wight that has y-gazing been,
> Kens the forth-coming Rod, unpleasing Sight I ween.

History of the Horn-Book

The following passage occurs in a letter from Mrs. Carter to Miss Talbot, dated Deal, 16th August 1741 :—" I am afraid this letter has begun under the influence of some very dull planet, for it has cost me at least half an hour's laborious study to compose the introduction. I believe too one cause of the difficulty may be, that I have almost forgot my alphabet, and if I keep sinking from one abyss of ignorance to another, with a velocity proportionable to what I have lately done, I must soon turn back again to the first foundation of all human learning, a horn-book."—*A Series of letters between Mrs. Elizabeth Carter and Miss Catherine Talbot from the year* 1741 *to* 1770, *etc., Lond.* 1809.

In a letter signed " Angell " in *The British Magazine, or Monthly Repository for Gentlemen and Ladies,* p. 131, vol. iv. Lond. 1763, the writer begins : " I keep a School for little children, and being ambitious to commence author, I was composing a new horn-book, etc." " Composmg a new horn-book " is vague. It might mean literally what it says ; it might mean a new battledore, or it might mean a new book on an unknown subject but dealt with in an easy or A B C fashion.

In De Foe's *Family Instructor* (Dialogue 3, Part II. vol. ii.), 12°, p. 272, rev. edit. 1766, Margaret tells a friend of the family in which she is an exemplary servant : " I have taught my little master to know his letters and spell a little, as well as I could, out of my Bible ; for they have given him neither horn-book nor primmer."

In his *Tirocinium, or a Review of Schools* (1784), the poet Cowper mentions a horn-book :—

In early days the conscience has in most
A quickness, which in later life is lost :
Preserved from guilt by salutary fears,
Or guilty, soon relenting into tears.
Too careless often, as our years proceed,
What friends we sort with, or what books we read,
Our parents yet exert a prudent care
To feed our minds with proper fare ;
And wisely store the nursery by degrees
With wholesome learning, yet acquired with ease.
Neatly secured from being soil'd or torn,
Beneath a pane of thin translucent horn,

History of the Horn-Book

A book (to please us at a tender age
'Tis call'd a book, though but a single page)
Presents the prayer the Saviour deign'd to teach,
Which children use, and parsons—when they preach.

We get an allusion in Parliament to the horn-book in *Sheridaniana,
or Anecdotes of the Life of Richard Brinsley Sheridan : his table talk and
bon mots.* Lond. 1826, pp. 89, 90 : "When the India Bill of Mr. Pitt
was brought up from the Committee, and read on the 26th of July 1785,
Mr. Sheridan observed that twenty-one new clauses were added, which
were to be known by the letters of the alphabet from A to W, therefore
he hoped that some gentleman of ability would invent three more for X,
Y, and Z, to complete the alphabet, which would then render the bill a
perfect horn-book for the use of the minister," etc.

There is a political allusion in Peter Pindar's *Advice to The Future
Laureat* (*Works*, 1812, vol. ii. p. 339), 1790—

Once more upon your letters look,
Go, find of Politics the lost Horn-book.

In chap-books the horn-book is seldom mentioned. We get it in
The Cutting Up and Scramble for an Apple Pie, which follows *The Trifle,
or Goody Goosecap's Toy* (Manchester : printed for A. Swindells, Hanging
Bridge), dateless but probably published late in the last century. The
writer has another edition published by Marsden of Chelmsford. In
modern versions of *An Apple Pie*—a very old story indeed, the origin of
which it would be difficult to trace—the horn-book, so far as concerns
the horn, is deposed.

"*THE TRAGICALL DEATH OF AN APPLE PIE," Which
was cut in Pieces and eat by Twenty-Five Gentlemen with whom all good
Children should be well acquainted.*

The letters on a time agreed
Upon an Apple-pie to feed,
But as there seemed to be so many,
Those who were last might not have any,
Unless some method there was taken
That every one might save his bacon :
They all agreed to stand in order
Around the apple-pie's fine border :

202

History of the Horn-Book

Take turn as they in Horn-books stand
From Great A down to little &
So being at their dinner sat
Some eat while others thus chit-chat.

In the song in *The Mysteries of the Castle: A dramatic tale in three acts.* By Miles Peter Andrews. Lond. 1795 (Act II. sc. 5), is the following verse :—

Thus do married men,
Knowledge to discover,
School-boy like, again
Con their Horn-book over.

The horn-book is mentioned by the Gentle One in his ever fresh and delightful "Rosamund Gray." (*Tale of Rosamund Gray and Old Blind Margaret.* By Charles Lamb. London : Printed for Lee and Hurst, No. 32, Paternoster Row, 1798.) The allusion is on p. 81, in a letter from Elinor Clare to Maria Beaumont : "Methinks, you and I should have been born under the same roof, sucked the same milk, conned the same horn-book, thumbed the same Testament together ; for we have been more than sisters, Maria ! "

She could have conned the book of horn
Within the month that she was born,

is from Ward's *Reformation*, Canto II. p. 155 (1815).

A writer in the *London Magazine* (1821) on "Alphabet Studies and Chinese Imitations " waxes indignant with imitators of the Chinese who confuse high-sounding names and terms with true knowledge. "It is now become fashionable," he complains, "in almost every branch of learning and philosophy, to esteem the acquisition of the mere rudiments, or horn-book Alphabet, as the consummation of perfection."

John Clare in his *Shepherd's Calendar,* printed in 1827 (*The Shepherd's Calendar ; with Village Stories, and other Poems.* By John Clare, Author of *Poems on Rural Life and Scenery, The Village Minstrel,* etc., London : Published for John Taylor, Waterloo Place, by James Duncan, Paternoster Row ; and sold by J. A. Hessey, 93 Fleet Street), speaks of the horn-book being in use at that time, probably in the vicinity of Helpstone in Lincolnshire, where he lived. Telling of village scenes during harvest season he says, on p. 77 :—

History of the Horn-Book

None but imprison'd children now
Are seen, where dames with angry brow
Threaten each younker to his seat,
Who through the window, eyes the street ;
Or from his *horn-book* turns away,
To mourn for liberty and play.

Bishop Warburton says in the *Monthly Review*, October 1831, p. 176 : " For they (Critics) cannot deny but the Christ-row in the horn-book has ever been esteemed by the ablest of them an inseparable part of the alphabet."

There is an allusion to the horn-book in *The Saint's Tragedy : or the true story of Elizabeth of Hungary*, etc., by Charles Kingsley jun. Lond. 1848, Act IV. sc. 1, p. 181:—

> Potentially—
> As every christened rogue's a child of God,
> Or those old hags, Christ's brides—Think of your horn-book—
> The world, the flesh, and the devil—a goodly leash !
> And yet God made all three.

In chap. i. part ii. of *The Caxtons* Lord Lytton mentions Dr. Herman, a learned pedagogue who hated the spelling-book with a holy hatred and treated with bitter contempt all mechanical methods of teaching, into whose mouth he put : " No wonder that the horn-book is the despair of mothers." And in his *Harold*, chap. vii. p. 154, he has, " Learn the horn-book of war."

Washington Irving in his biography of Oliver Goldsmith (London : H. G. Clarke and Co., 1850, pp. 22, 23) cursorily mentions the horn-book : " Oliver's education began when he was about three years old ; that is to say, he was gathered under the wings of one of those good old motherly dames, found in every village, who cluck together the whole callow brood of the neighbourhood to teach them their letters and keep them out of harm's way. Mistress Elizabeth Delap, for that was her name, flourished in this capacity for upward of fifty years, and it was the pride and boast of her declining days, when nearly ninety years of age, that she was the first that had put a book (doubtless a horn-book) into Goldsmith's hands."

Charlotte Brontë, in *Villette*, chap. viii. p. 72 (Lond. 1855), has : " Inadventurous, unstirred by impulses of practical ambition, I was capable

STUDIES.   *Miss Sambourne.*

History of the Horn-Book

of sitting twenty years teaching infants the horn-book, turning silk dresses, and making children's frocks."

" . . . walked abroad with ferule and horn-book" (1831, Carlyle, *Miscellanies*, vol. ii. p. 271, ed. 1857).

The *Spectator* of 4th June 1864, p. 647, has an article on "Danish Obstinacy" *apropos* of the Schleswig-Holstein War, in which the horn-book is mentioned : "Assertions will be made and believed, that some Dane unknown, has forced on some school, never heard of, some horn-book, which does not exist, and armies will be poured on Jutland to pillage its inhabitants into submission."

The following passage opens an address from Mary Ramsay, a school dame, "to er Scholards," and occurs in *The Dialect of the West of England*, by James Jennings, 2nd ed. p. 142 (J. R. Smith, 36 Soho Square, 1869): "Commether (come hither) *Billy Chubb*, an bring tha hornen book. Gee ma the vester in tha windor, you *Pal Came !*—what ! be a sleepid !—I'll wake ye. Now, *Billy*, there's a good bway. Ston still there, and mind what I da za to ye, an whaur I da point. Now ; criss-cross, girt â, little â-b-c-d. That's right, Billy, you'll zoon lorn the criss-cross lain—you'll zoon auvergit Bobby Jiffry—you'll zoon be *a scholard*. A's a pirty chubby bway—Lord love'n ! "

The horn-book applied to the very beginning or A B C of a subject is well illustrated in the following passage from *The Life and Death of John of Barneveld, Advocate of Holland*, etc., by J. L. Motley, vol. ii. chap. ii. p. 30—London, Murray—1874 : "He (Barneveld) relied much on Villeroy, a political hack certainly, an ancient Leaguer, and a Papist, but a man too cool, experienced and wily, to be ignorant of the very horn-book of diplomacy."

Mention of the horn-book is seldom made in these days, but the writer of an amusing paper, " My Pupils in the Great Karroo," in *Macmillan's Magazine* (No. 402, pp. 444-450), who went out to the Cape to seek health, and profitably filled up his time by teaching a family of Dutch lads and lasses, says : " I had pictured to myself three or four shambling farm-lads coming indoors for an hour or two every morning to do sums in long division, and to learn to read English out of a horn-book."

In Miss Charlotte M. Yonge's *Love and Life, an Old Story in Eighteenth Century Costume* (Macmillan, 1880), are some characteristic

History of the Horn-Book

allusions to the horn-book : "There were no children's books, properly so called, except the ballads, chap-books brought round by pedlars, often far from edifying, and the plunge from the horn-book into general literature was, to say the least of it, bracing." (vol. i. p. 38). "The dame who hobbled along in spectacles, dropping a low curtsey to the 'quality,' taught the horn-book and the primer to a select few of the progeny of the farmers and artisans, and the young ladies would no more have thought of assisting her labours than the blacksmith's " (vol. i. p. 68). "She had some notion of good manners, knew as much of her horn-book and catechism as little girls of five were wont to know. The other two were perfectly ignorant, but Mrs. Aylmard procured horn-books, primers, and slates, and Aurelia began their education in a small way" (vol. i. p. 137).

In *Punch*, 13th June 1885, the cartoon is called "That Forward Boy." Sir Stafford Northcote, dressed as an old woman, is teaching little yokels the political A B C from a book which the Forward Boy (Lord Randolph Churchill) is snatching away :—

Pooh ! pooh ! Goody Staffy, you talk about teaching,
It's really absurd.
Do you think an old Partlet who's taken to preaching
Is like to be heard ?
Do you think in these days of First Standards your horn-book
Is in it a mite ?
No, no, dear old Goody, the Dame's School is done with
Both obsolete, quite !

The "Horn-book" as a title in literature does not appear to have been much favoured. The earliest work in which the term is used as a title seems to be *The*  *Guls Horne-booke :* Imprinted at London by R. S. 1609. It is a satire taking the form of rules for the conduct of the gallant. The prologue is short and explanatory: "A Horne-booke have I invented because I would have you well schooled, Powles is your Walke, but this your Guid : if it lead you right thanke me ; if astray, men will beare with your errors, because you are Guls. Fare-well. J. D."

Cut 104.

History of the Horn-Book

A reprint of the Gul's Horn-book, published by Baldwin and Triphook of London in 1813, contains some initial illustrations, one of which, a donkey looking through a letter W at a horn-book at his feet, is reproduced in cut 104.

HORN-BOOK OF JACOBITE TOASTS

A. B. C.	A blessed Change !
D. E. F.	Drive every Foreigner !
G. H. I.	Get home Jamie !
K. L. M.	Keep Loyal Ministers !
N. O. P.	No oppressive Parliaments !
Q. R. S.	Quickly return Stuarts !
T. U. W.	Tuck up Whelps !
X. Y. Z.	'Xert your Zeal.

This Alphabet of Toasts, many times reprinted, would seem to have been handed down from the time—or about the time—of the expulsion of James II. from this country in 1688.

> By parents guided round the gulphs of Youth,
> He, o'er his horn-book, learn'd to lisp the truth,

is from *The Life and Lucubrations of Crispinus Scriblerus ; A Novel in Verse*, written by James Woodhouse, who was the *protégé* of Shenstone and of Dr. Johnson, and a poet who had a wide circle of readers in the last century. The *Life*, which has not before been published, appears with a reprint of his other poems, in a work recently issued from the Leadenhall Press, Limited, under the title of *The Life and Poetical Works of James Woodhouse* (1735-1820). It is edited by the Rev. R. J. Woodhouse, M.A., a descendant of the poet.

In No. 83, third volume, of *The Connoisseur* (London : Baldwin, 1757) is a proposal for a " Poetaster's Horn-Book," which may be set forth in full : " There are almoſt daily publiſhed certain Lilliputian volumes, entitled *Pretty Books for Children*. A friend of mine, who confiders the little rhymers of the age as only ' children of a larger growth,' that amuſe themſelves with rhymes inſtead of rattles, propoſes to publiſh a ſmall pocket volume for the uſe of our poetaſters. It will be a Treatiſe on the Art of Poetry *adapted to the meaneſt capacities*, for which ſubſcriptions will

History of the Horn-Book

be taken, and fpecimens may be feen, at *George's* and the *Bedford* coffee houfes. It will contain full directions how to modulate the numbers on every occafion, and will inftruct the young fcribbler in all the modern arts of verfification. He will here meet with infallible rules, how to foften a line and lull us to fleep with liquids and diphthongs ; to roughen the verfe and make it roar again with reiteration of the letter R ; to fet it hiffing with femi-vowels ; to make it pant and breathe fhort with an hundred heavy afpirates ; or clog it up with the thickeft double confo-nants and monofyllables : with a particular table of Alliteration, containing the choiceft epithets, difpofed into alphabetical order ; fo that any fub-ftantive may be readily paired with a word beginning with the fame letter, which (though a mere expletive) fhall feem to carry more force and fentiment in it than any other of a more relative meaning, but more diftant found. The whole to be illuftrated with examples from the modern poets. This elaborate work will be publifhed about the middle of winter, under the title of *The Rhymer's Play-thing, or Poetafter's Horn-Book ;* fince there is nothing neceffary to form fuch a poet, except teaching him his letters."

A political satire of little interest to the present generation, *The Battle of the Horn-Books* (Dublin : Printed by William Spotswood, College Green, 1774. Price, a British Sixpence), deals with more or less known public persons of the period, in connection with whose doings the horn-book prominently figures. Of the author nothing is known : ". . . In the mean time, notwithstanding the vigilance of *Warehawk* and others, everything that the Village could produce, made of Horn, was going off gradually ; combs, spectacles, razor hafts, handles of knives, etc., so that (as most of such things in the Village were of Horn) there was soon very little left, except the *Horn-books* of the *School Boys.* These *Horn-Books* were much coveted by the Curate. . . . There was a deeper design in this than barely to get *Jack* out of the way ; they wanted to get into their possession, the above mentioned *Horn Books,* which were no common alphabets, but of much greater consequence than they appeared. A complete set, in *number seventy,* were left to the Parish by an *old Lady,* an adept in the occult sciences ; to them she communicated certain properties and virtues of a peculiar nature, among which the most remarkable was, that each of them was a very just criterion of a Boy's

History of the Horn-Book

spirit, and shewed by infallible signs, whether he had in him the *Stamina* of a Gentleman or a Plebeian. A Lad of Blood might play at quoits, shuttlecock, or duck and drake, with his *Horn-book*, and it still continued bright and clean ; whereas the book of a mean-spirited little fellow, tho' kept with the nicest care, had always a soiled look, and the letters were hardly distinguishable. The *old Lady* used to say, that the books were made of the Horns which blew down the walls of Jericho. . . . When he found he had nothing else to give, he had the effrontery to ask their *Horn-Books*, or their holiday-sports should absolutely be discontinued. Some of the Boys were glad to part with theirs, as they could not keep them *clean* for their lives. To them he gave *Books* of *Gingerbread* in their stead, with which they were as well satisfied ; and he promised besides, to them, and such others as would be tractable a sight worth a cartload of *Horn-Books ;* for next Friday (God willing) they should see him *jump down his own throat !* . . . He began bitterly to inveigh against them for that want of *uniformity* in their appearance, some having *Books* of Horn, others of *Gingerbread.* He then proceeded to give the genealogy of his Ass, which he shewed plainly to be descended in a right line from the Ass of Balaam ;—that he was equally inspired with his famous Progenitor, only one small ceremony was wanting to give him power of utterance— namely to shoe him with Horn-Books.

". . . Therefore he humbly requested they would all give up their *Horn-Books* for this patriotic purpose. Some of them asked him where the *Horn-Books* were which he had already got. He told them he had cut them all into distinct Letters, which he had sent to a *Mill to make Verses* whence they would come out in Rebus's, Anagrams, Acrosticks, etc. etc. . . . The *Schoolmaster* at the head of the *Gingerbread Boys* pursued. *Watt* who expected this fled to a deep river—and threw the *Horn-Books* over in a Bundle to a Friend on the other Side."

Burns's *Death and Doctor Hornbook* need but be mentioned.

There is record of a prospectus, issued some time in the last century by a Mr. W. T. Playtes, relating to *The Horn-Book for the Remembrance of the Signs of Salvation,* in twelve vols. 8vo, with 365,000 marginal references, or 1000 for every day in the year. Mr. Playtes evidently found the task too much for him.

Milk for Babes : or a Horn-book for That Able Divine, Eminent

History of the Horn-Book

Lawyer, and Honest Politician, Mr. H——— and his Disciples, is the title of a polemical tract issued by "Orator" Henley, of the Oratory, Lincoln's Inn Fields, in 1729.

The nature of *A Horn-book for a Prince* (viz. the Prince Regent) *or the A B C of Politics* (in verse), London, 1811, seems sufficiently expressed in the title.

The Parson's Horn-Book, published with etchings in two parts in 1831, is a series of anonymous theological and political satires, in its day widely circulated.

The Horn-Book of Storms, for the Indian and China Seas, by Henry Piddington (Calcutta : Ostell and Lepage, second edition, 1845), is a guide to the tracks of storms in the Southern Indian Ocean and Arabian Sea. In a pocket at the end of the work are plates of horn faintly etched with what are known as Colonel Reid's storm circles. These plates are laid upon any part of a chart, and represent a storm circle in a given area.

A Horn-book for Diplomatic Beginners is the title of another political hand-book issued by Ridgway, Piccadilly, as late as 1860.

A recent use is in the heading "A Legal Horn-Book" to a review of a manual of Roman law, which appeared in the London *Daily Chronicle* 29th May 1893.

Punch headed a political skit (20th January 1894), "From a New Horn (Castle) Book."

Mr. George Potter possesses the *Highgate Horn-Book*, an interesting manuscript by T. Purland, being an account of a pilgrimage made by certain "lovers of antiquity" and old customs to the old gate-house at Highgate, with the intent of being sworn upon the horns.

CHAPTER XVI

More about the horn-book in literature—Hornbye's *Horn-Book*—"A Divine Horn-Book"—Tickell's *Poem in Praise of the Horn-Book*—*Sir Horn-book, or Childe Lancelot's Expedition.*

ABOUT the writer of an exceedingly scarce work, Hornbye's *Horn-Book*, nothing is known but what he chooses to tell us. Concerning his birth and death we are ignorant, but Hornbye says of himself that he was educated at Peterborough Free School. The only other book he is known to have written is *The Scovrge of Drunkennes*, in 1618 or 1619, which looks as if he might have been a reformed drunkard. Hornbye's *Horn-Book* has a cut on the title-page (cut 11) representing a boy learning from a horn-book, and well within view, to entice to learning, is an apple held by the schoolmaster. If that should fail there is a broad hint near at hand of more drastic measures. Over the cut is printed "*Hornbye's Horn-book.* Iudge not too rafhly, till through all you looke ; If nothing then doth pleafe you, bvrne the Booke": and under, " By *William Hornbye*, Gent. *London.* Printed by *Aug. Math.* for *Thomas Bayly,* and are to be fold at his fhop in the middle Row, neere Staple Inn, 1622."

213

History of the Horn-Book

Hornbye's *Horn-Book* seems to have had little right of birth, unless it be that it afforded an opportunity for separate dedications on as many pages to three different persons, with laudatory verse to each : " To the Honovrable and Hopefvl Yovng Gentleman, Sir Robert Carr, Barronet ; *W. H. wiſheth increaſe of all honourable vertues.*" " To the Worſhipfvll Young Gentleman, Thomas Grantham, Efquire, Sonne and Heire to Si: Thomas Grantham, Knight ; *W. H. wiſheth all Health and Happineſſe.*" " To the Worſhipfull and vertuous young Gentleman, *Mr. Rochester Carre ; W. H.* wiſheth increafe of all *Spirituall and temporall bleſſings.*" The final dedication is signed, " Yours as you like him, Cornu-Apes," which is probably meant to convince us that Master William Horn-bee considered himself possessed of a pretty wit.   It will be noted that the excerpts which follow are full of allusions to the horn-book :—

> My honeſt, humble, harmleſſe horning-book,
> From whence young Schollers their firſt learning took,
> To you I dedicate (true generous fpirit)
> Your early towardneſſe, and vertues merit
> A farre more worthy worke, then here I can
> Set out, that ne're was Accademian :
>
> .   .   .   .   .
>
> (The *Horn-book* is at firſt Arts Nurce fro whence
> We fuck the milk of our intelligence)
> We muſt be perfeĉt in our letters all,
> Ere we to fpelling and to reading fall.
> By this Originall, we win (indeed).
>
> .   .   .   .   .
>
> *The Horn-booke* of all books I doe commend,
> For the world's knowledge, it doth comprehend.
> There is no book vnder heavens copious cope,
> Of mightie volume, large and full of fcope,
> Compofde of the pure quintiſſence of wit,
>
> .   .   .   .   .
>
> But fure the Horn-booke full containeth it.
> Whatever can be written, read, or faid,
> Åre firſt of letters fram'd, compofde, and made ;
> Each word, and fentence are in order fet,
> Derived from the Engliſh *Alphabet.*
> Of all chiefe learning, litrature and Art,
> The *Horn-booke* is the ground, which doth imparte
> A world of Science ; and great Art and ſkil?
> Comes from the Horn-booke, be it good, or ill.
>
> .   .   .   .   .

WORK AND PLAY.

Ambrose Dudley.

History of the Horn-Book

And all that deeply politick are found,
Had firft their knowledge from the Horn-booke's ground.
Great learned Preachers of Divinitie,
Which with the heavens have neare affinitie ;
Profound found Doctors of the *Morral* Law,
Firft from the *Horn-booke* did their reafon draw.

. . . . . .

For three or fower yeares fpace, like to a lamb,
He fpends his time in fporting, and in gam :
His wanton courage fomewhat then to coole,
His Parents put him to a petty Schoole.
Then after that, he takes a pritty pride,
To weare the Horn-book dangling by his fide.

. . . . . .

And, was it not well arm'd with plate and horne,
'Twas in great danger to be rent and torne :
For, in his fport, fometimes he falleth out
With his Schoole-fellow, fo they have a bout
At Buff, and counter-buff ; the *horn-bookes* then
Are all the weapons for thefe ftout tall men.

. . . . . .

And, having fo the child's affection won,
(He faith) Sweet Lad, come, and thy *Horn-booke* con.
And fo the *A B C* he firft is taught ;
From that to fpelling, he is after brought ;
And, being right inftructed for to fpell,
He learns his *Sillables* and *Vowells* well.
Then, with due teaching he doth well confider
By's Mafter's rule how he may put together.
The *Horn-booke* having at his fingers end,
Vnto the *Primer* he doth next afcend.

. . . . . .

So, "from the *Horn-booke*" we muft firft incline
Before we can attain to things divine.
And, as the *Bible* is the well of preaching,
Even fo the *Horn-booke* is the ground of teaching.

. . . . . .

A fecond worthy ground there is in truth
Of learning, apter for more able Youth ;
But yet he cannot unto this attaine,
Before the *Horn-booke* doth direct him plaine.

. . . . . .

217

History of the Horn-Book

Even fo the *Horn-booke* is the feede and graine
Of fkill, by which we learning firft obtaine ;
And though it be accompted fmall of many,
And haply bought for twopence or a penny,
Yet will the teaching fomewhat coftly be,
Ere they attaine vnto the full degree
Of Schollerfhip and Art.

.   .   .   .   .

So the *Horn-booke* without God's grace guiding ftill,
May be an introduction vnto ill.
And now my *Horn-booke* I may rightly apply
Both to the *Clergie* and the *Laitie.*

.   .   .   .   .

Thefe kind of fcatter-graces right are found
Like him that hid his Talent in the ground,
For fuch as thefe I mourne, and make great mone
They better never had the Horn-booke knowne.
Yet many a *Citie,* many a *Towne* is bleft,
Here in our *Land* with *Paftors* of the beft
Who take moft earneft paines, and honeft heed,
Not for to fleece their flocks, but them to feede
And with a fpeciall care, and confcience caufe,
Reform the wicked to religious lawes :
So they which fit in *Ignorance* black night,
They doe enlighten with their fplendent light.
Thefe are true *Shepheards,* even to Chrift's defire
And Hee'l reward them with a *Heavenly* hire :
Bleffed are they, that ever they did know
The Horn-booke, and the happy Chrift-croffe-row
The great grave worthy Iudges of the Land,
That doe with care and confcience vnderftand
The poore men's caufes, be they right or wrong.
To give the right, where right doth true belong,
(I hope) will with my *horn-booke* free difpence,
Knowing that knowledge is deriv'd from thence.
Before we learne to know each letter,
Or elfe to learn to reade, is nere the better.
        And to all gentle Iuftices of Peace
Who doe their Talents (in their charge) increafe
In doing Iuftice with a fingle eie,
Without refpect of men, or briberie,
My *horn-booke* very humbly I commend,
Hoping that learning they will ftill defend.

History of the Horn-Book

To all Schoole-founders, that have ever been
Moft beneficiall vnto Schollers feene,
By Schooles errecting, and protecting thofe
Vnder their favours, which in learning growes
To full maturitie ; thefe doe fupport
Poore Schollers in a charitable fort,
Thefe happy Stewards have their Talents fpent
Pleafing to God, and for a good intent :
To thefe my *horn-booke* likewife I commend,
Knowing the Mufes they doe beft befriend.

    The bufie *Lawyers*, and the briefe *Atturneys*,
Which every *Term-time* take moft tedious ironies
To toyle and moyle, to ride through thick and thin,
And all to bring their fees more roundly in,
Whofe onely labours to this purpofe tends,
They would have all men rather foes than friends,
Becaufe by controverfie they doe gaine,
And concord makes the beggers, they complaine
Thefe from the *Horn-booke* firft did draw their fkill,
Good caufe have they to beare it great good will.

   .   .   .   .   .

    A conftable's a iudicious man,
If he performe his Office wifely can :
But if unlearnedly he doe amiffe,
(Ales) the *Horn-booke* was no friend of his.
    The learned *Poet* that in *Poetrie*
Doth mount aloft unto the loftie fkie
In high conceits, through divine infpiration
Who for his Art, is held in admiration ;
That which I write, will grant for to be true,
And give vnto the Horn-booke praife due.

   .   .   .   .   .

    The Free-Schoole Mafters, which paines doe take,
Good Schollers fit for *Cambridge* to mak,
Were Infants firft themfelves, and little Boyes,
Which did delight in trifles, and in toyes,
And at the Horn-book likewife did begin,
Before they do fuch good preferment win
(Where youth is brought to reverence and grace
I hold a very venerable place).

   .   .   .   .   .

As fure as I the *Horn-booke* firft did know
So furely is he named in this *Roe*.

   .   .   .   .   .

History of the Horn-Book

Now to my Horn-booke I returne againe.

To thefe the *Horn-book* proves not croffe.

And fo (indeed) the Horn-booke backwards learne.

My Horn-booke's honefty will their's affront

And though the Horn-book be my books right ftile

The *Horn-booke*, if it true be vnderftood,
Containeth nothing but is right and good.
Then wives and Maidens, this is my requeft,
Befriend the *Horn-booke*, for it is your beft.
Young hopefull Gentleman, that doe refort
By Art and learning to the Inns of Court,
Which doe through time and paines much vnderftand
To grow great men, and Iudges of the land :
All thefe I reverence with a due refpeft,
Whofe labours turne vnto a good effeft
(I hope their fplendent favours all will fhine
Vpon my *Horn-booke;* though that fome repine
And *critick*-like, doe my good meaning wreft
To the worft fenfe, though I conceive the beft ;
For (I proteft) I think not an ill thought,
Though I doe *itterate* the Horn-booke oft.)
Thefe learn'd the Horn-booke to a bad intent
Their time of learning was but vainely fpent.

Thefe from the *Horn-book's* honeft meaning fwerve,
And in their places right like knaves doe ferve.
Now ceafe (my *Mufe*) in quiet filence reft,
For of the *Horn-booke* thou haft faid thy beft.

"The former popularity of the Horn-book derives illustration," says Hone in an unpublished note, "from the title of a rare quarto tract of four leaves. 'A Divine Horn-Book, or the first Form in the true Theosophick School, wherein is taught the knowledge of God's Great Name Jeova in the House of Letters, etc., by H. L. London : Printed for the Author, 1688.' The author maintains that 'God, the Divine Nature, and this whole World' is truly discovered in the alphabet." He assigns a symbolical meaning to each letter, and thus carefully notices the cross :

220

History of the Horn-Book

"+ signifies The Free Gift of the Father in the offering of his Son for our offences" (see p. 76).

A copy of this rarity belongs to the writer. With the vowels A E I O V transposed, H. L.—about whom nothing can be learned—makes J E O V A, which he takes for his theme, and, although the arguments are weak, and, at times, untenable, the advice is good.

> A e i o u his Great Name doth spell,
> Here it is known, but is not known in Hell.

Following the poem is an *Explanation*, which thus opens :—

"A bcd E fgh I klmn O pqrst U wxyz. Note, *a e i o u* being taken from between the Consonants, the Consonants are found in five Divisions : the first two Divisions consist of three Letters, as appears, *b c d* and *f g h*. The third Division of four Letters, *k l m n*. The fourth of five, as *p q r s t*, and the fifth of four, as *w x y z ;* then take the Central Letters out of each Division, and they are *c g l m r x y*, when we find first the number seven and no more, then what remains are *b d f, h k m, p q s, t w z*, which are twelve in number and no more : the five Vowels being the Letters that spell the Great Name of God *Jeova* are thus placed, the Central Letter is I, and the first is A, put that which in the Alphabet is first last, and the Central Letters first, and then they stand in this order *Jeova*. . . . These things the Ancients no doubt did well understand who first devised the use of Letters, for it is unreasonable to believe that they were placed in this most Excellent and Significant Order by mere chance. . . ."

Thomas Tickell, M.A., the author of an oft-quoted *Poem in Praise of the Horn-Book*, was a contemporary of Addison and Steele, whom he assisted in the *Spectator*. He became Secretary to the Lords-Justices of Ireland, which post he held until he died in 1740, aged fifty-four. In his spare time Tickell was guilty of other minor poetical pieces, including "Kensington Garden" and "A Lament on the Death of Mr. Addison." His poem on the horn-book, "written by a Gentleman in England under a Fit of the Gout," first saw light in Dublin, where it was "Printed by and for J. Gowan at the Spinning-Wheel in Back Lane, MDCCXXVIII." George Bickham in the last century took this poem as "copy" for one of his writing lessons : he honoured it with a special title-page, which is reproduced in cut 105. The pamphlet is exceedingly scarce, and is here reproduced in facsimile :—

A Poem

In Praise of the Horn-Book,
and the Power of A, B, C.

Extracted from the Works of
Thos Tickel, Esqr

Written in a legible, expeditious, and
beautiful Running Hand, as a Copy fit
for young Clerks & Youth to write after.

To which are prefixt

Alphabets and Sentences in all the Hands now
Practised in Great Britain.

Engrav'd by G. Bickham, Senior.

LONDON: Printed for John Bowles at the Black-Horse in Cornhill.

Cut 105.

A

POEM

In Praife of the

HORN-BOOK:

Written by a Gentleman in *England,* under a Fit
of the G O U T.

Magni magna. Patrant, nos non nifi Ludicra.
——————— *Podagra bæc Otia fecit.*

D U B L I N:

Printed by and for *J.* G O W A N, at the *Spinning
Wheel* in Back-Lane. MDCCXXVIII.

A
POEM
In Praife of the HORN-BOOK.

HAIL *ancient Book,* moſt *venerable Code,*
Learning's *firſt Cradle* and its *laſt Abode!*
The Huge unnumber'd *Volumes* which we fee,
By *lazy Plagiaries* are ſtol'n from *thee* :
Yet future Times to *thy* fufficent *Store*
Shall ne'er prefume to add *one Letter* more.

THEE will I ſing in *comely Wainſcot* bound,
And *Golden Verge* enclofing *thee* around ;
The faithful *Horn* before, from Age to Age,
Preferving *thy invaluable Page* ;

Behind

Behind *thy Patron Saint* in Armour ſhines,
With *Sword* and *Lance,* to guard *thy ſacred Lines* ⁊
Beneath his *Courſer's Feet* the *Dragon lies*
Transfix'd ; *his Blood thy ſcarlet Cover dies* ;
Th' *inſtruɖive Handle's* at the Bottom fix'd,
Leaſt wrangling *Critics* ſhould pervert the *Text*.

Or if to *Ginger Bread,* thou ſhalt deſcend,
And *Liquoriſh Learning* to *thy Babes* extend ;
Or *Sugar'd plane,* o'er ſpread with *beaten Gold,*
Does the ſweet Treaſure of *thy Letters* hold ;
Thou ſtill ſhalt be my Song ; — *Apollo's* Choir
I ſcorn t' invoke. *Cadmus,* my Verſe inſpire.
'Twas *Cadmus,* who the firſtMaterials brought
Of all the Learning, which has ſince been taught,
Soon made compleat ; for Mortals ne'er ſhall know
More than contain'd of old the *Chriſt-croſs* Row ;
What Maſters diɖate, or what Doɖors preach,
Wife Matrons hence, ev'n to our Children teach.
But as the Name of ev'ry Plant and Flow'r,
(So common that each Peaſant knows its Pow'r)
Phyſicians in myſterious Cant expreſs;

T' amuſe

T'amuse their Patient and enhance their Fees,
So from the Letters of our native Tongue,
Put in *Greek* Scrauls, a Myftr'y too is fprung,
Schools are erected, *puzling Grammars* made
And artful Men ftrike out a gainful Trade;
Strange Characters adorn the learned Gate,
And heedlefs Youth, catch at the fhining Bait:
The pregnant Boys the noify Charms declare,
And *Taus, and †*Delta's* make their Mothers ftare,
Th' uncommon Sounds amaze the vulgar Ear,
And what's uncommon never cofts too dear.
Yet in all Tongues the *Horn-Book* is the fame
Taught by the *Grecian* Mafter, or the *Englifh* Dame

But how fhall I *thy endlefs Virtues* tell,
In which *thou* doft all other Books excell?
No *greafy Thumbs, thy fpotlefs Leaf* can foil,
Nor *crooked Dogs Ears thy fmooth Corners* fpoil;
In idle Pages no *Errata* ftand,
To tell the Blunders of the P R I N T E R's *Hand* :
No *fulfom Dedication* here is writ,

---

*Tau the Greek **T**, †Delta the Greek **D**.

Nor

(4)

Nor flatt'ring Verſe to praiſe the Author's Wit,
The *Margin* with no tedious Notes is vext;
Nor *various Readings* to confound the *Text*:
All Parties in *thy lit'ral* Senſe agree,
Thou perfect Center of Concordancy!
Search we the Records of an ancient Date,
Or read what Modern Hiſtories relate,
They all proclaim, what Wonders have been done,
By the *plain Letters* taken as they run.
Too high the Floods of Paſſion us'd to roul,
And rend the *Roman Youth's* impatient Soul,
His haſty Anger furniſh'd Scenes of Blood,
And frequent Deaths of worthy Men. enſu'd:
In vain were all the weaker Methods try'd,
None could ſuffice to Stem the furious Tyde,
Thy ſacred Line he did but once repeat;
And laid the Storm, and cool'd the raging Heat.

---

* Theſe Lines ingeniouſly deſcribe the Advice given to *Aguſtus* by *Athenodorus* the Stoick Philoſopher, who deſired the Emperor neither to ſay nor do any Thing, but to take Time, till he had firſt ſaid over the *Alphabet* or Letters of the *Horn-Book*; The ſtrict obſervance of this Rule would be the Means to make his Paſſion fall and prevent any raſh Words or paſſionate Actions.

Thy

Thy Heavenly Notes like Angels mufick eheer
Departing Souls, and footh the dying Ear.
An Aged Peafant, on his lateft Bed,
Wifh'd for a Friend fome godly Book to read.
The pious Grandfon, *thy* known *Handle* takes,
And (Eyes lift up,) this fav'ry Lecture makes.
Great A, he gravely roar'd, th' important Sound
The empty Walls and hollow Roof rebound :
Th' expiring Ancient rear'd his drooping Head,
And thank'd hisStars that *Hodge* had learn'd to read ;
Great B, the Yonker bawls : O heavenly, Breath!
What Ghoftly Comforts in the Hour of Death!
What Hopes I feel! *Great C*, pronounc'd the Boy ;
The Grandfire dyes with Ecftacy of Joy.

Yet in fome Lands fuch Ignorance abounds
Whole Parifhes fcarce know *thy ufeful Sounds* ;
Of *Effex* Hundreds Fame gives this Report,
But Fame I ween fays many Things in Sport.
Scarce lives theMan, to whom *thou'rt* quite unknown,
Tho' few th'Extent of *thy vaft Empire* own.

What

What ever Wonders, Magick Spells can do
In Earth, in Air, in Sea, in shades below;
What Words profound and dark wise *Mah'met* spoke
When his *old Cow* an Angel's Figure took ;
What strong Enchantments *Sage Canidia* knew,
Or *Horace* sung, fierce Monsters to subdue,
O *mighty BOOK*, are all contain'd in you.
All humane Arts, and ev'ry Science meet,
Within the Limits of *thy single Sheet*,
From thy vast Root, all Learning's Branches grow,
And all her Streams from *thy deep Fountain* flow.
And lo! while thus *thy Wonders* I indite,
Inspir'd I feel the Power of which I write;
The *gentler Gout* his former Rage forgets,
Less frequent now and less severe the Fits,
Loose grow the *Chains*, which bound my uselessFeet;
Stifness and Pain from ev'ry Joynt retreat ;
Surprizing Strength comes ev'ry Moment on,
I stand, I step, I walk, and now I *run.*
Here let me cease, my hobling Numbers stop,
And at *thy Handle*, hang my Crutches up.

FINIS.

History of the Horn-Book

By some strange blunder, the authorship of Tickell's poem is wrongly attributed to William Taylor of South Weald (1673-1750), in a work

Cut 106.

The first that came was mighty A
The last was little z.

entitled *Some Account of the Taylor Family* (originally Taylard), compiled and edited by Peter Alfred Taylor, M.P., London. Printed for Private Circulation, 1875.

Sir Horn - book, or Childe Lancelot's Expedition ; A Grammatico - Allegorical Ballad, by Thomas Love Peacock, was first published in 1814, and ran through a number of editions until the latest in 1843, issued by the late Joseph Cundall of 12 Old Bond Street. It also appears in the collected edition of Peacock's *Works*, 1875.

It will be noticed in the illustration (cut 106) that in the shield-shaped horn-book borne by the courtly knight the handle is curtailed.

Martin F. Tupper was acquainted with the horn-book. His poem "Of Life," in *Proverbial Philosophy* (18th ed., Lond. 1854), opens :—

A child was playing in a garden, a merry little child,
Bounding with triumphant health, and full of happy fancies.
His kite was floating in the sunshine—but he tied the string to a twig,
And ran among the roses to catch a newborn butterfly,
His horn-book lay upon a bank, but the pretty truant hid it,
Buried up in gathered grass, and moss, and sweet wild thyme.

CHAPTER XVII

Anecdotes, jests, and proverbs—Lord Erskine and the judge—How to keep one's temper —Tickell's story of the aged peasant—The adventures of Coquetilla—The boy who could not say " A "—The fable of the boy and his mother—A story about a horn-book in the British Museum—A couple of sayings, a couple of proverbs, and a single cry.

NECDOTES and jests and proverbs in which the horn-book is mentioned are few. Of anecdotes, here is perhaps the best known. It belongs to the last century. A case was being tried— Thomas Carman *v.* the Stationers' Company—relating to a dispute in connection with sheet almanacks. The judge put a question to Lord Erskine as to whether a printed sheet of paper like an almanack could be described as a book. Erskine, who had come prepared, held up something in his hand, and after a moment's pause said impressively, " The common horn-book, my lord ! "

In a note to his *Poem in Praise of the Horn-Book*, written in 1728 (see p. 227), Tickell mentions " the Advice given to *Aguſtus* by *Athenodorus* the Stoick Philoſopher, who deſired the Emperor neither to ſay nor do any Thing, but to take Time, till he had firſt ſaid over the *Alphabet* or Letters of the *Horn-Book ;* The ſtrict obſervance of this Rule would be the Means to make his Paſſion fall and prevent any raſh Words or paſſionate

History of the Horn-Book

Actions." And in the poem itself is a story which, being short, may perhaps bear repetition :—

An Aged Peasant, on his latest Bed,
Wish'd for a Friend some goodly Book to read,
The pious Grandson, *thy* known *Handle* takes,
And (Eyes lift up), this sav'ry Lecture makes.
Great A, he gravely roar'd, th' important Sound
The empty Walls and hollow Roof rebound :
Th' expiring Ancient rear'd his drooping Head,
And thank'd his Stars that *Hodge* had learned to read ;
Great B, the Yonker bawls : O heavenly Breath !
What Ghostly Comforts in the Hour of Death !
What hopes I feel ! *Great C*, pronounc'd the Boy
The Grandsire dyes with Ecstacy of Joy.

The story of the adventures of one Coquetilla, a woman, feather-brained and foolish, who flourished in the earlier years of the last century, is not of entrancing interest, but finds mention here because, on one occasion, she appeared in public with a horn-book at her side. Coquetilla longed to take part in a masquerade, the first of the season, at the *Haymarket.* "At Night she went with a select Company of her own. She was dressed like a Child in a Bodice Coat and Leading Strings, with a Horn-Book tied to her side." This extract is from p. 52, and on reading farther one learns that a nurse was provided to lead the "child" about and keep her out of mischief. But the experiment was a failure. The curious may read these adventures in a scarce sixty-paged tract, which for long I unsuccessfully sought, and found by a fluke in a "Satyr" aimed at vice and folly in general, entitled *A View of the Beau Monde,* or *Memoirs of the celebrated Coquetilla, a real History ; with Original Songs.* To which is added *The Masque of Life : A Ballad by a Person of Distinction.* London : A. Dodd at the *Peacock* without *Temple Bar,* 1731. Price One Shilling.

Children used to tell in English village schools of a boy refusing to repeat *A* after the master who was teaching him the alphabet from a horn-book. When threatened with the rod he whimpered, "If I do, I know you'll want me to say *B*." This jokelet was known to little German boys [Das A B C cum notis variorum (Leipzig und Dresden, 1695), p. 7] in the seventeenth century, and probably was current wherever the alphabet was taught. A late version appears on p. 30 in a

232

Harry Becker.

SO DIFFICULT.

History of the Horn-Book

Readingmadeasy, published by Norbury of Brentford, in which the " Horn-book " is displaced by a " book " :—

On a Boy that would not learn his Book.

A Boy that once to School was fent,
On Plays and Toys was fo much bent,
That all the art of Man, fay they,
Could not once make him fay Great A.

His Friends that faw him in thefe fits,
Cry'd out for Shame, leave off thy Tricks ;
Be not fo dull, make it thy Play
To learn thy Book ; come, fay Great A.
The Dunce then gap'd, but did no more ;
Great A was yet a great Eye fore,
The next Boys jog him, Sure fay they—
'Tis not fo hard to cry great A.
No, no, but heres the Cafe fays he,
If I cry A, I might cry B,
And then go on to C and D,
And that won't do, but ftill there's Jod
Lurks in the way with X. Y. Zod.
And fo no end I find there'll be,
If I but once larn A, B, C.
But as things ftand I will not do it,
Though fure I am one day to rue it.
At this crofs rate the Dunce went on,
Till one at length a Means thought on.
A Plant, fays he, grows near the Wood,
That will not fail to do him good,
And cure his Fits while in the Bud,
This Plant, adds he, will clear the fight,
And with a Touch, will make him bright.
At Eyes and Nofe will purge the fkull,
And drain off all that makes him dull.

Cut 107, *Of the Boy and his Mother*, is from Æsop's *Fables*, with their Morals in Prose and Verse, Grammatically Translated, Illustrated with Pictures and Emblems, Together with the History of His Life and Death, newly and exactly translated out of the original Greek. The Fifteenth Edition, exactly corrected by W. D. London : Printed for I. Phillips, H. Rhodes, and I. Taylor, 1703.

There is a longer version of this fable, numbered CXIX., in Croxall's

235

History of the Horn-Book

Æsop, 1722 (this is the rare first edition: the same cuts were used in later editions)—*Fables of Æsop and Others newly done into English with an application to each Fable.* Illustrated with Cuts. London: Printed for J. Jonson at Shakespeare's Head in the Strand, etc. (see cut 108).

F A B. 193.

Of the Boy *and his* Mother.

A Boy having ſtollen his Shool-fellows Horn-book at School, brought it to his Mother: By whom being not chaſtiſed, played the Thief daily more and more. In proceſs of time, he began to ſteal greater things; at laſt being apprehended of the Magiſtrate, was led to execution: But his Mother following and crying out, he entreated the Serjeants that they would permit him to whiſper in her Ear, who permitting him, the Mother haſtening laid her Ear to her Son's Mouth, he bites off a piece of his Mother's Ear with his Teeth; when his Mother and the reſt rated at him, not only as being a Thief but alſo un-gracious towards his own Mother, he ſaid, She is the cauſe of my undoing, for if ſhe had puniſhed me for ſtealing the Horn book; I had not proceeded to grea-ter things, nor been led to my Execution.

Cut 107.

FAB. CXIX.—THE BOY AND HIS MOTHER

"A little Boy who went to School, stole one of his School-fellows' Horn-books, and brought it home to his Mother, who was so far from correcting and discouraging him upon account of the Theft, that she commended and gave him an Apple for his pains. In process of time, as the

History of the Horn-Book

child grew up to be a Man, he accustom'd himself to greater Robberies ; and at last, being apprehended was committed to Gaol, he was try'd and condemned for Felony. On the Day of his Execution, as the officers were conducting him to the Gallows, he was attended by a vast crowd of people and among the rest by his mother, who came sighing and sobbing along, and taking on extremely for her son's unhappy fate ; which the Criminal observing, call'd to the Sheriff, and beg'd the Favour of him, that he would give him leave to speak a word or two to his poor afflicted Mother. The Sheriff (as who would deny a dying Man so reasonable a Request) gave him Permission ; and the Felon, while as every one thought he was whispering something of Importance to his Mother, bit off her ear to the great Offence and Surprise of the whole Assembly. What, say they, was not this Villain contented with the impious Facts already com-

Cut 108.

mitted, but that he must increase the number of them by doing this Violence to his Mother ? Good People reply'd he, I would not have ye be under a mistake ; that Wicked Woman deserves this, and even more at my Hands, for if she had chastis'd and chid, instead of rewarding and caressing me, when in my Infancy I stole the Horn Book from School, I had not come to this ignominious untimely end."

A horn-book seems a curious sort of thing for a boy to steal. Far more likely would he have hidden it away. As mentioned on another page, the preservation of more than one horn-book is due to the unpremeditated foresight of little boys.

In later versions of " The Boy and his Mother," a book naturally takes the place of a horn-book, and this may be cited as a small but by no means unimportant instance of the numerous changes these entertaining travesties of man's concerns have undergone since they were spoken—if they ever were spoken—by Babrius, the great Roman fabulist.

237

History of the Horn-Book

Hone's hitherto unpublished version of this story argues a good memory. Says he: "I remember that when I was a child I read in an old spelling book a story to this effect—A boy who stole a horn-book at school was forgiven by his mother, and then he stole again and went on stealing from that time till he was tried for his crimes of picking and stealing and sentenced to death, and going in a cart to the place of execution he saw among the mob his mother weeping for his untimely end ; upon which he procured the cart to be stopped and calling her to come to him he leaned over, and putting his mouth to her ear as if to whisper something privately, he cruelly bit her ear and called out ' Remember, mother, if you had whipped me for stealing the horn-book I should not now be going to be hanged.' "

There is a print-honoured legend to the effect that one of the horn-books now in the British Museum was found in Derbyshire, very many years ago, in a very deep closet built in the very thick wall of a very old farm-house. It is said that the labourer who unearthed it—or unmudded—unstoned—unbricked—or unflinted it, recognised this as the identical horn-book from which his father had learned his A B C!

A well-worn Joe Miller points to a dictionary as a book containing the sum of all knowledge, and Tickell follows, when he says of the letters of the alphabet in a horn-book :—

> All humane Arts, and ev'ry Science meet,
> Within the Limits of thy single sheet.

The saying, " he knows his book," and its French equivalent, " savoir sa croix de par Dieu "—to know one's cross-row or A B C—probably originated with the use of the horn-book.

" To break one's horn-book," [1] meaning to incur displeasure, peculiar to the South of England, irresistibly suggests an unruly youth banging his horn-book against form or desk, and the hot smart following the promptly-administered swishing.

A Cornish lady favours me with two proverbs she has heard her

---

[1] See p. 360 of Supplement to Grose's *Provincial Glossary*, by Samuel Pegge, F.S.A., which follows his *Anecdotes of the English Language*, chiefly regarding the local dialect of London and its environs (London : J. N. Nichols and Son, 1844, third edition).

mother quote. They are certainly worthy of preservation, more especially as trace of them elsewhere cannot be found : " A dame, a child, and a couple of horn-books do not make a school." " He who keeps a small shop must be content to sell horn-books."

"Come buy, come buy a horn-book," once a street cry, is mentioned in *Wit and Drollery*, p. 78, 1682.

CHAPTER XVIII

The horn-book in English prints and pictures—Portrait of Miss Campion, 1661 (see frontispiece)—Why the horn-book is not pictured in A B C books—A wild-goose chase for a horn-book depicted in a church window—A horn-book in the *Roxburghe Ballads*—A dunce with a horn-book—The horn-book in Bickham's *Universal Penman;* in a drawing by Lavinia, Countess of Spencer; in "The Country Schoolmistress"; in a drawing by Stothard; in a print of "Dick Swift, Thieftaker, Teaching his Son the Commandments"; in a drawing by Westall; in a Christmas card; in an *ex libris* plate.

Cut 109.

LTHOUGH the examples noted form by no means an exhaustive list, it is safe to say that the horn-book appears comparatively seldom in English[1] prints and pictures. The interest of the frontispiece to this work lies chiefly in its being engraved from one of the few pictures in which the horn-book plays a part. The portrait, from an unknown hand, and dated 1661, is that of Miss Campion,—according to the inscription, aged two years and two months,—of a notable Essex family, from which sprang Thomas Campion, chirurgeon by

[1] Examples of foreign horn-books, or horn-book tablets, in prints and pictures, are given on p. 141 *et seq.*

240

History of the Horn-Book

profession, musician and poet by choice and instinct. The sadly-dilapidated original painting, now the property of Miss Day of Enfield Wash, measures 34 × 46 inches. The old home of the Campions, near Great Parnden, where the portrait hung for generations, was pulled down in recent times.

It might be thought that in illustrations to the earlier spelling and reading books the horn-book would sometimes have had a place. But in frontispieces thereto (see cuts 110, 111, 112, and 113) the children are invariably holding a lesson-book and never a horn-book.

But there is at least one exception in the frontispiece to the third edition of *The Juvenile Preceptor ; or an Easy Introduction to Reading* (compiler John Blaymires ; publishers Lane and Whittaker of 13 Ave Maria Lane, London, date 1815). A mother is teaching a boy to read from a book; a smaller boy is conning his lesson also from a book, and a couple of tiny brats are sprawling on the ground, disputing over the letters faintly indicated on a horn-book, which the artist has represented of imposing dimensions. The moral—that is, the publishers' moral—seems sufficiently on the surface.

The spelling-book certainly did its best to choke the horn-book out of existence, and its producer naturally took

Cut 110.

Cut 111.

care that his, and not the other man's wares, should figure in the frontispiece. In a typical illustration of the Schoolmaster (cut 110) the artist seems to have thought the birch rod sufficiently telling without a book of any kind.

One careless person told another careless person, who, in a magazine article, carelessly repeated to the public that a stained-glass window in York Minster contained the figure of a female holding in her hand a

Cut 112.

horn-book. The statement of this careless pair was the cause of a vicarious examination with a binocular of every window in York Minster, in addition to which officials both high and low were needlessly worried about something which never existed. The myth is probably due to a paragraph in *Notes and Queries* (second series, 9, 17th March 1860), signed by one M. G., who says: " There is, or was, a few years ago, a most interesting stained-glass window

History of the Horn-Book

in All Saints, North Street, York, at the East end over the Communion Table. It had been grievously mutilated, but the remains were very beautiful. It represented St. Anne teaching the Virgin to read out of a horn-book with pointer. Parts of this group had been patched with pieces from other windows so that at first there was some difficulty in making out the subject, but the horn-book was entire as well as the figure of the Virgin, a lovely little girl with golden hair, and crowned with a wreath of lilies. I should imagine that it was the work of the fifteenth century."

In recent years this window has been restored, but fortunately a drawing made some twenty years before "M. G." inaccurately described it is reproduced in the first part of Weale's *Quarterly Papers*, which appeared in 1843, and shows the window as it originally stood (cut 12, p. 26). The artist in glass has sought to deipct a child's

Cut 113.

243

History of the Horn-Book

Cut 114.

book,—not a horn-book, but an ordinary volume—a fescue being used to point out the words. The lettering—haphazard and meaningless—seems intended to indicate a child's lesson.

The *Roxburghe Collection of Ballads*, edited by that painstaking and erudite antiquary, Joseph Woodfall Ebsworth, has but one 'cut (114), in which the horn-book figures—a tailpiece to "Great Boobee," lines popular before the Civil Wars began. This woodcut had done duty in ballads of an earlier date. The Great Boobee is in two parts : the first has six verses and the second ten. Its second verse in the first part, sung by the way "To a pleasant new Tune or *Sallengers Round*," is as follows :—

> I went to School with a good intent and for to learn my book,
> And all the day I went to play, in it I never did look,

Cut 115.

244

History of the Horn-Book

Full seven years or very nigh, as I may tell to thee,
I could hardly say my " *Christ-Cross-Row* " like a *great Boobee.*

Cut 115 is curious, because all the children have ordinary lesson-books except the boy on the left, who holds a horn-book. He, and the boy behind him, are probably a couple of dunces. The cut is copied from one of those in a quarto volume entitled *Specimens of Early Wood Engraving*, being Impressions of Woodcuts in the possession of the Publisher, Newcastle upon Tyne, William Dodd, No. 5 Bigg Market, 1862. It is the only cut in a collection numbering some hundreds in which a horn-book appears, and what

Cut 116.

book it helped to illustrate I do not know. In the introduction Mr. Dodd says that these wood-cuts were first gathered together by John White, a citizen of York, who came to Newcastle in 1708. In 1711 he started the *Courant* newspaper, and printed and sold to chapmen and the public a " large variety of small books, ballads and songs." John White lived to the age of eighty-one (till 1769), and was succeeded at his house in Pilgrim Street by Thomas Saint (mentioned in another page), who also published and sold horn-books and battledores.

In the *Universal Penman*, Engraved by George Bickham (London : Printed for and sold by the Author at the Crown in James Street, Bunhill Fields, 1741), a horn-book is shown in the right hand of a boy forming part of a headpiece on p. 4 (cut 116). The work is signed *G. Bickham, sculp.* 1733.

Cut 117.

" The Naughty Boy," a child

with a birch rod seated on a punishment stool, a cracked horn-book at his feet (cut 117), is from a drawing (afterwards engraved in stipple) by Lavinia, Countess of Spencer ; date about 1780.

A pretty oval print, stippled in colours and published 1st January 1797, by S. W. Fores, of 50 Piccadilly, is entitled " The Country School-mistress." The subject, a school dame and a boy holding a horn-book, is outlined in cut 118. There are some amusing lines under the title :—

> " Come, my Dear, begin, what's first ? "—" I don't know."
> " Why what's on the Window ? "—" A Bee."
> " Very well, that's Right, what's next ? "—" I don't know."
> " Look at me then, what do I do ? "—" Squint."
> " No Billy, C."

In a small oval, engraved by Knight, after Stothard, of a school scene, a little boy dissolved in tears—the dunce—is standing on a stool, holding in his hand the reminder of painful trouble to come,—a birch rod ; a little girl, seated on the left, holds a horn-book, but so covered with her plump little fingers that two or three only of the opening letters of the alphabet can be read.

A characteristic print, with a horn-book as the theme, entitled " School," engraved by Godby after Metz, is reproduced on a small scale on p. 175.

A vilely-executed illustration (119), " Dick Swift, Thief-taker, Teaching his Son the Command-ments," which doubt-

Cut 118.

246

STUDIOUS COUPLE.

Robert W. Allan.

less decorated a book of the blood-and-thunder order, is facsimiled from the original copperplate. It comes in here because the boy is holding a horn-book, the handle of which may just be made out. The reader's

Cut 119.

sharp eyes will not fail to note that with the other hand Master Dick is picking the pocket of his papa, whose forefinger wickedly blots out the "not" in the eighth commandment. An extended account of Dick and his doings is given in the last volume of the *Newgate Calendar*. Dick, who in literature figures as Richard, ostensibly kept, about the middle of the last century, "The Barley Mow," a dirty disreputable alehouse in Old Street, but his real business was receiving stolen goods.   He also ran a thieves' school, and it is said that during his career twenty at least of

Ye Hornbooke of
Chriſtmaſſe Greetynge
. ; ' , , ? + a e i o u + ! ( ) ? - ; . ,

+ I Wishe you +

Alle · Open a
Bleſsynges · Path of Peace & never
Content that Cheerelh ye Quit you but give you
Darkeſt Dayſ · No · Reſt &
Enemy but many · Sunneſhine In
Friendes · Trial may you bee
Good luck & good · Onceaſynglie
Health to · Victorious. & attaine
Inspire · Weallhe & Wiſdom &
Joye Bee happy as a · Xcellence Bee .
Kynge through a · Younge in hearte, with
Longe Lyſe · Zeſt to enjoy theſe
May Mirlhe · & all other good thyngs
Amen

Cut 120.

his pupils had the honour of being hanged and still more transported beyond seas.   Swift, after several more or less successful attempts to escape, finally got fourteen years' transportation, which knocked the non-sense out of him.

If we are to believe the picture (cut 109), copied from a print, " drawn and engraved by Richard Westall, R.A.," entitled "Grandma's Pet," there were horn-books with half the alphabet on one side and half on the other. While this is more than likely, we must remember that an artist would be tempted to take liberties with the arrangement, number, or position of the letters in a horn-book.

The illustration (1 20) headed "Ye Hornbooke of Chriftmafse Greetynge" is a Christmas card issued on a larger scale to her friends by Mrs. E. M. Field, the authoress of *The Child and his Book*, of which mention is made on another page. This is probably the only Christmas card where a horn-book forms the leading idea.

The design for an *ex libris* plate (1 2 1), where the theme is a child with horn-book, was sent to the writer as a complimentary Christmas card by a clever artist friend of the Birmingham School—Miss Georgie Cave France, now Mrs. Gaskin.

Cut 121.

CHAPTER XIX

The horn-book and William Hone—Hone begins a shilling tract on the horn-book—
His reasons for abandoning it—His hitherto unpublished notes on the horn-book
—Hone's title-page—Facsimile draft of placard—Hone advertises for horn-books.

ILLIAM HONE, born at Bath in 1779,
the intimate of Charles Lamb, the compiler of the *Every-Day Book* and *Year
Book*, on which, by the way, some of us
were suckled, and the author of sundry
attacks on the Government, one of which
landed him in prison, projected in 1832
a shilling tract on the horn-book, but
alas! that delighting and painstaking
literary rag-bagman never got further
than rough notes scrawled on the white
portions of circulars and any odd scraps
of paper that came in his way. (How
I obtained these rough notes is told in
a later page.) Hone had not proceeded far before he changed his mind ;
why, let him tell :—

"This little work is in the nature of notes concerning my life and
opinions at different ages. I had intended an article upon an obsolete
instrument of instruction—the Horn-book of the village school-mistress, and
had purposed so to write that students in archæology might be instructed
and even grave antiquaries might incline to read my dissertation ; not as

252

History of the Horn-Book

in the form of an important five shilling quarto suitable to a volume of the Archæologia. But while thinking upon the Horn-book I thought upon the venerable dame who first put a horn-book into my infant hands to learn my letters by, and seeking to honour her memory by mentioning something of her innocent old age and her childlike death, my proposed account of the horn-book deviated into a tone of feeling which I was unwilling to suppress, and seemed so ill-suited to typographical dignity that I abandoned the notion of assuming it and determined not to."

For his projected work Hone drafted several title-pages, all varying and more or less scored through and altered. From these it has been possible to make one embodying his intentions, but omitting the cut of a horn-book referred to farther on. It will be seen that his book was to have been divided into eight heads, but beyond the rough notes already alluded to there is no scrap of writing concerning the old school-dame. Hone appears to have stopped his work before it was well begun.

SOMETHING NEW:
THE
HORN-BOOK, &c.

By William Hone.

———

Introduction.

The Horn-Book	Knowledge & Ignorance
An Old School Dame	The Great Secret
A World of Wonders	Explanations
A Singular Man	Postscript

I am most anxious that this little work should go into the hands of every person who ever heard my name. I earnestly hope it will be read by all who are acquainted with anything I ever wrote.

LONDON
13 Gracechurch Street
1832

(One Shilling)

253

History of the Horn-Book

The two facsimiles (122 and 123) are drafts of placards evidently intended for the use of book-sellers.

"The title-page," says

One Shilling

Strange Things on the Horn Book & By W. Hone.

Something New By William Hone Sold by all Booksellers

Cut 122.

"Many things that I would not confess to any one in particular, I deliver to the public; and refer my lost friends to a bookseller's shop, to know what are my most secret attainments and thoughts"

The Shilling

Sold Here

Cut 123.

Hone, alluding to his unpublished tract, the complete MS. of which if ever finished has gone astray, "bears a representation of a Horn-book which I possess and purpose to describe. This horn-book is of the exact size of the engraving.[1] Upon a piece of Dutch oak, called wainscot, something less than a quarter-inch thick, is pasted a small page of paper printed with the alphabet in Roman lower-case. The alphabet is preceded by

[1] Amongst Hone's notes is a roughly-outlined sketch of a horn-book of the ordinary type, but no engraving.

History of the Horn-Book

a cross ✠, which is followed by a capital A before 'little a.' The lower-case alphabet concludes in the second line with ' &.' Then there follow, also in lower-case and in the same line, the vowel letters, which fill up the first two lines. The third line begins the alphabet in Roman capitals, which concludes in the fourth line, but leaves a blank space to the end of that line. The fifth line contains repetitions of the vowels. Then follow three lines of syllables of two letters, 'ab,' etc., in double columns ; after these, there is 'In the Name of the Father,' etc., in two lines, and then ten lines con-sisting of the Lord's Prayer conclude the page. These contents will be seen within the present page, line for line, word for word, and letter for letter, as they are printed. Upon the page is laid a leaf of horn a little larger than the page. Upon the edges of the horn are narrow slips of a kind of thin brass called latten which make a border to the horn ; and the metal border and the leaf of horn, through which is seen the printed page, are securely nailed upon the oak wainscot. Every horn-book I have seen is made exactly in the same manner with the printed contents precisely the same,[1] and at the bottom, as in mine, there is left from the wood of the back, a handle suited to the tiny fingers of a little child for holding the horn-book while conning the page seen through the horn. Such is, or rather was, the horn-book, and from such a one I learned my letters."

Referring to my copy of the *Table Book*, which has bound up with it the original wrappers and advertisements, I find on the fourth page of the cover of Part VI. for June 1827 the following paragraph :—

"After much enquiry in town for a '*Horn-Book*' and a '*Battle-door*,' I cannot meet with either—will some good-natured friend who has leisure attempt the discovery of these old steps to learning and oblige me by sending them to my Publishers : a '*Horn-book*' I especially wish, and if forwarded from the country will gladly pay its carriage."

In Part X., published in September,[2] Hone again utilises the wrapper in appealing for horn-books :—

"A Horn-Book consisted of the Alphabet and the Lord's Prayer, printed and pasted on a small board with a handle, over the printed

---

[1] Hone knew of the Bateman horn-book in black letter, but when this statement was written he probably had not seen it.

[2] The *Table Book* was published in monthly parts, but in June two numbers were issued, on the 1st and 23rd, which explains the apparently incorrect sequence.

History of the Horn-Book

paper was nailed a thin transparent horn, from beneath which the letters appeared. Formerly, by this contrivance, children were taught their letters. I shall be particularly obliged by *every* reader who will take the trouble to seek for one and send it to me. I am very desirous of specimens of different *Horn-books ;* and each that I have the pleasure to receive will be regarded as a private favour. They are doubtless to be met with among the obsolete stocks of stationers and booksellers in towns remote from London, and perhaps at old turners and toy-shops, or at chandlers, or hucksters, or general dealers. Probably too, there are a few preserved in the clothes box or drawers of many a village school-mistress—

> " Goody, good woman, gossip, n'aunt, forsooth,
> Or dame, the sole addition she did bear.

" These were her appellations in former times, nearer to our own and nearer our metropolis, this now venerated and always venerable female was known as the ' Ma'am ' or ' governess.' How much should I be indebted to one of these ancient ladies for a *Horn-book !* I would crave it in the name of one, who, through such a device as I have described, first ' taught my young idea how to shoot '—she has long since deceased from their matronly sisterhood. W. HONE."

Hone quotes what is said of the horn-book in Johnson's and in Bailey's dictionaries ; he quotes from Shakespeare, Shenstone, Tickell, and Cowper. Notes referring to matters other than the horn-book may possibly have been destroyed, but one or two have been preserved. " (Opinions)—Vessels going by steam—London streets lighted by smoke—tunnel—presumption against God Almighty to attempt going under the water—Dame Redfearn at Millpond Bridge—remembers old horn-books—formerly manufactured them forty years ago—had some unfinished ones—produced boards."

Another note takes the form of a soliloquy. " Ah ! what fond recollections I have of my Horn-book age when in my infant breast there was perpetual summer ; or if my mind was ever clouded, and there followed some droppings of tears, the sunshine of my heart gleamed beneath, and turned them into heat-drops ; and my sorrows were short

Thos. R. Beaufort.

and my days long, and no hour was without its happiness and no day without its joy."

In the Preface to the Fourth Edition of *Aspersions Answered*, dated 12th February 1824, Hone says: "I now declare publicly, what I have frequently affirmed in private, that, with the exception of finishing one work at my entire leisure, I withhold my pen from every purpose but that of cataloguing books." Alas! for such promises ; in the same year a tract appeared written by him entitled "Another article for the *Quarterly Review.*" The work referred to could hardly have been that on the horn-book, but probably related to a long-deferred project referred to years afterwards in a note to his account of the early life and conversion of his father : "The History of my Mind and Heart, my Scepticism, my Atheism and God's final dealings with me, remains to be written. If my life be prolonged a few months, the work may appear in my lifetime. William Hone, 3rd of June, 1841. My Birthday. Now entering my sixty-second year. Church Road, Tottenham."

William Hone left behind him a vast quantity of unsorted MSS., which, according to his catalogue announcements for 1869, Mr. John Camden Hotten, the Piccadilly bookseller and publisher, contemplated publishing under the title of "*Hone's Scrap Book, a Supplementary Volume to the Every-Day Book, the Year Book and the Table Book.* From the MSS. of the late William Hone, with upwards of One Hundred and Fifty engravings of curious and eccentric objects. Thick octavo, uniform with *Year Book*, pp. 800. In preparation." The energy of Mr. Hotten was vast and untiring, but unfortunately his fire was not quite big enough to heat all the irons he put into it, and Hone's *Scrap Book* has never seen the light. In fact, it has not even been prepared. The material, or much of it, passed to Messrs. Chatto and Windus, who it is hoped may some day or other see fit to collate and publish it. If Mr. Hone's transcription of his first rough notes on the horn-book, which he may have licked into shape, is still in existence here it is that it may be looked for. And here I take the opportunity of heartily thanking Messrs. Chatto and Windus for the trouble they have taken in rummaging amongst the chaos of Mr. Hone's papers for the MS. relating to youthful experiences in which the horn-book played a part, and my thanks are not the less hearty because the search has proved fruitless. Mr. Hone was not in the habit of destroying MSS., and it may be that the one I have vicariously hunted for has got into other hands. Thirty and odd years ago Mr. Hotten bought, for fourteen shillings, lot 307 in a sale at Puttick and Simpson's (16th December 1863), catalogued as "Hone's (William) MS. Memoranda, Collections, Correspondence, Cuttings, Sketches, etc., for the *Every-Day Book, Year Book, Table Book*, and other publications, including many useful Selections not printed in either of the Above, Architectural Memoranda, Plan of Windsor, etc., 7 parcels." It is known, however, that other parcels of Hone's MSS. became more or less widely distributed.

CHAPTER XX

Dr. Mackenzie accepts a commission for a work on the Horn-book—He comes into possession of Hone's rough notes—He reads a paper on the Horn-book at the Society of Antiquaries—The paper is suppressed—Horn-books acquired by him—Mackenzie's paper *in extenso.*

BOUT 1860 Dr. Kenneth Mackenzie, F.S.A., accepted a commission from Mr. William Tegg, the veteran publisher, to write a work on the Horn-book, and in hunting about for material he came into possession of Mr. William Hone's rough notes.

Dr. Mackenzie, a man of considerable attainments, had always many irons in the fire. He did some good work, but he commenced a great deal more which was never finished. He contributed largely to literary papers, and amongst other works he wrote a *Life of Homer* (Bohn), *Discoveries in Egypt* (Bentley, 1852), *Burmah and the Burmese* (Routledge, 1853), *Schamyl and Circassia* (Routledge, 1854), *Life of Count Bismarck* (Hogg, 1870), besides editing numerous translations.

For Mr. Tegg, Dr. Mackenzie wrote two poetical and imaginative chapters containing much food for thought, but unfortunately little or nothing about the horn-book. He did, however, write an interesting paper on the subject, which was read before the Society of Antiquaries on

History of the Horn-Book

7th May 1863. It was understood that this paper would be printed in the *Transactions* of the Society, but in view of his relations with Mr. Tegg it never was, and as Dr. Mackenzie died in 1866, all trace of it seemed to be lost. After much inquiry, Mrs. Mackenzie was found, from whom I obtained the two chapters in manuscript which the doctor had left behind, a proof of his unpublished paper read before the Society of Antiquaries, and some of Mr. Hone's original rough notes.

Dr. Mackenzie acquired some horn-books which were exhibited when he read his paper. These, ten in all, were afterwards lent to the South Kensington Museum, and are now the property of Mrs. Mackenzie, who very kindly gave me authority to remove them, so that I might examine them at leisure. They are noted in other pages, and have since been returned to the Museum.

Neither Kenneth Mackenzie nor William Hone, on whose rough notes Mackenzie has largely drawn, seemed to have suspected that away from English-speaking countries the horn-book, as we know it—that is, a tablet covered with horn—never was in use.

The printing here of Dr. Mackenzie's paper on the Horn-book *in extenso* must necessarily lead to repetitions, or rather what seem to be necessary extensions, to which it is hoped the reader will be indulgent :—

NOTES TOWARDS THE HISTORY OF THE HORN-BOOK.

By Kenneth R. H. Mackenzie, Esq., F.S.A.

Read 7th May 1863.

In drawing the attention of the Society of Antiquaries to so homely a subject as the history of the Horn-book, and in laying some specimens of such objects before them, I feel sure that English Antiquaries will be generally pleased at the fact that so many of those humble but important instruments of education have been preserved. I must, however, state that it is not to me that any merit either in their accumulation or preservation is to be imputed. I have only acted as the focus to the joint efforts of many others, and the slight claim which I may prefer upon your attention to the few remarks with which I propose to accompany your examination of the objects, is grounded upon my great desire that some record should exist, so far as is possible, of their early introduction and general history.

Before proceeding to a general review of such facts as I have been able from various sources to gather together, I will briefly refer to the objects before you,

History of the Horn-Book

and state whence each reached me, observing a chronological sequence in mentioning each article. The notes from books, and the reference to the use of the Horn-book, may be reserved till afterwards.

First, however, I will describe the Horn-book and its usual appearance. The back is formed of a piece of Dutch oak, technically called "wainscot," something less than a quarter of an inch thick; upon this is pasted a small page of paper, on which is printed the alphabet in Roman "lower case"; this alphabet is usually preceded by a Greek cross, whence the alphabet was called the Christcross row, or cross row. Next to the cross came a capital A before little a, and the alphabet is succeeded by the sign " &." Next came the vowels, after these the alphabet again in Roman capitals, and then the vowels, and their simplest combinations with the consonants. The formula, " In the name of the Father, etc.," stands next in order, and ten lines containing the Lord's Prayer filled up the page. Over the paper is nailed a leaf of Horn, whence the term Horn-book, secured by narrow strips of thin brass, called latten; a small handle for the scholar to hold by at the bottom completes the object.

The Horn-book is also termed the Battledoor, from the larger specimens being shaped like a battledoor for outdoor games, or for women to use in beating clothes in washing. The battledoor is also used in country places for affixing parish notices on the church door, and the parish clerk detached it when it was his duty to read such notices to the congregation. It is probable that in early times the alphabet may have been *cut* in the wood of the battledoor, as almanacks were cut upon walking-sticks before the invention of printing. The term battledoor was widely spread, and we find the famous founder of the Society of Friends, George Fox, using the word in the title of one of his publications, viz. : *A Battledoor for Teachers and Professors to learn Singular and Plural,* small folio, 1668. Each page of this work is formed into the shape of a battledoor by printers' rules. The first page begins thus : " This Battledoor is for you to learn that you may speak *thou* to one singular, and *you* to many plurall," etc. And the English Battledoor requires you to "read the Battledoor that you may come to the Accidence, Grammar, and Bible." In the compilation of this work, which is in a number of languages, illustrating the same topic, Fox was assisted by Benjamin Furly and others.

Before the final disuse of the Horn-book it was made and sold without horn, as you will perceive by some of the specimens submitted this evening. In place of the horn the printed page is covered with varnish, and of course the *latten* strips are unnecessary. The cross at the commencement was omitted, and the Letter X substituted. I need not enlarge upon this, as the specimens before you sufficiently show the gradual changes which the Horn-books underwent.

The first and earliest record of the Horn-book I have been able to discover, is in one of the engravings to the famous *Margarita Philosophica* of Gregorius Reisch, the prior of Freiburg Carthusian Monastery. The first edition of this book, which

History of the Horn-Book

was often subsequently reprinted, was published at Heidelberg in 1486. The photograph containing a Horn-book was taken from the edition of 1503, from a copy kindly lent to me by our esteemed Fellow, Mr. Robert Cole. We may therefore date the use of the Horn-book in Germany as anterior to 1486, and from the perfect shape of the instrument, it was no doubt extensively in use and well known. It is a curious fact, that the Horn-book represented in the engraving varies in a very slight degree from the one[1] presented to the British Museum by Mr. Halliwell,[2] either in shape or contents. In his *Notices of Chapbooks*, Mr. Halliwell assigns the date of 1570 to this object, but I have since understood that the specimen in question, of which several copies exist, was more likely to have been printed in the time of Queen Anne. It is however worthy of remark, that the handle of this Horn-book or Battledoor is much better than the ordinary one, being so formed that a child could not easily snatch it from a master's hand.

For the benefit of those who may not see this early German print, I will attempt some description of it.

The Goddess of Grammar, ever kind to the youthful aspirant, is here represented in the costume of the period in which the illustration was executed, and with a semi-stern, semi-hopeful countenance. She holds out to him the object to which our present inquiry refers. Satchel by his side, this young gentleman does not seem at all by the expression of his face to typify the schoolboy creeping unwillingly to school. Let us hope he subsequently anticipated the application of the learned Kennicott, who is said to have not only read, written, and construed Hebrew at seven years of age, but to have spoken it with ease ; with eager, outstretched hands, if we may trust the perspective, he is apparently contemplating the golden side of that shield of learning which, like the dream-gates of Hellenic Mythology, has the true material of horn, as well as the golden reverse useful for shuttlecock. Had our young friend been acquainted with a poet, who flourished in a subsequent age, Mr. Thomas Tickell, to whom I shall afterwards refer, he would no doubt have exclaimed with him :—

> Hail, ancient book, most venerable code,
> Learning's first cradle, and its last abode !
> The huge unnumber'd volumes which we see,
> By lazy plagiaries are stol'n from thee :
> Yet future times to thy sufficient store
> Shall ne'er presume to add one letter more.

The key of learning in her hand, the goddess attempts to insert it in the lock, situated, as were no doubt all locks in the middle age, near the extreme top of the door. Evidently, from her towering stature, it is intended to convey that she has no intention of following the acolyte's example, or else in satiric vein, the artist depicted the learned men of his time as very little fellows.

---

[1] Spurious. See page 181.   [2] The donor was Mr. George Offor.

History of the Horn-Book

Armed with the Horn-book, we will suppose the young gentleman to have passed the portal of Agricola, and entered upon the fashionable curriculum of his time. On the lowest storey we perceive Donatus busy in his school, and, as the course of time must be presented, the scholar is mounting higher towards the academy of Priscian; thenceforth we lose sight of him, as he no doubt becomes bewildered in the colleges where Aristotle, Cicero, Pythagoras, Euclid, Ptolemy, and other worthies, who all *head* (a quaint type of the artist's for intellect, perchance), peep from windows in the temple, surmounted at last, thank fortune, with the head and shoulders of that intellectual giant, Peter Lombard, theologian, Metaphysician, and master of sentences. This may complete the outline of the picture, and I would only request, in conclusion, that gentlemen interested in photography should note how the faithful sun has even given a faint adumbration of the black letter type on the reverse page, on the upper part of the photograph.

The second object to which I would refer is, the small oblong plate, seemingly intended for the page of a Horn-book. It is the work of a German artist of the sixteenth century, D. Hopfer. It is three and a half inches high by five and a half inches wide, and contains an alphabet of Roman capitals in three lines, but without the cross at the commencement and the little & after the last letter. The whole is surrounded by an ornamental scroll, adorned with fantastic faces. At the bottom, in the centre, immediately above where the handle of the wooden back would come, is an arch of cherubs over a Triune head, symbolical, we may suppose, of the Trinity. In one lower corner is a crowned head, and in the other a turbaned head. Hopfer, it has been presumed, was himself a Lutheran and a strenuous partisan of the Reformation. Hence, perhaps, some religious feeling prompted the omission of the cross at the commencement. It may be interesting to note that in engravings from various old paintings, the alphabet, or Horn-book, when introduced, is always displayed as in Hopfer's alphabet, viz. the long lines the wide way of the wood. There are engravings from a celebrated picture called the Virgin of the Horn-book, because it represents the infant Saviour with a Horn-book alphabet; but after much inquiry, both public and private, I have not as yet been able to see a copy of that engraving.

Of Continental Horn-books I have not been able to procure any originals; but, from a description given me by M. Octave Delepierre, I have attempted an outline to serve as an idea of those used in Flanders. It will be noticed that the Greek cross surmounts the letters, and these are followed by the ordinary Arabic numerals. Whether any prayer filled up the space, I have been unable to learn. The only other Continental Horn-book of which I can offer any description is the A B C Ballbret, or Ballboard, analogous to our Battledore. The form shown in the outline is common to Germany, Bohemia, Sweden, Norway, and Denmark. Here the three crosses are placed at the end, no doubt as a triple invocation to God, in His threefold character, against the machinations of evil spirits.

History of the Horn-Book

I have next to draw your attention to a celebrated Horn-book known as the Middleton Horn-book, now in the collection of antiquities made by the late Mr. William Bateman, at Lomberdale House, at Youlgrave and Bakewell, in Derbyshire, and completed by his son. When, in 1860, I began to make inquiries into the subject of the Horn-book, the *Athenæum, Notes and Queries, Critic*, and other newspapers, did me the favour to publish a short letter in which I asked for facts. Among the many interesting letters I received was one from Mr. Thomas Bateman, whose recent and untimely decease is so much to be regretted. In the kindest way he placed the engravings of the Middleton Horn-book at my disposal, and I have had several printed, exact facsimiles of those in the catalogue of the Bateman Museum. Mr. Bateman expressed a cordial desire to promote the publication of my proposed history of the Horn-book by any aid from his stores ; and his sudden demise only arrested the execution of his purpose. I shall have occasion subsequently to refer to a curious relic analogous to the Horn-book, for which I was also indebted to Mr. Bateman.

The Middleton Horn-book was discovered on the 10th of March 1828, in the thatch of an old farmhouse at Middleton, by Youlgrave, in the county of Derby. Its length is $3\frac{1}{4}$ inches by $2\frac{7}{8}$ inches, exclusive of the handle, which is an inch long. The wood-engraving is, therefore, the exact size of the original. The page contains the big A and little a to the end of the alphabet, but no cross at the beginning. The vowels succeed with the capitals and syllables. Next comes the formula : "In the name of the Father, and of the Son, and of the Holy Ghost, Amen"; and the Lord's Prayer, down to the words "and deliver us from evil, Amen," fills up the page. The whole is in black letter. The most remarkable peculiarity of the Middleton Horn-book consists, however, in the device upon the reverse, which in ordinary cases is of wood only, but in this instance is entirely covered with calf, originally red, but now faded. Upon the leather is impressed, in silver foil, a figure of Charles I. on horseback, and bareheaded, dressed in armour. A single-line border runs round the entire device. At the upper corner facing the king is a large celestial crown, issuing from what appears to be a cloud over his head. Behind the cloud is a cherub with extended wings ; under the crown are the letters C.R., and beneath the horse's feet the letters T.H. As books (for instance, Harrington's *Oceana*, in the time of the Protector) and horn-books and schoolbooks continued to be printed in black letter down to the time of Queen Anne, there is nothing remarkable in the use of that type in the reign of Charles. It is probable that it was printed only a short time after the execution of the king, and was concealed in its hiding-place during the supremacy of Cromwell. Just over the handle is a device of a quaint nature.

I next beg to draw your attention to the small series of plain Horn-books which have been mounted upon the cardboard. They do not require any special comment ; their probable date is about the middle of the last century.

266

The Adjutant, the Infant and the Hornbook

Sir Arthur Clay, Bart.

History of the Horn-Book

More interesting is the Scottish Horn-book, which bears the date 1784. It is a curious fact that William Hone the Antiquary, to whose diligence we are in the present instance indebted for bringing together the major portion of the present collection, failed all his life to find a copy of a Scottish Horn-book. It was known to exist, but no traces of it could be found when Hone made his researches. Mr. Williamson of Glasgow, to whom I am indebted for the loan of this specimen, has had the page mounted upon horn, thus reversing the order of things in this case. Indeed so highly prized were these objects, that in one instance a gentleman residing near Bristol has had his Horn-book mounted on a silver plate, having, somewhat to its detriment I should think, taken it off the old wooden back which constituted a portion of its integrity and added to its value as a relic. Nevertheless the circumstance is a proof of the estimation in which the object is held.

I have also had a woodcut of a Horn-book printed for exhibition with the remainder of the series; it is a facsimile of the Horn-book depicted some years since in the *Illustrated London News*, and there described by Mr. Timbs, who subsequently inserted it in his gossiping little book, *School Days of Eminent Men*, p. 144. It is unnecessary to refer further to the woodcut, which differs in no respect from the others now on the table.

Among the documents illustrative of Horn-book literature which I have to submit, is one of which I exhibit two pages out of twelve. The subject is the birth and education of young Harlequin, and in a homely and somewhat coarse way depicts the trouble which Harlequin has in bringing up his eldest son. The work is dedicated to Rich the actor, " Harlequin General of Great Britain," and the last page contains an illustration of a Horn-book from which Harlequin is being taught his letters. In this instance the cross precedes the letters, as is generally the case. This constant prefix is alluded to by Bishop Warburton in a letter to Garrick; condemning the pedantic criticism of critics, he says : " They cannot deny that the Christ cross in the Horn-book has been ever esteemed by the ablest of them an inseparable part of the alphabet." Passing from the Horn-book proper, covered with horn, we next come in point of date to those Horn-books merely covered with varnish or mucilage. These are probably of more recent origin, and date from the beginning of this century only. The price of these varied from one penny to twopence each, and the chief printers of those were a firm in Long Lane, Smithfield. Mr. Offor told me that on the introduction of the spelling-book to a greater extent these objects became obsolete, and upwards of a Million and a half of these common Horn-books were destroyed, on account of there being no longer any demand for them, on clearing out the warehouse of his brother and himself. Still they seem to have lingered on in use down in country villages till about 1820, many persons with whom I have conversed having been taught their letters from them. The central northern and western counties abounded in them until the spelling-book became more common.

History of the Horn-Book

In Scotch parlance they were called Ah Bay Broads or A B Boards, and traces of their use are still recoverable in various districts of the Scottish Lowlands and Border counties. Between the introduction of the spelling-book generally, however, there was a transition period in which folding cards called Battledores specially were used. Of these I beg to exhibit several specimens. They contained more than the ordinary Horn-book, as may be seen, and were adorned with rude woodcuts. But they in turn have passed away and are no longer in use. The copies on the table were mostly printed in the Midland Counties, and bore prices varying from twopence to fourpence.

Before the Horn-book was completely in use, it was common to inscribe the alphabet at the commencement of MSS. and Psalters. Mr. Offor showed me a book of Latin prayers, of the fifteenth century, consisting of eight leaves in twenty-fours, at the head of which a criss-cross alphabet of four lines, containing after a cross a great A, a small and large alphabet, and some other signs. In Mr. Bateman's collection a similar manuscript begins in this way.

There is yet one kind of Horn-book to which I might be allowed to refer, although unhappily I have not been able to produce one for the inspection of the Society. Perhaps among youthful students this form of the Horn-book was the most popular and welcome. It was not expensive, and the munificent patrons of learning who published and sold it combined amusement and instruction in a very successful manner. It was rather larger than the ordinary horn-book and there were two editions. The superior edition, a fine tall copy with good margin, splendidly gilt, was to be had for one halfpenny, and the ordinary edition cost one farthing. The colour was of a rich dark brown, and the material was thick. These editions were highly prized and rapidly consumed.

A gentleman who mentioned this edition to me, said that in his early days he had frequently purchased several copies of it, but he had never preserved one. Mr. Tickell, from whose poem I have once already quoted, thus refers to the edition in question :—

> Or if to gingerbread thou shalt descend,
> And liquorish learning to thy babes extend,
> Or sugared plane o'erspread with beaten gold,
> Does the sweet treasures of the letters hold ;
> Thou still shalt be my song.

The method of tuition adopted by professors of education in the employment of this edition was, to promise the pupil for every letter guessed the letter itself; and thus the scholar was doubly able to gratify his taste for learning. Prior mentions this mode of teaching, thus :—

> To Master John, the English maid
> A Horn-book gives of gingerbread ;
> And that the child may learn the better,
> As he can name he eats the letter.

History of the Horn-Book

I have now, in as brief a manner as possible, referred to the various objects I have had the honour to submit to you. Many points of interest the brief limits of this paper will not allow me to name. Of the collateral documents illustrative of the universal esteem in which the Horn-book was held, I produce two: one a poem written by Thomas Tickell in 1728, in praise of the Horn-book, a *jeu d'esprit* worthy of preservation; the other a tract in eight pages which I have mounted, and which is entitled "A Divine Horn-book, or the First Form in the True Theosophick School," wherein is taught the knowledge of God's great name, Jeova, in the House of Letters, as a good help to know God in Nature and Creature, through the Chief of Sinners, the unworthiest of all God's servants, his Majesty's Loyal Subject and Every Man's Brother, by H. L. Gloria in Excelsis. Am I not he that filleth all things? London: printed for the Author, 1688.

Tickell's poem is a passable piece of mock-heroic rhyme, wherein the glories of the Horn-book and its elevated mission to man are sufficiently extolled; but the other document is of an entirely different and fanciful character. As the papers are on the table, I need not detain you by perusing any portions of them.

Having merely termed this paper "Notes towards the History of the Horn-book," I am not necessarily obliged to overweight these remarks with a number of quotations with which you are mostly well acquainted. References to the Horn-book abound alike in our early dramatists and our early poets, and are easily accessible. With Dekker's *Gull's Horn-book*, especially now that it is reprinted in a commodious form, all can render themselves familiar. I will, therefore, in concluding my paper, thank you for your kindness in listening to it, and terminate my paper with an extract from a less-known production, the Horn-book of William Hornbye, in 12mo, published in 1622, and dedicated to the "honorable and hopeful young gentleman, Sir Robert Carr, Baronett":—

> The Horn-book of all books I doe commend,
> For the world's knowledge it doth comprehend,
> Whatever can be written, read, or said,
> Are first of letters framed, composed, and made,
> Each word and sentence are in order set,
> Derived from the English alphabet.
>
> The little infant that receives his birth,
> To pass his pilgrimage upon the earth,
> Takes first a respite, and a time to grow,
> Before he comes unto the Christ-cross roe.
>
> For three or fower yeares space like to a lamb,
> He spends his time in sporting and in gam;
> His wanton courage somewhat then to coole,
> His parents put him to a petty school,
> Then after that he takes a pretty pride
> To weare the horn-book dangling by his side,
> And was it not well armed with plate and horne,
> 'Twas in great danger to be rent and torne,

History of the Horn-Book

For in his sporte he sometimes falleth out
With his schoole-fellow, so they have a bout,
And buffs counterbuff, the Horn-bookes then
Are all the weapons for these stout tall men.

Hornbye tells us that a mustard-seed is the least of all seeds, and yet becomes a great tree and of large value :—

Eke so the Horn-book is the seed and graine
Of skill by which we learning first obtaine,
And, though it be accounted small of many
And haply bought for twopence or a penny,
Yet will the teaching somewhat costly be,
Ere they attain unto the full degree
Of scholarship and art.

I may be permitted, in closing this sketch of the present information existing as to the Horn-book, to say that I should be greatly indebted to any gentleman who could add in any way to the numerous stray notices and facts in my possession, who could indicate to me any further sources whence to gather together materials, or who could inform me of the existence of other specimens, to add to the list, now numbering some forty, of this early instrument of education.

Only two chapters (all that he ever wrote) of Mackenzie's projected work on the Horn-book, commissioned by Mr. William Tegg, were written. They are merely preliminary flourishes, and as they add absolutely nothing to the reader's knowledge, I refrain from printing them here. The title-page of this projected volume was planned as follows :—

THE HORN-BOOK

its

Origin, Progress

and

Decline.

By

Kenneth R. H. Mackenzie

Fellow of the Society of Antiquaries.

Hail ancient book, most venerable code,
Learning's first cradle, and its last abode !
The huge unnumber'd volumes which we see
By lazy plagiaries are stol'n from thee :
Yet future times to thy sufficient store
Shall ne'er presume to add one letter more.

Tickell's *Poem in Praise of the Horn-Book*, 1728.

LONDON :

William Tegg : 85 Queen Street.

MDCCCLX.

272

CHAPTER XXI

The horn-book in use in some form through long ages—Scratched tiles—Why the letters in the Hebrew, Greek, and Latin alphabets follow the same illogical order—Early pens—When the horn-book was first made—An impossible nut to crack—Egyptian and Arabic tablets—Tabellæ—An opinion on the Horn-book from Professor Petrie—Dr. Lepsius's Greek terra-cotta horn-book—Professor Dr. George Stephens's ox-horn horn-book—An early A B C tablet—Perkin Warbeck's A B C or "Crosse Rowe"—Caxton horn-books queried—A block-sheet horn-book by Wynkyn de Worde—When the horn-book was in general use—The syllabarium and the horn-book—An assertion exploded—A savant's theory regarding "ba-be-bi-bo-bu"—The girdle—The ampersand—The horn-book in Shakespeare—Halliwell on the Horn-book.

E know that our alphabet was of gradual growth, and that it is traced back to the Egyptian hieratic or sacerdotal characters in use perhaps twenty-five centuries before Christ. Hand-tablets, somewhat akin to horn-books, were probably known all through these long years. The signs were originally ideographic or pictorial, and from them came phonograms, symbols, or what we call letters, representing sounds, the development of which need not be here discussed. Perhaps the earliest alphabetic writing known (approximately 4000 B.C.) appears on a tablet preserved in the Ashmolean Museum at Oxford, of the time of Sent, an

History of the Horn-Book

Egyptian monarch of the second dynasty. From the signs or letters then in use, amongst them the letter n, as we have it, was developed the Phœnician alphabet, whence came the Greek and its offshoot the Roman.

Tiles, scratched or incised with alphabets before being baked, may be classed with the earliest of children's lesson " books." Amongst the many treasures recently excavated with much thoughtful labour at Silchester is a tile bearing a writing lesson in Roman cursive hand, probably of the first or second century. Later tiles, impressed with separate letters of the alphabet, are generally of red clay inlaid with coloured clay of another kind. The designs were stamped from wooden, moulds and in tiles manufactured so long ago as the fourteenth century, the grain of the oak is plainly traceable. In the ruins of Dale Abbey, a Premonstratensian house near Derby, founded towards the close of the twelfth century, some beautiful old decorative tiles have of late years been unearthed, amongst them being one marked off into a series of small squares containing therein the complete alphabet in Lombardic capitals. Curiously enough, although the letters are in sequence, they must be read from right to left (see cut 124) instead of from left to right, the mistake being that of the mould-cutter, who forgot to reverse his work.

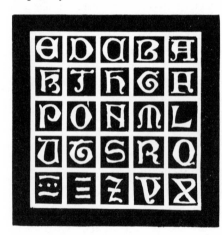

Cut 124.

Mr. John Ward, in his *Dale and its Abbey*, suggests that the kilns often attached to the monastic houses where these tiles were made and baked, were used by the skilled artisans forming travelling companies of tile-makers, who carried with them their stamps, otherwise it is difficult to understand how a small abbey like that of Dale could have had a tilery attached. This opinion is borne out by the fact, otherwise extremely puzzling, that armorial tiles relating to a family in one county are found in distant counties.

But we are wandering a little too widely. The fact that the characters in the alphabets of the principal literary languages—Hebrew, Greek, and

History of the Horn-Book

Latin—follow each other in the same illogical order, must suggest that there is probably a cause explaining this conventional juxtaposition. Dr. Pleyte of Leyden provides an ingenious solution of the problem, agreeing in the main with Lepsius.

The learned doctor points out that the Egyptians, previously to the eleventh dynasty about three thousand years before our era, were accustomed to write in vertical columns, and that if the Hebrew, Greek, and Latin alphabets—all derived from the Egyptian—are compared, it is found that upon dividing the letters into vertical columns of the vowels, labials, sibilants, gutturals, and dentals, according to the natural method, and reading them in horizontal lines, very nearly the conventional sequence results :—

Vowels.	Labials.	Sibilants.	Gutturals.	Dentals.
a	b	c		d
e	f	g	h	
i j			k	l
	m		n	
o	p		q	r
		s		t
u	v			
	w		x	
y		z		

If we bear in mind the additions and omissions required to adapt the original Egyptian alphabet to suit the requirements of the languages which have successively adopted it, Dr. Pleyte's explanation would seem reasonable.

The pen is by no means so late an invention as is often supposed. One of the earliest must have been that used by the Ostrogoth Theodoric, who, by means of a stencil plate, on which were cut the first four letters of his name, ingeniously followed the openings with a pen, and was thus enabled to write his signature. According to the *Nineteenth Century* of May 1891, a metal pen, slit and shaped like a quill pen, was recently found in the so-called tomb of Aristotle at Eretria.

When the first horn-book was made—it was certainly written, not printed—and who made it, nobody knows, but obviously its origin was in the tabellæ or tablets on which wax was smeared for writing or scoring upon with a stylus, as tabellæ had their origin, born of convenience, in writing, or scratching on bone, stone, metals, horn, clay, wood, leaves, bark, skins, or anything that would take a mark and retain it. Sir Edward Maunde Thompson, K.C.B., in his *Handbook of Greek and Latin Palæography*, points out that, as the skins of animals for writing purposes had been in very early use, "the introduction of parchment, or vellum, as it is more generally termed—that is to say, skins prepared in such a way that they could be written upon on both sides—cannot properly be called an invention ; it was rather an extension of or improvement upon an old practice." Perhaps Sir Edward, who so ably controls the fortunes of our National Library, may one day be induced to give us his promised account of early Greek and Roman writing used for educational purposes.

For teaching children in schools the Egyptians used tablets of various kinds, of which specimens are in the British Museum. They are generally coated with wax or other composition, on which an impression could easily be made with the stylus. In others of a more permanent kind the writing was done with ink on the wood itself. The stylus might be of iron or other metal, ivory or bone, the letters being scratched or incised by the point. The other end was made flat for smoothing the wax and for obliterating. To this day an Egyptian child is instructed from a horn-book-shaped tablet of wood (cut 125), painted white, on which its lessons are written. When the little fellow is supposed to have mentally absorbed what is before him, the lesson is washed off and another written on the white surface. The children also use the tablet, in which it will be noted the handle is at the top, for practising writing.

Cut 125.

The tablet, reduced to quarter size, shown in cut 126, containing the Arabic alphabet, is in the museum attached to the Sunday School Union,

THIRST FOR KNOWLEDGE.   *Ambrose Dudley.*

to which it was presented by Mr. J. Gadsby.   Another Eastern tablet of this description is in the Biblical Museum of the Church of England Sunday School Institute.

Cut 126.

Tabellæ, Greek and Roman, were of varying size, single, double, or made up of several separate leaves held together by ring hinges.   The wood was lowered by cutting, so as to leave a raised rim or frame all

279

History of the Horn-Book

round for the reception of the wax which had been previously mixed with a dark pigment. Quintilian mentions wooden tablets with incised letters for teaching children reading and writing.

In some tablets taken from Pompeii, the outer leaves were devoid of wax and bore inscriptions in ink. In July 1875, during excavations at Pompeii, a great haul of waxen tablets was made, no less than 127 being discovered in a box. They were, however, of no great interest, being *perscriptiones* connected with sales by auction, etc.

In the Lübeck Museum are two school writing-tablets of uncertain age. They were discovered during the demolition of the oldest National School in Lübeck which stood next to the Church of St. Jacob. These tablets, about 8 × 5 inches, are enclosed in a wooden frame, and are covered on both sides with black wax.

In a letter to the writer, Professor W. Flinders Petrie, whose intuition is keen as his knowledge is profound, says : " So long as writing was on wax tablets in Roman and Byzantine times there was no inducement to use horn-covering. Parchment would be none the worse for handling. So until paper came into common use it is not likely that horn-covering would be desired."

When papyrus was superseded and paper came into "common use" it is difficult to exactly determine. While known in China ages before, it was not common nearer home until the tenth or eleventh century, and it was in the twelfth that the first paper was made in Europe. In this country rag-paper was not in common use until the fourteenth century.

Included by some writers amongst horn-books is the Greek terra-cotta ink-bottle in the Gregorian Museum in the Vatican, unearthed in a tomb of ancient Caere, on which is scratched a Pelasgic alphabet and syllabarium, which Dr. Lepsius of Berlin is inclined to regard as the oldest known alphabet thus extended. It is difficult, however, to follow the reasoning of those who would dub an ink-bottle a horn-book simply because little Pelasgians drew ink from the inside to write the letters they learned from the outside.

The late Professor Dr. George Stephens, in *The Runes, Whence came They ?* (Williams and Norgate, Henrietta Street, W.C.), mentions a small ox-horn, not intended for drinking from, found at Erga, Stavanger Amt, Norway, now in the Stavanger Museum, on which is engraved a Runic

History of the Horn-Book

alphabet. The learned doctor, who catalogues between ten and eleven thousand examples of Runic remains, describes it as "the oldest horn-book in Europe." For what "oldest" here means the author vexatiously compels us to refer to another of his works, *Old Norse Runic Monuments*, where we find the relic ascribed to the twelfth or thirteenth century. An alphabet for teaching children the A B C is certainly incised on a horn, but whether it can be classed as a horn-book is a matter for individual opinion.

Reference to a very early example of the A B C being fastened to a board, "a brede of tre," which may or may not have been protected by horn, is found in Harl. MS. 3954 in the British Museum. The date is late fourteenth century :—

> Quan a chyld to scole xal set be,
>   A bok hym is browt,
> Naylyd on a brede of tre,
> That men callyt an abece,
>   Pratylych i-wrout.
> Wrout is on the bok without
> .V. paraffys grete and stoute,
>   Rolyd in rose-red ;
> That is set withoutyn doute
>   In tokenyng of Cristes ded.
> Red letter in parchemyn
> Makyth a chyld good and fyn
>   Lettrys to loke & se.
>
> Be this bok men may dyvyne
> That Cristes body was ful of pyne
> That deyid on rode tre.
> On tre he was don ful blythe,
> With grete paraffys, that ben wondes. V.
>   As ȝe mon understonde, etc.

Much more of this interesting verse might be quoted, the whole of which forms the introduction to a poem of nearly two hundred lines, each paragraph beginning with the different letters of the alphabet in succession.

In the Fifty-Third Annual Report of the Deputy Keeper of the Public Records (C. 6804) something which may have been a horn-book is mentioned in connection with the trial in 1499 of a number of persons implicated in a conspiracy to release the Earl of Warwick and Perkin

History of the Horn-Book

Warbeck. According to the indictment, one "Luke Longford feloniously sent to the said Peter a closed letter in which was enclosed a long white thread, by which he could receive through the said windows letters from the said Luke and other traitors touching their treasonable intentions. And the said Peter feloniously and treasonably delivered to the said John Audeley a certain book called A B C, otherwise called a Crosse Rowe, and under each letter in the said 'Crosse Rowe' was written a character or sign, to the end that the said Audeley should write back to him by the said character or sign his felonious and treasonable purpose, so that in case any persons unused to such characters should see the said letters, they should not understand their purport; which book the said Audeley for that purpose feloniously received from the said Peter." The characters used by these conspirators may have been symbols, ciphers, or even the letters of the alphabet transposed. The episodes connected with this interesting trial having been fully set forth by Mr. W. E. A. Axon in the *Phonetic Journal*, led an anonymous paragraphist to suggest shorthand as the characters employed. But although a system of abbreviations is known to have been practised in the fourth century B.C. or earlier, for such a purpose shorthand would have been useless if not impossible. No form of modern shorthand was practised in this country until some three-quarters of a century later than the date of this trial for conspiracy.

Herodotus records the successful conveyance to the Lacedæmonians of a message written on the under or wooden surface of a tablet which was afterwards covered with wax. Here the message was concealed and symbols would be unnecessary.

There is no reason why Coster of Haarlem, to whom the honour is accorded of having printed in 1438 the first stylographic or block book, *Speculum Humanæ Salvationis*, should not have multiplied alphabets for the use of children by rubbings from engraved wooden blocks. He probably did. As horn-books were certainly in use long before the time of Caxton, it is quite likely that he printed them, and if examples should turn up they will probably be found, as other typographical treasures have been found, embalmed as binder's waste in books printed by himself or by those who followed him.

In the library of the Society of Antiquaries of London is an engraved oaken block with a Lombardic alphabet in relief, from which the im-

282

pression shown in cut 127 is reduced in size to one-quarter. This alphabet, in which the V and W have disappeared, would seem to have a special interest, as suggesting more nearly than either the Latin or Greek the hieroglyphics from which every alphabet is derived. The P (from hieroglyph ⊟) is less corrupt in form than what now prevails, and the K (from hieroglyph ⊐ written cursively ⨭) can hardly be looked upon as incomplete. But alas for theorising! An examination of the

Cut 127.

block itself shows conclusively that while the greater part of both letters has been broken away, sufficient of the original work remains to restore their shapes. The block shows signs of wear, and from an impression it is easy to construct a perfect horn-book such as might have been, and probably was, supplied to schoolmasters and dealers; cut 128 shows such a horn-book full size, with the missing letters restored. The imprint at foot is the tripartite device (shorn of its upper and lower divisions) that Wynkyn de Worde most frequently used, the initials W C (the W interlaced—a form which Caxton did not affect) and the date indicating, it will be remembered, his connection with William Caxton. The contraction ⅋ is made up, it will be noted, of the numerals 7, 4 in their old form 7 ⅄, giving the year 1474, the 14 being omitted.

Wynkyn de Worde is supposed to have adopted Caxton's device

History of the Horn-Book

about 1504, but it is reasonable to suppose that work of an ephemeral character bore the central lettering as a stamp or merchant's mark from about 1496 when he succeeded him. It may be fairly assumed that this alphabet block, in which the absence of the cross will be noted, was cut by Wynkyn de Worde, or by some one in his employment, between 1496 and 1534, the date of his decease. It is of course possible that it may be the work of some modern engraver, say of the beginning of the last century ; it can hardly be later. We must remember that at whatever date the block was cut, the horn-book was in use, and so far as one can judge, there can have been no motive in comparatively modern times for adding Wynkyn de Worde's mark. This extremely interesting and valuable relic—for a *cliché* of which thanks are due to the Society of Antiquaries—has every appearance of age, and if it is to be accepted as genuine, is the only direct evidence of block-printed horn-books—if horn-books were ever made from it—preserved to us.

When readers were few the copyist reigned supreme, but as they increased, their wants were met by engraving his work on wood page by page and stamping impressions therefrom, the natural transition being printing from separate types, a development born of the wants of the people. If Coster of Haarlem, Gutenberg of Mentz, or one of the dozen or more printers for whom the honour of being first in the field has been claimed, had not, some time between the first and second quarters of the fifteenth century (1438-50), come to the rescue—well, somebody else would ! We know positively that horn-books were made by the copyist, and we know intuitively that, as with playing cards, a large demand would be met by impressions from engraved blocks.

No example of a written or printed horn-book on parchment or vellum appears to have been preserved to us. The costliness and comparative difficulty of manipulating these materials may have influenced the makers of block books in using paper, the notable exception being the Donatus or Latin Grammar, which, to get even with the destructive schoolboy, was printed upon parchment. It is probable that all horn-books from movable type, as well as those worked at an earlier period from wooden blocks, were printed on paper. But as block books continued to be manufactured after the invention of printing, " at an earlier period " must not be taken too literally.

Cut 128.

History of the Horn-Book

The Stationers' Company, a power long before the invention of printing, was not incorporated until 1557. In October 1587 "the horne A B C" was licensed to John Wolfe, and in 1605 the Company granted three pounds a year to Alice Wolfe during her lifetime for relinquishing her claim to the "A B C horn-book." Another entry relating to the "Horne A B C" occurs in 1619-20. In 1655, information being received that letters were cast to print the horn-book, "Mr. Warden Foster was desired to commence a suit for the irregular printing of that and against all others who incroached on the privileges of the Company." Although there is evidence that it was known earlier, it is probable that the horn-book was not in general use until somewhat late in the sixteenth century.

The Will of Dame Thomasine Perceval, dated the Vigil of the Feast of Christmas, 1510 A.D., directs "that a chantry with cloisters, should be built near the church of Wike St. Marie, Cornwall, which she endowed with thirty marks a year, and further directs that there shall be established therein a schole for young children born in the parish of Wike St. Marie; and such to be always preferred as are friendless and poor. They are to be taught to read with their fescue (pointer) from a boke of horn, and also to write, and both as the manner was in that country when I was young."[1] The age of the Dame we do not know, but we learn from Hawker that John Bunsley took her to London in 1463. Say she was eighteen in that year, and that she was taught the A B C when five years old, then we have the date 1450 when the horn-book was in use.

Bequests of horn-books have not been specially looked up, but they could not have been common. In addition to that previously mentioned is another, later, in the Will of Francis Pynner of Bury, Gent 1639 (*Wills and Inventories from the Registers of the Commissary of Bury St. Edmund's, and the Archdeacon of Sudbury*. Edited by Samuel Tymner. Printed for the Camden Society, 1850, p. 176): "The same overplus shall from tyme and to time, by the said new elected ffeoffees of the said messuage for the time then being, be employed to and for the buyeing and provideing of horne bookes and primers to be giuen to poore children of the said parish of St. Maries, in Bury aforesaid."

---

[1] The *Prose Works* of the Rev. R. S. Hawker, Vicar of Morwenstow. London : Blackwood and Sons, 1893.

History of the Horn-Book

In the minutely-detailed inventory of the goods of Mr. John Wilkensone (an opulent Newcastle Merchant, Sheriff of Newcastle in 1555, and Mayor in 1561), "at the howse off his deathe and praysed by iiij honest men John hudson M'chaunt, John gybson, Alexander lawson M'chaunts, and antonye Sympson gowldsmythe, the 4 of May A° 1571," appears " Xiiij doss'pap^r latten abeesees iij^s vj^d—iiij doss'abeesees in p'chment ij^s" (*Wills and Inv. North Count., Surtees Soc.,* ii. 362).

More than one writer has stated that some evidence that the syllabarium was first added to the horn-book about 1596 is to be found in the Preface to the Reader of *The English Schoolmaster,* an extraordinarily popular book, first published in that year, which ran into nearly fifty editions, and was compiled, according to the title-page, by Edward Coote (Christian name really Edmund—why the change no one knows), then Master of the Free School in St. Edmund's Bury. The writer's copy is the "thirty time imprinted . . . by William Leybourn for the Company of Stationers, 1661," but from carelessness the last page has on it " Printed for the Company of Stationers, 1655." " I have so disposed," says Coote, " the placing of my first book that if a child should tear out every leaf as fast as he learneth yet it shall not be greatly harmful, for every new chapter repeateth and teacheth again all that went before." So broad a hint may in a measure account for the large number of editions into which this manual ran.

Here is one of Mr. Coote's spelling lessons : " Boy, go thy way to the top of the hill, and get me home the bay Nag, fill him well and see he be fat, and I will rid me of him, for he will be but dull as his dam ; if a man bid well for him, I will tell him of it ; if not, I do but rob him : and so God will vex me, and may let me go to hell, if I get but a jaw-bone of him ill."

To get at the so-called evidence that the syllabarium was first added to the horn-book in Coote's time, we must read carefully what Coote himself says in his Preface : " But to return to my teaching Trades-men, if thou desirest to be informed how to teach this Treatise, work diligently the directions given in all places of the book, and as this scholar is in saying his lesson, mark what words he misseth and them note with thy pen or pin, and let him repeat them at the next lecture, and so until he be perfect, not regarding those where he is skilfull. And let his fellows

"DON'T YOU KNOW?"   Everard Hopkins.

History of the Horn-Book

also remember them to appose him in their propositions. But methought I heard thee say, that my Reasons have perswaded thee to be willing to teach this, but thou canst not move all their parents to be willing to bestow so much money in a book at the first. Tell them from me that they need buy no more, and then they shall save much by the bargain ; but they will reply that this little young childe will have torn it before it be half learned. Then answer them that a remedy is provided for them also, which is this ; First, the Printer upon sight hereof, framed the Horn-book according to the order of this book, making the first part of my second page the matter thereof, which in my opinion he did with good reason, for a child may by this treatise almost learn to spell perfectly in as little time as learn well the Horn-book. But this latter being first learned, being the ground-work of spelling, all the rest of this work will be gotten with small labour."

The first page, which backs the last page of Preface, has but the alphabet several times repeated in black and Roman letters, and under all, the vowels. The second page has directions to the teacher, the vowels, and a syllabarium of twenty lines in double column, every line in the first beginning with the letter A.

If Coote's printer, as he says, "framed the Horn-book according to the order of this book, making the first part of my second page the matter thereof," it would have the following matter, which is the upper part of the page shorn of directions to the teacher :—

a	e	i	o	u		a	e	i	o	u
Ab	eb	ib	ob	ub		Ba	be	bi	bo	bu
Ad	ed	id	od	ud		Da	de	di	do	du
Af	ef	if	of	uf		Fa	fe	fi	fo	fu
Ag	eg	ig	og	ug		Ga	ge	gi	go	gu
Ah	eh	xx	oh	xx		Ha	he	hi	ho	hu
Al	el	il	ol	ul		La	le	li	lo	lu
Am	em	im	om	um		Ma	me	mi	mo	mu
An	en	in	on	un		Na	ne	ni	no	nu
Ap	ep	ip	op	up		Pa	pe	pi	po	pu
Ar	er	ir	or	ur		Ra	re	ri	ro	ru

Several of the pages which follow in Coote's book contain more

History of the Horn-Book

directions to the teacher and the syllabarium further extended. Although every example seems to have disappeared, there is no reason for absolutely disbelieving Coote's statement that his printer made so extraordinary and useless a horn-book, but that he did so cannot of course be accepted as evidence that the syllabarium was first introduced into the horn-book by him. In fact, no such claim is made. The syllabarium, as we know it in the horn-book, figures in the earliest primers, and if not quite as old as the hills, must go back in some form or other to the time of the invention of a written alphabet and simple words formed therefrom.

The horn-book recommended by Mr. Coote being insufficient for teaching a child to read, a parent would naturally be led on to invest in a copy of *The English Schoolmaster.* Mr. Coote would appear to have been an exceedingly astute person, and with this to his credit, we may leave him.

Ba, *pueritia*, with a horn added.

This dialogue (*Love's Labour's Lost*, Act V. sc. 1) is constructed, says Halliwell, on the actual mode of the elementary education of the time, which has been partially continued to the present day. That this is the case is seen by the following instructions given in the *Ludus Literarius, or the Grammar Schoole*, 1627, p. 19 : —" Then teach them to put the consonants in order before every vowel and to repeat them oft over together—as thus : to begin with b, and to say ba, be, bi, bo, bu. So d —da, de, di, do, du ; f—fa, fe, fi, fo, fu. Thus teach them to say all the rest, as it were sounding them together—la, le, li, lo, lu ; the hardest to the last, as ca, ce, ci, co, cu, and ga, ge, gi, go, gu, in which the sound is a little changed in the second and third syllables. When they can doe all these, then teach them to spell them in order thus. What spels b-a ? If the childe cannot tell, teach him to say thus b-a, ba ; so putting first b before every vowel, to say b-a, ba, b-e, be, b-i, bi, b-o, bo, b-u, bu. Then ask him againe What spels b-a, and hee will tell you ; so all the rest in order. By oft repeating before him hee will certainly doe it. After this, if you will ask him how he spels b-a, he will answer b-a, ba." So in all the others.

The scene in the text appears to have been imitated by Ravenscroft in his comedy of *Scaramouch a Philosopher*, 1677. " *Mist.*—How, open your book and read. *Harl.*—A-b, ab, e-b, eb, i-b, ib, o-b, ob, u-b, ub.

History of the Horn-Book

B-a, ab. *Mist.*—How's that? b-a spell ab? *Harl.*—Yes. *Mist.*—A-b spells ab. B-a spells—what? What says the Sheep? *Harl.*—What says a sheep? Ha! ha! he! he! *Mist.*—What says the Sheep. *Harl.* —The Sheep says, ha! ha! he! nothing can a Sheep speak. *Mist.* —Did you never hear a Sheep cry *ba*? *Harl.*—Ba, yes. *Mist.*—Well b-a spells ba. This is the third fault. Come, a sound whipping will quicken your apprehension."

One whose acquaintance with the classics is as close as his knowledge of babes and their prattle is remote, insistently maintains that a mother's talk " ba-ba-ba," " boo-boo-boo," is a survival of horn-book days when the infant mind was educationally deluged with the sounds of " Ba-be-bi-bo-bu." The labial " b " naturally finding expression from infant lips when infants were first invented, the ingenious theory of a learned friend who may have had in his mind the stuttering Comte de Boissy d'Anglas nicknamed " Babe-bi-bo-bu," will not be taken too seriously.

It is improbable that vellum or parchment horn-books—that is, horn-books covered with horn and not merely tablets—were ever much used if at all, but if examples turn up we should expect to find the handles pierced for a ribbon or string to suspend them from the girdle. The earliest horn-books left to us are printed on paper and are so pierced, but as the girdle disappeared very soon after the introduction of printing from movable letters, most of the later examples are unpierced.

The girdle must naturally be one of the oldest parts of a woman's attire : " A good name is better than a golden girdle" (Proverbs xxii. 1). There is an allusion to " a horn-book hanging at the girdle of a girl," in the comedy of *Sir Courtly Nice*, 1685, p. 14 : and " You shall stay here and hang at my girdle like a horn-book till I have learnt ye through," is found in Dogget's *Country Wake*, 1696, p. 14.

> An your v ist, mistress, were as slender as my wit,
> One o' these maids' girdles for your waist should be fit.
>
> *Love's Labour's Lost*, Act IV. sc. 1.

Florio gives " Centurola, a horne-book for children to learne to reade hanging at their girdle." " School-boys," says Halliwell, " were accustomed to carry their horn-books to school, suspended from the girdle, and sometimes to use them without detaching them from it." It would appear that horn-books were also suspended from the neck.

History of the Horn-Book

In his comedy, *Love for Love*, "acted at the Theatre in Little Lincoln's Inn Fields, by His Majesty's Servants," and "Printed and sold by H. Hills, in Black Fryars, near the Water-side," undated, but probably 1695, Act I. sc. 14, the author, Mr. Congreve, mentions the horn-book. Scandal, speaking of his pictures, says : " I have another large Piece too, representing a School, where there are huge proportion'd Criticks, with long Wigs, lac'd Coats, Steinkirk Cravats and terrible Faces, with Cat Calls in their Hands, and Horn-books about their necks." It was not uncommon for ladies to carry books of devotion slung from the waist. In the Tudor Exhibition, held in 1890, a portrait of Lady Petre was exhibited, in which, suspended from a gold chain encircling her waist, is a book of prayers ; and there is a note of such a book in the privy purse expenses of Princess (afterwards Queen) Mary.

The English black-letter (a term not generally used until about 1600) horn-book, probably the earliest left to us, reproduced in cut 129, may have seen the light about the middle of the sixteenth century, but its age, like that of all horn-books, is impossible to arrive at with certainty. It is in the collection of the late Hon. Granville Leveson-Gower, and was found in the winter of 1870-71 behind the panelling of a Tudor house in the village of Limpsfield in Surrey. It is unfortunately much dilapidated. The base is of roughly-shaped oak, quarter of an inch thick, about two-thirds of the lettering has disappeared, and owing to the combined effects of dirt and damp, what horn there is left has lost much of its translucency. The two or three pieces of metal rimming still remaining are oxidised almost out of existence. The types are identical with those by William, the son or the younger brother of Robert Copland, one of Wynkyn de Worde's [1] servants.

Robert Copland, who printed from 1515 to 1540, was a man of some knowledge. He was painstaking in his work, consistent in his spelling, and it is to him we owe the modern form of the comma. The date of the birth of Robert Copland is unknown, and the first heard of him is in

---

[1] An enthusiast attributes this horn-book to Wynkyn de Worde, but an examination of the type in a few representative volumes due to him, say his *Scala Perfecconis*, printed in 1494, *Vitas Patrum*, 1495, *Polycronycon*, same year, *The Meditations of Saint Bernardz*, 1496, *This present boke shewyth the manere of hawkynge and huntynge*, etc., same year, and *a full deuoute and gostely treatyse of ye Imytacio* and *following*, etc., 1503, *Thordynary of Crysten Men*, 1506, shows conclusively that the horn-book figured in cut 129 could not have been printed by him.

History of the Horn-Book

the Prologue to *Kynge Appolyn of Thyre*, which he translated for his master, Wynkyn de Worde. It has been supposed that he worked for Caxton, as in this Prologue he says he is "gladly followyng the trace of my mayster Caxton, begynninge with small storyes and pamfletes, and so to other." But it seems improbable that he had any connection with the great printer, as further on he begs the reader "to pardon myn ignorant youth"; and Caxton had died in 1491, or nineteen years before the publication of *Kynge Appolyn*. He is also known as the author of two pieces of verse : *The Hye way to the Spyttal Hous* and *Jyl of Breyntfords Testament*. Wynkyn de Worde must have had a good opinion of his servant Robert Copland, for in his will he leaves him ten marks. His first dated book seems to have been in 1515, and the last dated is 1540 ; but he is believed to have lived till 1548, when his successor, William Copland, succeeded to his business and published his first book. Whether William was the younger brother or the son of Robert is unknown ; indeed, little is known of him except that he was one of the original members of the Stationers' Company, and is named in their Charter. His last dated book is 1561, but *A Dyaloge between ii Beggars* is registered for him by the Stationers' Company between 1567 and 1568. He died some time between July 1568 and July 1569, and his Company did special honour to his funeral, for there is an entry in their accounts of "Payd for the buryall of Copland vjs."

A number of books printed by William Copland, in which the type closely accords with that used in this horn-book (cut 129), are in the British Museum.[1] If, as supposed, Robert Copland died in 1548, the date 1550, assigned in the Museum Catalogue to most of these books, must be too early.

---

[1] *Sir Isumbras.*—Here begynneth the history of the valyent Knyght Syr Isenbras (Lond. 1550 ?).
R. Hood.—A mery geste of Robyn Hoode and of hys lyfe, wythe a newe playe for to be played in Maye games, very plesaunte and full of pastyme (Lond. 1550 ?).
Tryamoure.—Syr Tryamoure (Lond. 1550 ?).
Bevis (Sir) of Southampton.—Syr Bevys of Hampton (Lond. 1550 ?).
Degore.—Syr Degore (Lond. 1550 ?).
Squire.—The Squyr of lowe degre (Lond. 1560 ?).
Guy, Earl of Warwick.—Title wanting. (The booke of the most victoryous Prynce Guy of Warwick) (Lond. 1560 ?).
Elias, Chevalier au cygne.—The Knight of the Swanne. Here beginneth the History of ye noble Helyas Knyght of the Swanne, newly translated out of the Frensshe into Englysshe at th' instygacion of the Puyssaunt and Illustryous Prynce Lorde Edwarde Duke of Buckyngham (Lond. 1550 ?).

✠Aabcd
qrilstv
A.B.C.D.E.
O.P.Q.R.S.
a e i o u
ab eb ib ob ub
ac ec ic oc uc
ad ed id od ud
In the name of the
Sonne, and of the ho
Ur father w
heauen hall
name. Thy kingdo
Thy wil be done
it is in heauen. Gi
day our daily bread. A
giue vs our trespasses as we
forgiue them that trespas a
gainst vs. And lead vs not
into temptation. But deliuer vs from all. Amen.

Cut 129.

History of the Horn-Book

With a cut in facsimile before him of the horn-book itself, it seems almost wasting the reader's time to say that a portion of the printed sheet has disappeared, that the "u" consistently takes the place of "v"[1] (as it does in books printed by Copland), that the word "will" in "Thy wil be done" is spelt with one "l," that "hallowed" has but one "l," and that in the alphabet the "u," which had not then settled down into the position it now occupies, comes after the "v."

The tacks confining the horn have disappeared, and it will be noted that the handle of the oaken base is pierced at the foot to admit of a string for suspending the horn-book from the girdle. Horn-books of this class are *rarissimæ* in any condition ; perfect examples are unknown.

The sixteenth-century horn-book, which need hardly be engraved, found in Paternoster Row[2] and now in the collection of the Rev. S. M. Mayhew, is indeed an interesting old scarecrow. The oak base, fully quarter of an inch thick, is devoid of ornamentation. The almost perfect horn-covering is blackened and opaque through long exposure to dirt and damp, and the once spotless printed black-letter sheet long ago mouldered into dust. The width of this relic, which may have been identical in character with the horn-book figured in cut 129, is three and three-eighths, and the length, without the handle, five and one-eighth inches ; the handle, of the usual shape, is two and seven-eighths, giving a total length of eight inches. Three-quarters of an inch from the bottom of the handle is a hole a full eighth of an inch in diameter. The rimming, which in this horn-book is fixed close to the outer edge, is of tin, and the iron tacks keeping it in place are ten in number, instead of the usual eight—three at top, three at bottom, two at the right-hand side, and two at the left. As tin-plating was not practised here until 1670, this horn-book should be of foreign manufacture. If home-made, the tin rimming must be a late "repair." The unusual number of tacks would favour the latter surmise.

With the English black-letter horn-book, shown full size in cut 130, belonging to Mr. Robert White of Worksop, damp has made havoc. As in horn-book (129) the "v" precedes the "u" in the alphabet of small letters, and in the capitals the "V" is absent. Peculiarities in spelling need not be

---

[1] The letter "v" in the word "us" will be noted.

[2] In the Middle Ages, and later, Paternoster Row was, as now, the booksellers' abode, and thence issued horn-books in countless thousands.

pointed out. The oaken base, from which the handle has at some time been bodily wrenched off, is three-sixteenths of an inch in thickness, and with the exception of a small piece, weatherworn and stained with dirt and

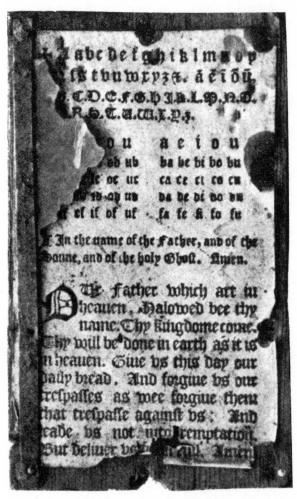

Cut 130.

age, the horn has disappeared. Only one strip of brass latten, running from top to bottom at the left-hand side, remains. The type is the same as that seen in Grafton's *Chronicles*, printed by Henry Denham in 1569, and there is no reason why this horn-book should not have been printed

THE CHAPMAN.

Ambrose Dudley.

History of the Horn-Book

about that time. In general character it is much the same as the Raban horn-books (see cut 50), which are known to be fifty years later. It must be remembered that in printing these horn-books Raban simply did something which had been done before.

Little scholars appear to have been allowed to gabble through the alphabet "a per se a," *et seq.*, without explanation from the teacher, and as to the ampersand, they were left to form their own conclusions. "It has been remarked," says Hone, in an unpublished note, "that in every horn-book I have seen the alphabet concludes with '&,' a contraction for 'and.' I was taught by my mistress of the horn-book to call it 'little and—anpersand.' I had attained many years of manhood before I discovered what her pronunciation never intimated, that 'anpersand' signified 'and *per se* and.' In village schools this character is still called 'little and—anpersand.'"

Hone continues : " The capital letter A standing in the horn-book next after the cross + the child was taught to call 'great A' and likewise ' A by itself A.' It may be imagined that every vowel letter being also sometimes 'by itself' a syllable, the old mode of teaching may have required the scholar in the alphabet on coming to each vowel letter to express its substantive power, and the like of the pupil in spelling on coming to a word in which a vowel by itself formed a syllable, and hence children would say 'A by itself A—E by itself E—I by itself I,' etc. However that may be, in the horn-book 'great A' comes immediately after the cross, and is followed by little 'a' and then by 'b' and 'c' and the other small letters of the alphabet in consecutive order. Why the interpolation of 'Great A' between the cross and the lower-case alphabet, I am unable to form a notion. But while fruitlessly pondering upon it, I have derived pleasure from unexpectedly discovering the propriety of a line in *Pierce the Plowman's Creed;* he says—

A, and all myn a, b, c, after have I lerned.

This seemed absurd until acquainted with the fact, that in the alphabet of the horn-book 'A' for some reason or other stands by itself, and 'a, b, c' after. This line establishes the antiquity of 'A by itself A,' between the cross and the lower-case alphabet which uniformly appears in every horn-book I know of."

History of the Horn-Book

In one of the earlier numbers of *Notes and Queries*, a correspondent, who signed himself F. C. H., stated that the word never puzzled him, because his venerable instructress pronounced it quite intelligibly. He was taught to say after the letter Z "and-pussy-and." He understood that the abbreviation was called "pussy" from its resemblance to a cat in a sitting posture. In a later issue, Professor Skeat comes to the rescue with the true meaning—a corruption of "and per se &," meaning that the character "&" standing by itself (Lat. *per se*) spells *and*, "merely a rough and ready way of writing the Latin word *et*, which occurs repeatedly in the Rushworth MS. at Oxford, or any tolerably old Latin MS." But F. C. H. was not satisfied, and alas! rushed to his own destruction by later on accusing the learned professor of dogmatic assertion, and so far as he is concerned, closes the discussion by sticking to the old-dame-and-pussy-cat explanation as "more plausible and much more natural than by representing it as a fanciful way of writing *et* in Latin."

In a note to "He teaches boys the horn-book" in *Love's Labour's Lost*, Halliwell says in his folio Shakespeare:[1] "No very ancient specimen of one (a horn-book) has, however, yet been discovered, the earliest known belonging to the seventeenth century," which does not actually tally with what he says in an earlier work,[2] where a horn-book afterwards suspected, and now known to be spurious, is described as "printed about 1570." Mr. Halliwell continues: "The horn-book of Shakespeare's time, as is gathered from various contemporary notices, generally consisted of a small rectangular plate of wood, from the bottom of which projected a handle with which it was held by the child. The book itself consisted of a single printed page, fixed on the wood, on which was first a large cross, the criss-cross (corrupted from Christ-cross), the alphabet, vowels, combinations of the consonants and vowels, a short and familiar Scriptural piece, the Lord's Prayer and a mark, consisting of three dots placed triangularly which denoted conclusion."

In a short dissertation on what he calls the "formost" vowels an old

[1] *The Works of William Shakespeare*, the text formed from a new collation of the early editions, to which are added all the original novels and tales on which the plays are founded; copious archæological annotations on each play, and essay on the formation of the text, and a life of the poet, by James O. Halliwell, Esq., F.R.S., vol. i., folio London; 1853, vol. xvi.; (and last), folio London, 1865.

[2] *A Catalogue of Chap-Books, Garlands and Popular Histories*, in the possession of James Orchard Halliwell, London. For Private Circulation, 1849.

History of the Horn-Book

writer[1] says : " A is thought to bee the first letter of the row because by it we may understand Trinity and Unity : The Trinity is that There bee three lines, and the Unity, in that it is but one letter. And for that cause, in the old time they used three prickes at the latter end of the Crosse row, and at the end of their books which they caused children to call tittle, tittle, tittle : signifying that as there were three pricks and those three made but one stop, even so there were Three Persons and yet but one God."

" It was the practice," says Halliwell, " to learn each letter by itself, the letter being emphatically repeated, e.g.—a per se a, b per se b, &c. A per se, con per se, tittle est, Amen ! Why he comes uppon thee, man, with a whole horn-book " (Nash's *Have with you to Saffron Walden*, 1596).

It will be noted that three dots or tittles follow the alphabet of small letters in three of Raban's horn-books (cut 50). The latest survival of this triplet of dots or tittles, the mediæval symbolism of three Persons in one God, is seen in cut 2, which was probably used for printing both battledores and horn-books. The date is approximately 1830-35.

Mistris Arthur.—" When that is done, get you to schoole againe."

Pip.—" I had rather plaie the trewant at home then seeke my M at school : let me see, what age am I ? some foure and twentie, and how have I profited ? I was five year learning to crish Crosse from great A and five yeare longer comming to F. There I stuck some three yeare before I could come to Q, and so in processe of time I came to e perce e and com perce, and tittle, and then I got to a, e, i, o, u, after to Our Father," is from *A Pleasant Con- ceited Comedie, Wherein is shewed how a man may chuse a good wife from a bad. As it hath been sundry times Acted by the Earle of Worcester's Servants, London : Printed for Mathew Lawe, and are to be solde at his Shop in Paules Church Yard, near unto S. Augustines gate, at the signe of the Foxe*, 1602, p. 34.

Interpolated in pen and ink in the British Museum copy is " Written by Joshua Cooke." Joshua Cooke is unknown, but there was a Jo. Cooke, a dramatist of the early seventeenth century, who is best known by his play,

---

[1] *A new Booke of new Conceits, with a number of Novelties annexed thereunto.* Whereof some be profitable, some necessary, some strange, none hurtful, and all delectable. By Thomas Iohnson, London : Printed by E. A. for Edward Wright and Cuthbert Wright, 1636.

History of the Horn-Book

Greene's Tu Quoque, or the Cittie Gallant, and this play is probably by him. Dates of his birth and death unknown.

In Morley's *Introduction to Music,* which appeared in 1608 and is referred to more fully in another page, we get—

> Christes crosse be my speede in all vertue to proceede,
> A. b. c. d. e. f. g. h. i. k. l. m. n. o. p. q. r. s. & tt.
> double w. v. with y. ezod. & per se, con per se.
> tittle. tittle. est. Amen. When you have done
> begin againe, begin againe.

CHAPTER XXII

Horn-books of the middle period—Black letter elbowed by the Roman—Horn books in the time of Elizabeth—The Caslon foundry—Enschedé, the Dutch founder— A depraved shoemaker—Known black-letter horn-books described and illustrated —Charles II. horn-books—" u " as a capital letter—The bird initial " O "—Sir John Evans and the " duck's egg "—Ducks and drakes—Known horn-books in Roman type described and illustrated—An utterly demoralised horn-book.

THE middle period of horn-books may be placed from late in the reign of Elizabeth until the eighteenth century was well opened. When black letter began to be elbowed by the Roman character, horn-books were made, printed in both, of a kind which may be described as the standard of the middle period (see cut 131 and others). As the clearer Roman letter advanced in estimation, black-letter horn-books gradually gave way and eventually disappeared. After the end of the sixteenth century, few, if any, new black-letter punches were cut, and if black type were required, old was used, or new was cast from old matrices. Roman-letter horn-books of the middle period were usually a little smaller than the black. An incalculable number—very many millions—must have been manufactured. Horn-books of this description, both home-made and imported, found favour from the reign of Elizabeth right up to the time of George I. The type, of Continental origin, used in the printing of the Lord's Prayer, alphabets, vowels, and syllabarium, was nearly always of the size known as small pica.

Theodore L. de Vinne, in his *Historic Printing Types*, notes that Joseph Moxon, Hydrographer to His Majesty Charles II., was the first

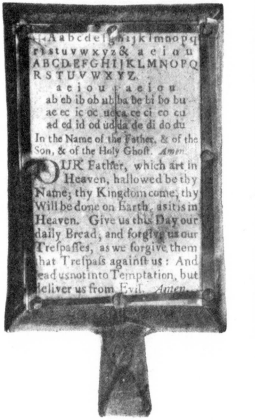

Cut 131.

English type-founder of note from 1659 to 1683, but that his types cannot be compared with those of his French and Dutch rivals. They were, however, better than the types of other English founders of the seventeenth century. Both before and after his time, publishers and men of letters preferred foreign types. The University of Oxford in 1672

History of the Horn-Book

paid four thousand pounds for foreign-made types, punches, and matrices; and even as late as 1710, Thomas James, the type-founder, had to go to Holland to buy matrices and moulds not to be had in London. Hansard tells us that "the glorious works of English literature which immortalised the reign of Queen Anne, were originally presented to the public through the medium of Dutch types."

The celebrated William Caslon, whose foundry is still ably continued by his successors in London, was the first to shake the faith of his countrymen in the superiority of Dutch type-founders. Before his advent type-founding in England was in a parlous way. The founders were careless and their moulds bad. In fact, the best English type was cast from Dutch matrices, and the best paper in use in this country was imported from Holland. Printers who achieved good work used Dutch type and Dutch paper. Writers on typography are silent as to the models selected by the first Caslon, and it has been generally surmised that he fell back upon what he admired in printed books that came in his way. In recent years, however, a very dirty and much used copy of the first book of founts of the celebrated Dutch founder Enschedé was found in the Caslon offices, which seems to prove that Caslon took Enschedé's Elzevir [1] types (designed by Cornelius van Dyck) for his models. He certainly could not have done better. Caslon's earliest specimen book (dated 1720, but printed later) was produced after the first specimen book of Isaac and John Enschedé of Haarlem, whose still flourishing foundry was based on the acquisition of that of R. Wetstein of Amsterdam, and the absorption of many old but minor foundries. In the loose sheets of Caslon's types which preceded his first specimen book, it may be noted that in the procession of letters the capital U comes after the V. In noting horn-books of the middle period still preserved, those printed in the older letters may have priority. It must not be taken, however, that those noted first are necessarily the earliest. *That* sequence the writer long ago gave up in despair.

Perhaps the best-known horn-book, which now belongs to history, is the interesting example depicted in cut 17. But the Bateman horn-book has a chapter to itself.

---

[1] The Elzevirs, like nearly all the celebrated printers of their time, cut their own punches and struck the matrices, which was done in order to keep the types to themselves.

History of the Horn-Book

A black-letter horn-book is depicted in Dr. Blunt's *Annotated Book of Common Prayer*.[1] The author said in his Preface : " The following is an engraving made from one of the two horn-books which were found by the present writer under the floor of Over Church, near Cambridge, in 1857. It is of late date, and has ' In the Name of the Father and of the Son, and of the Holy Ghost' in the place of the Angelic Salutation, but it is given as an illustration of the traditional practice and because it is of special interest as being found in the Church."

The Rev. C. F. S. Warren tells me that the actual finder of the horn-books was his father, the Rev. Charles Warren, to whom Dr. Blunt then acted as curate. As the doctor says distinctly that he found them himself, the probability is that they were found independently during the progress of repairs which were then proceeding. The hiding-place was under the joists of some seating. This horn-book was presented by the Rev. Charles Warren to the Library of Trinity College, Cambridge, where it is now preserved. (Over is a Trinity living.) The second horn-book mentioned by Dr. Blunt was the oak base only of one resembling the first, but whatever had been on its face had disappeared. This was retained by Mr. Warren, but in course of time was lost.

In connection with the horn-book, Dr. Blunt has some interesting notes :—" But in days when books were scarce, and few could read, little could be done towards giving to the people at large this intelligent ac-quaintance with the Services except by oral instruction of the kind indicated. Yet the writing-rooms of the monasteries did what they could towards multiplying books for the purpose, and some provision was made, even for the poorest, by means of horn-books on which the Lord's Prayer, the Creed, and the Angelic Salutation were written. While these horn-books were thus provided for the poor, the scriptorium of the monastery also provided Prymers in English and Latin for those who could afford the expensive luxury of a book. The latin Prymers are well known under the name of *Books of Hours*. Vernacular Prymers exist which were written as early as the fourteenth century and many relics of Old English devotion of that date still remain. These English Prymers contained

---

[1] *The Annotated Book of Common Prayer*, being an historical, ritual, and theological commentary on the devotional system of the Church of England, edited by the Rev. John Henry Blunt, D.D., F.S.A. Rivingtons, London, MDCCCLXXXIV.

"NOT B; LOOK AGAIN, SWEETHEART."

J. Walter West.

History of the Horn-Book

about one-third of the Psalms, the Canticles, the Apostles' Creed, with a large number of the prayers, anthems and perhaps hymns. They continued to be published up to the end of King Henry VIIIth's reign and in a modified form even at a later date ; and they must have familiarised those who used them with a large portion of the Services even when they did not understand the Latin in which those services were said by the clergy and choirs."

The cut (132) of the Blunt horn-book is due to the courtesy of the Rev. Dr. Sinker, the Librarian of Trinity College, Cambridge, who kindly lent the original, which is reproduced in facsimile. The engraver of the cut in Dr. Blunt's book did his work most carelessly and inaccurately, as any one can see who has the opportunity of comparison. Since this horn-book was copied for Dr. Blunt, a little more of the very scanty lettering that was left has disappeared, and some one has fastened down with brass tacks in the centre of the wooden base what remains of the horn and printed sheet. The holes round the edges, once occupied by iron tacks, long since rusted away, can easily be made out. The unusual shortness of the handle will be noted.

In the Bagford collection in the British Museum is an undivided sheet of paper, on the face of which are printed in black letter sixteen horn-books. This certainly argues a large consumption. The set is shown on a reduced scale in cut 133, and one is given full size in

Cut 132.

cut 134. The type appears to be worn, which, coupled with a blurred impression, due to careless printing, makes the sheet look older than it is. The date is probably about 1700. John Bagford was born in 1650 in the parish of

Cut 133.

St. Anne, Blackfriars, and began life as a shoemaker, but having a taste for literature, he not only collected for himself but bought and sold books on commission. He developed the curiously depraved taste of collecting title-pages of books, and the fruits of this ill-timed iconoclastic industry are contained in nine large volumes, which, with his other collections of ballads and printed matter, amounting in all to sixty-four volumes, were bought by the Earl of Oxford and are now in the British Museum. Bagford was a Fellow of the Society of Antiquaries, and got together a quantity of material for a History of Printing, proposals for publishing which were

Cut 134.

Cut 135.

issued in 1707, but the work progressed no further. He died on 15th May 1716, and must at that time have been poor, for he was one of the brethren of the Charterhouse.

Cut 135 is facsimiled from another printed horn-book sheet in the Bagford collection. It looks old, but as Bagford is supposed not to have begun amassing his amazing stores of title-pages, ballads, and other small deer until towards the end of the seventeenth century, this borderless specimen can hardly be very much earlier than the example previously noted. It may be from type set up at an earlier date.

The base of an uncovered black-letter horn-book in the British

History of the Horn-Book

Museum approximates in size to cut 138; the lettering is on a somewhat large scale, and is without the ornamental initial in the Lord's Prayer. The latten is carried close to the edge of the oaken base, or another way

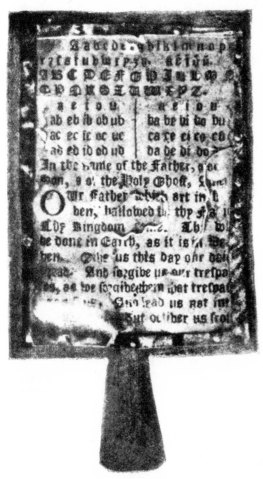

Cut 136.

of putting it, would be to say that the oaken base is smaller than usually prevailed in a horn-book of this size. The date is queried in the B. M. Catalogue as 1700, but it is probably earlier. The printed sheet, latten, and old tacks are perfect, but before it reached the Museum some one abolished the horn.

The horn-book in the Bodleian Library (cut 136), the oak base of which is bare of covering, has a neglected if not dilapidated air about it. Three only of the original tacks remain, and of the brass latten about one-third is wanting. What is left is kept in place with ordinary pins—a clumsy device of a former owner. It is labelled at back in the autograph of Mr. Falconer Madan, M.A., of Brasenose College: "This horn-book was found in the process of clearing the ground for the new buildings of Brasenose College in the summer of 1881 and was presented to the Library on April 26, 1882, by the Principal and Fellows of the College. The date seems to be about the time of Charles I." Mr. Madan may be right about the date, but I should take it to be earlier. With this horn-book was found a framework or base of another of corresponding size, but beyond the oak there is nothing left except tack-holes discoloured by oxidised iron.

History of the Horn-Book

A brown leather-covered black-letter horn-book (reproduced full
size), in the collection of Sir John Evans, K.C.B., etc., is shown in

Cut 137.

cut 137, which, it will be noted, in matter and general appearance
somewhat resembles 136. The leather has entirely disappeared from
the handle, which is pierced about half an inch from the end for

History of the Horn-Book

the insertion of a string for suspending the horn-book from the girdle. On the back is lightly stamped the device of St. George and the Dragon. In the Catalogue of the Caxton Exhibition of 1877, where it was exhibited, this horn-book is assigned to the time of James I., but I see no reason why it should not be earlier.

The fine black-letter horn-book belonging to Mrs. Jerome Mercier of Kemerton Rectory, Tewkesbury, is reproduced full size in cut 138, and it will be noticed that as regards the printed matter it is absolutely perfect. The oak backing is one-eighth of an inch in thickness ; unfortunately the horn and brass slips are entirely wanting. The worm-ravaged covering is red skiver leather, with a crudely-executed device stamped thereon representing St. George and the Dragon. The date might be the middle of the sixteenth century or later. The type used in the printing is English, and there can be little doubt that the horn-book itself was made in this country. This interesting example was found by a workman many years ago in the crevice of a wall at Beckford Hall, Gloucestershire. Commenting, the Rev. Jerome J. Mercier writes : " I believe that printed matter, especially religious print, was frequently secreted in walls because it was supposed to act as a beneficial charm on the inhabitants of the house." There is evidence of such a practice, but in this instance the secreting of the horn-book may have been due to an A B C-detesting child.

An interesting black-letter horn-book, somewhat reduced in cut 139, belongs to Mrs. R. Waddy Moss of Didsbury College, Manchester, whose grandmother used it at school. It is headed " Old English Print," and would seem to have formed one of a series. The back and rimming

Cut 139.

consist of a single piece of sheet-iron, turned over at the edges, which grip the printed sheet and horn. The full measurement is $6\frac{5}{8} \times 2\frac{5}{8}$.

Of the horn-book, shown in cut 140, in St. Asaph Cathedral Library,

Cut 140.

Archdeacon Thomas is good enough to send me some interesting notes : "In my *History of the Diocese of St. Asaph* (p. 612), I have told the story of the discovery and briefly described it as follows : During some alterations in the old church of Treyddyn (in the county of Flint) in the year 1866, one of the early Horn-books (Llyfr corn) was found under a pew in perfect preservation. It consisted of a small sheet of paper, having printed on it in Black Letter characters the letters of the alphabet, small and capitals, the vowels and monosyllabic words representing the simplest sounds, the formula ' In the Name of the Father and of the Son and of the Holy Ghost, Amen,' and the Lord's Prayer. This paper was laid upon a small oaken tablet, over which a sheet of horn was fastened, as we now put glass, and bound with a narrow rim of copper ;[1] and in the handle was bored a small hole for the string, by which to suspend it on the wall when the lesson was done. Unfortunately it became a little damaged on exposure. On the removal of the then vicar, the Rev. D. Davies, to another living, he took the horn-book with him, and subsequently lent it me to be photographed. On his death in 1887 a representation was made

[1] Brass.

BATTLEDORE AND SHUTTLECOCK.   *Ambrose Dudley.*

History of the Horn-Book

to the executors, claiming the horn-book for the parish church or the cathedral as its representative; but it was found that one of the domestics had selected it as a memorial of her old master. A pound was offered as a solatium under the circumstances, but the offer was rejected, and five pounds demanded. An official demand was thereupon made for its restoration, and after some demur it was given up without any compensation at all." The brass rim securing the horn has been lost, but the marks of the nails by which it was fastened are easily made out. When in late days the sheet of paper was gummed to the oak tablet, it was carelessly placed upside down. With the exception of the mistake in the spelling of the word " Father," and a slight difference in the arrangement of the capital letters of the alphabet, the St. Asaph horn-book is almost identical with cut 136, and would appear to belong to the same period.

A black-letter horn-book, described as hexagon-shaped, not long ago passed through the hands of a Teddington bookseller. Unfortunately it cannot be traced, and no dependable description of it can be obtained.

Horn-books of the middle period in Roman letter are fairly numerous. It would almost seem, from the number of examples left to us stamped with the device of Charles II., that decorated horn-books were not largely in vogue until his time. They may have been equally popular in the time of the first Charles and have become scarce in the days of the Commonwealth. Of horn-books decorated with the effigy of an earlier monarch than Charles I. there appears to be no record.

The brown leather-covered horn-book, cut 141 (reproduced full size), was found, in pulling down an old building in Hemel Hempstead in 1886, by Mr. H. Wyman, who presented it to its present owner, Sir John Evans, K.C.B., F.R.S. The left arm of the conventionally-designed mermaid stamped on the back is uplifted, and in the hand is the usual oval mirror, level with the top of the head. With the other hand the maiden, or mermaiden, is passing a brush through her abundant tresses. At foot is stamped the letter R, enclosed in a square, and in the mirror is a faint trace of the letter C. Probably it was printed in the time of the first or second Charles, and as likely as not from a type-forme of Elizabeth's time, which had passed from one maker to another. This interesting horn-book is unfortunately dilapidated. The front of the handle appears to

319

be stamped with some slight ornamentation, which may or may not be repeated on reverse, now covered out with a label.

It will be noted that the letter "u" in the opening word of the Lord's Prayer, and also in the alphabet of capitals, is a lower-case or small letter,

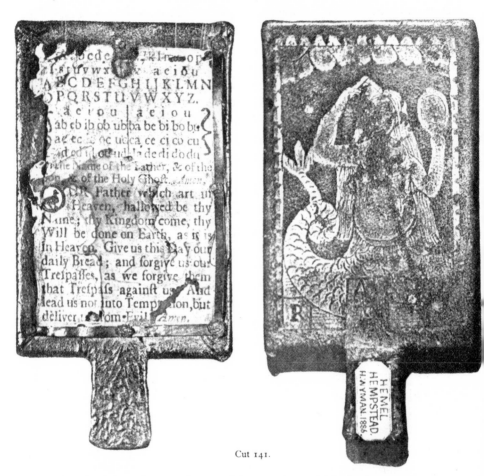

Cut 141.

apparently taken from a fount of larger size, which looks as though the printer had run short of "sorts" and had to make shift as best he could. But it may also mean, and probably does, that the lower-case "u" was cast in the fount for use as a capital letter (see p. 45). It will also be noted that the large capital letter opening the Lord's Prayer has a bird depicted in the centre, which Sir John Evans, the owner of this interesting

320

History of the Horn-Book

horn-book, surmised might possibly have before done duty in print, perhaps in something relating to one of our oldest games [1] the initial O symbolising a "duck's egg." But for an irrepressible twinkling of the eye, this mendacious suggestion from one prone to epigram rather than *espièglerie* might for the moment have been received with becoming gravity.

If we accept the pedigree—a pedigree apparently unimpeachable—of Lord Egerton of Tatton's beautiful horn-book (see cut 19), in which the printed sheet is of the same character as No. 141, belonging to Sir John Evans, though they are apparently by different printers, we should be fairly safe in assigning both examples to the time of Queen Elizabeth. The use of the bird initial O was probably at first a mere whim of a printer who had the block by him. It may be assumed that dames and dominies got accustomed to and asked for horn-books thus distinguished. Then followed supplies from other makers, whereon, according to the fancy of the engraver, the bird appeared sometimes solid, sometimes outlined, sometimes looking one way, and sometimes another. Differences in the various examples of this type of horn-book tend to show that it was in use for a considerable time. The bird O appears in cut 94, which represents a "British Battledore"—really a horn-book—made probably late in the last century.

Mr. C. H. Read has pointed out to me that in the two Sir Francis Drake horn snuff-boxes in the British Museum, the ornamental border of both contains a bird of the size and character of that in the initial, one being surrounded by a small circle. This seems to be something more than a coincidence, and it is probable that the symbolic O in the horn-book is a play upon the word "Drake." In Queen Elizabeth's reign flourished Sir Francis—El Draco, the dragon—and the historian, Arthur Duck. Other Ducks and Drakes there were in plenty, amongst them a physician, author, satirist, antiquary, and poet, but they were of later broods. In what earlier form this initial O was used may yet perhaps be traced, but in the horn-book it probably conveyed no special meaning, and was intended simply as an ornament. There is, of course, the bare possibility

---

[1] A game with a crooked stick called a *cryc* was played about the middle of the thirteenth century, and *criquet* is mentioned in 1478, but games with ball, bat, and stump must have delighted and invigorated still earlier generations.

that the printer may have meant the teacher to accept his duck as a dove, hoping that he would prove complacent because of the opportunity afforded of evolving mildly interesting discourses touching the animals which filed into the Ark. Though no English child was ever gammoned into believing that bird to be aught but a quack-quack, its presence may have helped to sell the horn-book.

A horn-book, evidently from the hand of the printer of cut 141, is shown in cut 20. Here we have the lower-case "u" repeated in the alphabet of capitals. There has been another tack just under the "e" in "evil"; the hole is there, and the marks of the tack head are distinctly visible. The covering is stout red leather stamped with the device of King Charles on horseback, crown on the left of the head, and initials C. R. underneath; in the right-hand corner is a winged cherub. It will be noted that there is some attempt at ornamentation on both sides of the handle. This interesting horn-book, now in the collection of the writer, was formerly the property of an aged lady living in Seacombe, Cheshire, whose father used to tell her that he learned his letters from it, and that before his time it was turned out of an ancient box and considered a great curiosity.

Mr. Walter L. Nash of the Grange, Northwood, was until recently the possessor of a horn-book stamped with an equestrian portrait of Charles I. But it passed to a French collector before the writer had an opportunity of seeing it.

A horn-book in the Bodleian Library, Oxford, is covered with bright red paper stamped on the back in black ink with the device of Charles I. on horseback, the design closely following that in cut 20. The crown is not quite of the same shape, and the wings of the cherub are on a somewhat larger scale, but it is evident that the designs are meant to accord, the differences being due to the brass stamping blocks having been cut by different engravers. Another horn-book in the Bodleian is covered with paper of faded brickdust hue, and is stamped at back in black ink with a representation of Charles II., as in cut 131. Here, again, due to the same cause, are slight differences in the carrying out of the designs. In the Lord's Prayer the full point after the word heaven—" as it is in Heaven "— is wanting, the "*stamp*," as a printer would term it, having, prior to working, dropped from the forme. In regard to date, it is catalogued " c. 1680 ? "

History of the Horn-Book

which obviously leaves nothing to be said, except that it might be earlier or later. To the first example no date is assigned. The paper edges in both are a little frayed, but horn, brass latten, and old rose-head tacks are perfect.

A fine horn-book, indeed, in condition almost perfect, is that shown in cut 131, owned by Mr. Robert White of Worksop. The reader can judge of its beauty from the illustration. The back is covered with faded brown leather, turned over at the edges, and stamped with an equestrian portrait of Charles II. The lettering at foot looks like a monogram of the letter C reversed with an R in the centre. The reversed C, however, resolves itself into the tail of the letter R, which takes a long and symmetrical sweep to the right. The impression, sharp and clear, is from a block which has seen little wear. This clearly points to the horn-book having been made in the days of Charles II. and not at a later period, when it might have been stamped from a worn block.

A friend, whose opinion is to be respected, thinks that the type used in the printing of this horn-book may not be contemporary with the leather cover. Doubt may be set at rest by comparing its lettering with the type in a work by George Wither, the poet (born 1588, died 1667), which appeared about 1625, entitled, *The Scholler's Pvrgatory discouered in the Stationers Commonwealth, And Discribed in a Discourse Apologeticall, as well for the publike advantage of the Church, the State and the whole Commonwealth of England as for the remedy of priuate iniuryes. By George Wither, Imprinted for the Honest Stationers.* As an examination will show that the printer who produced one could have produced both, a reference to other works is unnecessary.

A well-preserved horn-book, which has been several times exhibited, is owned by Mrs. Smith-Dorrien of Great Berkhamsted. It is covered in brown leather, backed with the equestrian portrait of Charles II., stamped in silver foil, most of which by age has become oxidised to a dull leaden hue. The whole of the horn has disappeared, and portions of the printed sheet have been eaten by the book-worm. The brass latten and old tacks are quite perfect. With this horn-book is a card, used for exhibition purposes, on which is written " Horn-book with figure of Charles I. stamped on leather back, found in the wall of an old public-house, the 'Anvil and Hammer,' at Ashley Green, Bucks, when digging for site of

History of the Horn-Book

new Vicarage 1875." "Charles I.," which should be Charles II., is evidently a clerical error. Mrs. Smith-Dorrien's horn-book is exactly like cut 142.

A very covetable example indeed is that in the collection of Sir A. Wollaston Franks, K.C.B., of the British Museum. It is covered with paper of a brickdust hue, which, through handling, has become slightly frayed at the edges. The back is stamped with the device of Charles II. on horseback, and between the horse's legs is a boldly-cut thistle, which seems to point to Scottish origin, but it is reasonable to suppose that the use of horn-books in which the thistle formed part of the ornamentation would not be confined to the Land o' Cakes. Sir A. W. Franks has the reputation of having been fortunate in the acquisition of many of his countless treasures. For this horn-book he, many years ago, gave half a crown at a naturalist's shop in London. The seller, thinking he had the better of the bargain, threw in a couple of odds and ends in the way of curiosities by way of make-weight! The printed sheet, the rose-head iron tacks, the horn, and the brass latten are all perfect. As a rule, the iron tacks in horn-books of this period are so oxidised that some, or even all, of the heads have disappeared.

An example of a "Charles" leather-covered horn-book, considerably smaller than the Bateman and printed in Roman type, has been lent to me for engraving by Mr. S. Richards of the Old Friary, Nottingham, and is represented in cut 142. It is covered in stout brown leather of the usual dingy red hue. The rimming and tacks are perfect, but about one-third of the horn has gone. The stamping of the device on back has been done over silver foil, some of which still remains. It will be noticed that while the design generally accords with that in the Bateman horn-book (cut 17) there are points of difference. The letters under the crown, C. R., are not quite of the same shape, and the king wears a spur. There are also minor differences in the treatment of the design, and in place of the letters T. H. amongst the horse's feet in the Bateman horn-book, there is the figure I. twice repeated (Charles II.).

An example of a "Charles" horn-book in fair preservation is owned by Mr. Carnegy Johnson, who for some time left it on loan at the Burlington Fine Arts Club. It is printed in Roman letter and covered with leather of a red hue paled by age and worn somewhat at the edges. Two-

"DO YOU THINK YOU KNOW IT?"   *Charles H. M. Kerr.*

History of the Horn-Book

thirds of the brass latten and one or two of the tacks are wanting; the horn is perfect. The device on back, exactly the same as that in cut 142, is sharply impressed.

In the Warrington Museum, whose curator is Mr. Chas. Madeley, a horn-book in fine condition, similar to that in cut 131, has found a home.

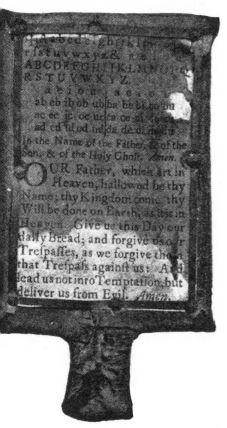

Cut 142.

With the exception of a single crack in the horn, the front is perfect. The back is covered with red paper of the usual dingy hue, stamped in black with the device of Charles II. on horseback.

A sadly mutilated, in fact, utterly demoralised, horn-book in Roman type is that in the British Museum, the date of which is queried as 1750. About two-thirds of the printed sheet has crumbled away and what

327

History of the Horn-Book

remains of the horn is unsecured. The little cardboard case containing this horn-book is open at the end, and one day or other when an attendant is carrying it to a curious reader, the horn will drop out and be lost. Three only of the old tacks remain ; an attempt at cobbling with modern

Cut 143.

ones seems to have been made in recent years, probably—nay, certainly— before the horn-book was acquired by the Museum.

A horn-book, covered in stout brown leather, faded, and somewhat frayed at the edges, and with the old tacks, latten, and horn quite perfect, was recently sold at Sotheby's for sixteen pounds to Mr. Henry Griffith

328

History of the Horn-Book

of Brighton. The back is stamped with the effigy of St. George and the Dragon, at the foot of which are the initials of the engraver, M. P. D.

A horn-book (uncovered) is mentioned in a letter (dated 23rd April 1853, and addressed from 52 Bolsover Street) from the late Robert Cole, F.S.A., its owner, to Mr. Walter Hawkins, from which we gather that it had been exhibited at the Society of Antiquaries (see p. 394). The sketch of it, shown at the same time (7th April 1853), is possessed by the writer, and is facsimiled in cut 143. The "duck" initial O will be noted. A second horn-book, or rather the carelessly-made reduced sketch of it,—the 9 would certainly not be omitted in the figures—depicted in cut 143a was also shown by Mr. Cole at the Society of Antiquaries. It is unfortunate that no particulars were recorded. The paper or card appears to have slipped into a groove, and it seems probable that there was wording of some kind on the other side.

Cut 143a.

Since the foregoing pages were written, a black-letter horn-book, similar to that shown in cut 136, has come into the possession of the writer. It is covered with brown leather, frayed and somewhat dilapidated. Part of the brass rimming and all the horn have disappeared ; the printed sheet is torn and worm-eaten. The back is stamped with the device of St. George and the Dragon in silver, the lustre of which in some parts is fairly well preserved.

CHAPTER XXIII

Horn-books of the late period—A persistent type described, and when it ceased to be manufactured—Horn-books from stereotypes—Stereotyping an old invention rediscovered—Horn-books of the late period in libraries, museums, and in private hands, described and illustrated—Their owners—A horn-book "price three halfpence."

NE type of horn-book—in which it will be noticed that the symbol of Christianity is sometimes *pattée* or *formée* ✠ ("the extremities spreading like dovetails," *Berry*), and that the printers, besides economising space, have added a border, to the pattern of which they have through many generations unanimously adhered—is very persistent, and may be described as the standard horn-book of late times. So economical were the printers in the matter of space that the typographically ornamental border was always covered out by the brass latten. This will be seen in cut 144, and in others where the metal strips are partly broken away. It is, of course, open to question whether the printed border served any purpose beyond acting as a guide to the horn-book-maker in fixing the brass latten. Perhaps it was this hankering to get rid of what was considered superfluous which induced our grand-

History of the Horn-Book

fathers to cut off the margins of prints before putting them in frames or scrap-books. Would they had been less considerate!

It is questionable whether such horn-books, which in dames' schools in out-of-the-way places were used within living memory, were made earlier than the first quarter of the eighteenth century. As one type of horn-book overlaps another, it would be unreasonable to suppose that a new kind at once ousted its predecessor.

The manufacture of the standard horn-book of late times would appear to have been continued well into the first quarter of the present century. The type used for the Lord's Prayer, alphabets, vowels, and syllabarium, is known as longprimer, while the Invocation, always set smaller, is in brevier. The type itself is of English make, and in the earlier examples is probably from the James foundry. But the splitter of hairs may dispute its nationality, inasmuch as Mores, in his *Dissertation upon English Typographical Founders and Founderies, London,*

Cut 144.

1778, tells us that the James foundry was equipped with matrices bought in Holland. The metal types themselves, however, from which standard horn-books of the late period were printed, were certainly cast in this country. There is every reason to suppose that the manufacture of these horn-books, the latest examples of which (referred to in the next chapter) were printed in what is known as " modern " type (see cut 145), was by many English printers carried on simultaneously with the production of books for children.

331

History of the Horn-Book

Four late " standard " horn-books are in the Mackenzie collection in the South Kensington Museum ; the S. K. M. has also one which it prides itself on having purchased some years ago for ten shillings ; the British Museum has another ; the writer owns that represented in cut 144, bought for five shillings at Oxford ; another was disposed of in the Bateman collection at Sotheby's, and purchased by Mr. Quaritch for £14 : 10s. ; Sir A. Wollaston Franks has one ; and since this paragraph was written many other examples have turned up.

In the latter half of the last century, when stereotyping, or casting in lead from standing type, was first practised in this country, both " black " and Roman types were commonly in use. In order to release type for fresh work printers made stereotypes, which, after serving their purpose, were put away until again required. Horn-books were probably printed from both type and stereotypes right up to the time of their disappearance.

Cut 145.

In an unpublished note, Hone says : " Mr. Abraham Hancock, printer, of Middle Row Place, Holborn, possesses the stereotype plate for a Horn-book, which appears by the character of the letter to have been executed a century ago, and may have been one of Ged's attempts at casting for stereotype printing " (William Ged of Edinburgh practised stereotyping about 1730). Middle Row was long ago pulled down ; it is probable that Mr. Hancock long ago died, and his descendants, who might be in possession of the horn-book stereo, a curiosity which many would like to possess, cannot be traced. But duplicating by moulding is only an old invention rediscovered. Mr. C. R. Redgrave has pointed out that in books printed by Ratdolt, the fifteenth-century printer of Venice, certain decorative initial letters are repeated several times on a page, and that the defects or peculiarities in one initial are exactly reproduced in another, which proves beyond doubt that they were printed from casts multiplied

History of the Horn-Book

from the original block. In a religious work, *The Garden of the Soul* (*Der Seele Wurzgarten, Conrad Dinckmut, Ulm,* 1483), cut blocks are repeated on the same sheet with the imperfections, damages, and batters, in facsimile, proving beyond doubt that the printing was from stereotype plates. In the Germanische Museum of Nuremberg are preserved stereotypes dating from the beginning of the seventeenth century, and alas! for the claims of Senefelder, in the same curious storehouse are etchings on stone three hundred and fifty years old.

The curiously interesting horn-book owned by Mr. Samuel Sandars[1] of De Vere Gardens, Kensington, is that which was figured in Quaritch's catalogue some three years ago, and was purchased by Mr. Sandars for twelve guineas. It is covered with red paper of the usual brickdust tint and stamped at back with the device of St. George and the Dragon. The pestilent restorer has been busy on it, but his doings can be easily undone. It is surmised that he found the horn and brass rimming nearly gone, and that he procured an immaculate piece of new horn, on which, of course, there is not the slightest trace of the dulness produced by much wear. For the brass rimming, of which enough was probably left to indicate the width, he substituted thin sheet-iron. In nailing it down he was careful to use the old rose-head tacks as far as they would go, and for those that had disappeared he substituted modern flat-heads. He sought to improve matters by adding an extra tack at each of the four corners, making twelve in all instead of the usual eight. Were it not more interesting in its present condition, it would be easy to make this horn-book perfect by taking it to pieces and substituting brass for the iron rimming, and putting in the usual eight tacks in their proper places.

A horn-book (cut 146) presented by Mr. Joseph Clarke to the Museum at Saffron Walden, whose curator is Mr. G. N. Maynard, is in good preservation. It is entirely covered with paper of a brickdust hue, and the back is embossed with the device of St. George and the Dragon. A good pair of eyes can distinguish the horse's head, St. George's body and head, and the lance, but the Dragon is very shadowy. The heavy raised work following the lines of the horse's head and mane, and also that below the Dragon's body, is due to the stamp being applied while the paper

---

[1] Mr. Sandars died after this paragraph was written. He has bequeathed a great many valuable books, amongst them his horn-book, to the University Library, Cambridge.

covering was damp. The printed sheet, horn, brass strips, and hand-forged tacks are all in perfect preservation.

For many years an uncovered horn-book, perfect in condition, was in the collection of Mr. Thomas Quiller-Couch, of Bodmin, Cornwall, who

Cut 146.

in 1869 exhibited it at the Royal Archæological Institute. At his death it passed to Mr. Jonathan Rashleigh of Menabilly, Cornwall, in whose possession it now rests. There is nothing to distinguish this horn-book except that the opening cross is shaped like this ‡. No mystery is here. The printer had not a cross by him of the proper size, so he took a couple belonging to a smaller fount and placed one on top of the other. This horn-book was originally obtained from an old man of Polperro, a Cornish

A DULLARD.   *J. R. Miller.*

History of the Horn-Book

fishing village, who learned his A B C from it, and who died in 1850 at the age of ninety.

A well-preserved horn-book, perfect except that one half of the strip of latten on left-hand side is missing, the old hand-forged nails intact, and the uncracked horn scratched and dulled by much wear, is owned by Mrs. Hesketh Gower of Ealing, who had it from her father, Major John Bent, of the Fifth Regiment, Northumberland Fusiliers, who died in 1873 at the age of ninety-two. Major Bent used to show this horn-book as a great curiosity.

A horn-book in a moderate state of preservation belongs to Mr. Pearson of Pall Mall Place. The printed sheet and horn are perfect, but the brass rimming has gone, and the tack heads have suffered by corrosion. The back was originally paper-covered and bore a device of conventional scroll-work, but most of it has disappeared.

Lot 119 in the Bateman sale (see p. 39) was a horn-book in fine fresh condition and complete, the tacks unrusted, and the brass rims and horn perfect. When in the Bateman Museum this horn-book bore a label describing it as belonging " apparently to the close of the seventeenth century, but certainly—probably a hundred years—later." Mr. Quaritch was the purchaser for £14 : 10s.

A very fine horn-book is that in the Huth Library. It was purchased in 1875 from Mr. Quaritch for ten pounds, and is in excellent preservation. The latten, the original rose-head tacks, and the horn-covering are quite perfect. At some time or other the inevitable restorer (who never can be got to understand that in his dreadful craft uncleanliness is next to godliness) has been at work. Dissatisfied with the grimy appearance of the rough old oak, he has subjected it to a scrubbing with soap and water, and the wood has paled under the treatment. There was a price, 1½d., marked on the oaken back, but under the onslaught the figures were nearly obliterated, and the restorer sought to mend matters by going over them with writing ink, which, being good of its kind, has turned jet-black. In the catalogue of the Huth Library (Ellis and White), 1880, vol. ii. p. 737, it is described : "*Horn-book.*—A specimen of this once popular mode of teaching children in village schools. This copy is probably not older than the middle of the last century. It consists of a single leaf fastened on to a piece of oak, three inches broad by two inches long and

337

covered by a piece of horn which is secured to the board by tacks driven through strips of thin brass which go round the edges of the horn. The contents of the page are simply : — 1. The alphabet in small roman characters. 2. The same in capitals. 3. The vowels with the variations of ab, ba, etc. 4. The invocation to the Holy Trinity. 5. The Lord's Prayer. The price, 1½d., is marked in ink on the back."

Cut 147.

In the Museum at Northampton is a horn-book, which was kindly sent me for examination by Mr. T. George, the curator. It has undergone trial by fire and water, with the result that the horn-covering and fastenings have partly disappeared, and the device of St. George and the Dragon on the dingy-hued leather back is nearly obliterated. The museum ticket says : " This Horn-book was found in a ceiling in Mr. G. Nichol's house in the Drapery, and is lent by him to the Northampton Museum."

The horn-book in cut 147 is interesting on account of the ornamentation, quite unusual, of the handle achieved with a gouge, which would appear to have been done at the time the base was shaped.

This particular horn-book is interesting to me personally because some abnormally intelligent person, after having read a letter of mine in the *Athenæum*, asking for references to horn-books, immediately went off to a Miss Page, living in Brighton, whom he knew to possess one which had been used by her mother and grandmother before her. He persuaded the owner to let him have this horn-book to dispose of, but instead of sending it to me, he straightway sold it to a Brighton bookseller. This is the sort of thing which makes a collector feel good and at peace with all mankind. However, such is the fortune of war, and I heartily thank Mr. J. Eliot Hodgkin, who was afterwards lucky enough to purchase it, for allowing me to reproduce his treasure.

The absolutely immaculate horn-book, shown back and front in cut 148,

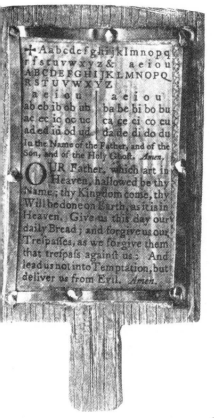 

Cut 148.

is in the collection of Mr. Robert Drane of Cardiff. On the back, as on the back of that in the Huth Library, is the price, three-halfpence, written in ink in figures, $1\frac{1}{2}$d. This horn-book was found wrapped up with two others of the same kind, whose whereabouts has long ago been lost sight of—one of them may be that in the Huth Library,—in the drawer of a Bath bookseller in 1820, when the business changed hands.

History of the Horn-Book

A horn-book, without device on back, stated to be the property of a lady, was some time ago exhibited in the window of a Folkestone tradesman. It was purchased by a dealer in Paris.

Mr. T. N. Longman, of Paternoster Row, has a horn-book which came

Cut 149.

to him from his father. It is covered with brickdust-coloured paper stamped with St. George and the Dragon. About half the brass rimming is absent, but with the exception of one, the old hand-hammered tacks remain. The horn is slightly cracked. There is a hole through the handle, evidently made in recent times. This horn-book is looked upon

History of the Horn-Book

as precious, and reposes in a bed of hollowed velvet in a snap-case covered with red morocco.

The four uncovered horn-books—all of about the same period—forming part of the Mackenzie collection in the South Kensington Museum are in good preservation, and are labelled by the doctor as belonging to a period between 1750 and 1770. The oak base of one is very much darker than the others, and the handle is pierced with a hole, which would seem to point to an earlier period than that assigned. The depth of colour is, however, due to wear and exposure, and the hole has evidently been drilled in late times.

General Sir Anthony Stransham, K.C.B., of Ealing, has a fairly well-preserved horn-book which has been in his family from the later days of the last century. Most of the horn is wanting, and the worms have taken liberties with the text. The brass rimming and the original tacks are quite perfect.

An uncovered and covetable horn-book, quite perfect, which has evidently been little used, is owned by Mr. Harry Praill of the Cannock Chase *Courier*.

Cut 149 is a horn-book belonging to the writer, perfect as to condition, covered with brickdust-coloured paper printed in black ink from a block roughly engraved with the device of a vase of flowers.

A nearly immaculate horn-book—although the horn is scratched and dulled by use, and the base darkened by age and much handling—is owned by Miss Yockney of South Hampstead. It belonged to her grandfather, Mr. Luke Hansard, printer of the Journals of the House of Commons, who died in 1828, aged seventy-eight. Miss Yockney thinks that it belonged to his father before him.

A horn-book in a fair state of preservation is in the Mayer Museum, Liverpool. Mr. Mayer gave his collection of curiosities and works of art to Liverpool in 1867. The printed sheet of this horn-book is perfect, but the horn is badly cracked, and one or two small pieces are missing. A piece of the brass latten at the top right-hand side as far down as the first tack, and the piece on the opposite side from the middle tack to the bottom one, are wanting, and the tacks themselves (rose-heads) are much oxidised. Some one has written on the back of this horn-book in pencil, " 17th Century," which is of course much too early.

History of the Horn-Book

Sketch 150 represents the back of a horn-book belonging to the Rev. Canon Whitelegge of Long Ditton. The cover is paper of a dingy red, and on it is faintly stamped the effigy of the Duke of Cumberland. (A cut of the duke, treated in a different manner and used for decorating book backs, and probably the backs of horn-books also, is numbered 151.) The front of this horn-book is quite perfect. Of the horn-book itself

Cut 150.

Cut 151.

Canon Whitelegge writes : " In regard to its antecedents I can only say that I can remember it as an object of much interest in our family from my earliest years, and I am now in my eighty-first year. My father, to whom it belonged, was born in 1766—that is going back 128 years— and I have no doubt that he received it from his predecessor."

Mr. George A. Plimpton, of New York, owns a carelessly-put-together but well-preserved and almost perfect horn-book which he obtained from Quaritch of London.

THE REVERIE. *Ida Lovering.*

History of the Horn-Book

A good example, like the one shown in cut 144,—except that the handle is more attenuated—is that belonging to Mr. R. West Manders of Casamsize, Naas, County Kildare. Horn and rose-head tacks are perfect, and the lower half only of the piece of latten on the right-hand side is wanting.

The Rev. Canon Jones, of Staunton Rectory, Coleford, Gloucestershire, owns an undecorated and uncovered horn-book, which was found some thirty years ago behind a skirting in pulling down an old cottage (probably once used as a dame's school) at a place called Bolloe, in the parish of Westbury-on-Severn, Gloucestershire, where at that time its owner was vicar. About two-thirds of the brass rimming has been broken away, nearly all the horn is gone, and about one-third of the lower portion of the printed sheet has been raided by mice.

Miss A. M. Dodd, of Holmesdale Road, Sevenoaks, owns a horn-book in which the worm has been at the printed sheet, but his ravages were discovered and put a stop to before many of the letters had disappeared. The horn and brass latten, which is unusually narrow, are perfect, and so are all the rose-head tacks. The handle has, unfortunately, been broken off. The back is covered with stout brown leather stamped with a conventional floral design without much merit, surmounted by an exaggerated full-blown tulip.

Cut 144 is a carelessly-made, crooked-backed, uncovered horn-book, picked up by the writer at Oxford for five shillings. One of the original rose-head tacks only is missing; the horn is perfect, but about one-half of the ornamental border is exposed by the disappearance of some of the slips of latten.

Judging from a rough pencil sketch, which need hardly be engraved, the undecorated horn-book owned by Mr. John Gibson, of Newcastle-upon-Tyne, is perfect. Mr. Gibson keeps his treasure, together with some early school-books, in a frame which he says it would be very inconvenient to take to pieces. This horn-book was knocked down for half a crown at the sale of antiquities belonging to the late John Bell of Gateshead dispersed about forty years ago.

Mr. John H. Chipchase, of Pontefract, owns a very roughly finished uncovered standard horn-book, with the original printed sheet, horn, latten, and tacks perfect. Mr. Chipchase writes: " I have not been able to trace it further back than my grandfather John Chipchase, who was a teacher of mathematics at Stockton-on-Tees and died in 1816."

The Grosvenor Museum, Chester, contains an uncovered horn-book in excellent preservation. It has been there for many years. There is no history whatever attached to it.

The horn-book in the Ashmolean Museum, Oxford, was found in 1877 when clearing away old buildings for the new wing of Brasenose College. Both back and front are identical with cut 149, and illustrations are therefore unnecessary.

An uncovered horn-book in good preservation was some time ago lent to Mr. Hockliffe, a Bedford bookseller, but where it is now I cannot trace.

CHAPTER XXIV

The latest horn-books—Change in character—Cardboard horn-books—Horn-books printed in "modern" type—The cross loses its significance and is superseded by the letter X—"Scratch cradle"—A handleless horn-book—An imaginative little history—A quartette of horn-books—William Hone's recollection of the horn-book —Living persons who remember and were taught from the horn-book.

HE horn-book in the early years of the present century altered materially in character. The wooden base was superseded by a piece of stout card or millboard, covered on one side with embossed and highly-coloured Dutch or tinted paper, and on the other with the printed sheet. The reading side was protected by ugly varnish of a dirty gray or muddy orange-brown tint, due perhaps to a desire to imitate the colour of horn ; but it is more likely that the crudely-made varnish of those days, preserved to us on framed but glass-less prints of the period, was always more or less "off colour." The brass strips and horn-covering were discarded. The selling price of the cardboard horn-book was a halfpenny.

The latest horn-books (see cut 145) are printed from type of "modern" cut due to Bodoni, a French founder, from which the majority of English newspapers are now printed. This type came into use here about 1804.

347

History of the Horn-Book

From the ledgers of Neill and Co., Edinburgh, probably the oldest established Scotch printing-house now in existence, it appears that a complete outfit of "modern" type was ordered from the founders in 1812, and the change from "old style" to "modern"—in which the *Transactions of the Royal Society* and the *Acts of the General Assembly of the Church of Scotland* were the first works printed by them—was made in the following year.

In days when the horn-book was in full swing, the alphabet on cardboard—whether with or without handle one cannot tell—appears to have been in use. The Criss-cross-row on card is mentioned on p. 606, paragraph H, in the *Works of Sir Thomas More, Knyght, some time Lorde Chancellour of England, wrytten by him in the Englysh tonge. In London at the costes and Charges of John Cawode, John Waly, and Richard Tottell.* Anno 1577: "Now, what Tindall must nedes answere vnto this, he can tell well ynough I warrant, when he loketh in his carde vpo those letters in his crosse rowe. For there he must nedes see, that though his faith fayleth neuer after while it fayled not, yet before whyle it fayled, it fayled parde. Whereof the prose is so playn upon his crosse rowe y^t he must nedes se it."

Speaking of the card horn-book, Hone says in one of the notes for his projected tract : " There was also a remarkable alteration at the beginning of the printed page ; the cross + which had given the name of the Christ-cross Row to the alphabet was omitted and the letter X[1] inserted in its place. This substitution must have sorely perplexed many an aged school dame who having taught that + was *cris-cross* found an unhorned horn-book with X which she could make nothing of but ' eks.' The cross was placed before the alphabet in Catholic times when the lips of infancy were required to name ' Christ's Cross,' while its fingers were forming the sign upon the bosom. After the Reformation the Cross continued to be printed before the alphabet, and children were still required to name the ' Christ's Cross,' but were not taught to sign themselves. The act of devotion had ceased and become forgotten, and the corrupt pronunciation *Cris-cross* soon rendered the cross unmeaning. The + naturally was transformed to X. Children who learned the horn-book were taught to know the *cris-cross* but not to know that it signified Christ's Cross.

[1] See cut 152.

348

" Little girls with thread upon their fingers play at what they call *scratch cradle*, and while they alternately lengthen and shorten the threads they say 'cris-cross, cris-cross.' This pastime is a conjunction of two different amusements which engaged children of bygone centuries.   In one of these recreations threads were arranged upon the extended fingers into

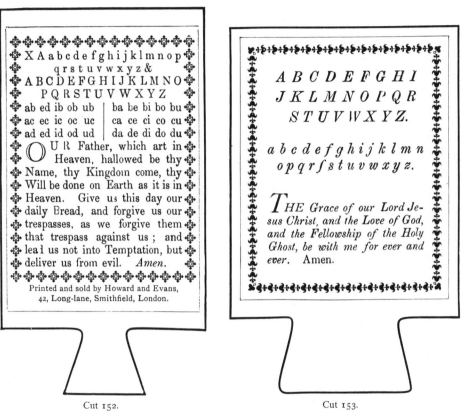

XAabcdefghijklmnop
qrstuvwxyz&
ABCDEFGHIJKLMNO
PQRSTUVWXYZ
ab ed ib ob ub | ba be bi bo bu
ac ec ic oc uc | ca ce ci co cu
ad ed id od ud | da de di do du
OUR Father, which art in Heaven, hallowed be thy Name, thy Kingdom come, thy Will be done on Earth as it is in Heaven. Give us this day our daily Bread, and forgive us our trespasses, as we forgive them that trespass against us ; and lead us not into Temptation, but deliver us from evil. *Amen.*

Printed and sold by Howard and Evans,
42, Long-lane, Smithfield, London.

ABCDEFGHI
JKLMNOPQR
STUVWXYZ.

abcdefghijklmn
opqrfstuvwxyz.

THE Grace of our Lord Jesus Christ, and the Love of God, and the Fellowship of the Holy Ghost, be with me for ever and ever. Amen.

Cut 152.

Cut 153.

the form of a manger, which anciently was called a *cratch*, and this form of the threads purported to represent the manger or cradle wherein the infant Saviour was laid by his Virgin Mother.   The other amusement was the adjusting of the threads upon the fingers in the form of Christ's cross.   It is doubtful whether any female who reads this and remembers to have played at *scratch cradle* and said 'cris-cross,' either intended to form or knew that her words implied *cratch cradle* of Jesus and Christ's cross."

349

History of the Horn-Book

In the *Archæological Journal,* vol. vi. p. 295, Professor Westwood speaks of the cardboard horn-book in the Bodleian Library (cut 153) as an *Abece.* The covering is marbled paper both back and front, over which the printed sheet has been mounted and afterwards varnished. This horn-book is of about the same period as cut 145, when old-style type was giving way to modern. The date suggested in the Bodley Catalogue

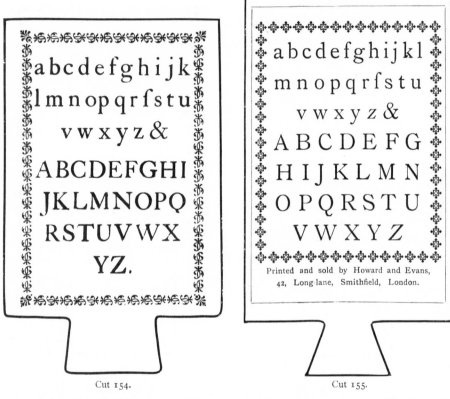

Cut 154.   Cut 155.

" c. 1780 ? " is, I think, too early by a quarter century or so. The long f has not yet been discarded, but it only appears in the alphabet of italic small letters.

The varnished cardboard horn-book (cut 154) was purchased not very long ago by the writer at Sotheby's with some other odds and ends. While the types are earlier than those in cut 153, both horn-books belong to the opening years of the present century.

History of the Horn-Book

Five examples of card horn-books are in the Mackenzie collection. Two of them are as cut 155, and three as cut 152. Dr. Mackenzie has variously labelled them "1800-1810," and "circa 1820." The printers of these card horn-books, Howard and Evans of 42 Long Lane, Smithfield, appear in the London Directory of 1800 as proprietors of a medicinal warehouse ; but in 1807, and for some few years later, they are described as "printers and Medicine Vendors." In regard to this firm, Dr. Mackenzie, in his paper on the Horn-book, makes the statement on the authority of Mr. George Offor, that upwards of a million and a half of varnished cardboard horn-books were destroyed by them as obsolete and worthless.

The handleless horn-book on card, facsimiled in cut 156, formed lot 120 in the Bateman collection mentioned on p. 39. The back of the card is covered with wire-laid paper of a grayish-blue tint, and on it is pasted a written label : "Battledore, a modern horn-book, about 1760-1770, curious and very scarce." On the front is another label, evidently written at an earlier period : "A modern horn-book, 1600." The later date would seem to be the more correct. This horn-book is now in the collection of Mr. George A. Plimpton of New York. Included in the lot—bought by Mr. Quaritch for two guineas—were two late battledores (see p. 414). But the old wooden horn-book, with its protective horn and brass latten rimming, was not easily ousted. In fact, it never was ousted, for it went hand in hand with its frailer and cheaper brother of card until both finally disappeared.

An interesting horn-book—that is, a horn-book proper of wood, with horn, latten, and tacks—of a late date is seen in cut 145.[1] It is the property of Miss Elizabeth A. Croker of Bovey Tracy, Devon, who had it from her father, Dr. John Gifford Croker, the antiquary. This horn-book is printed in "modern" type, a term used in contradistinction to "old face." It will be noted that the long ſ which a little later was entirely discarded is still used, but the compound ſt (compare "against" with the same word in cut 144) has disappeared. The cross at the opening is a creditable makeshift formed from a great primer dagger slightly shortened at the foot. Miss Croker's horn-book, which is quite perfect, is uncovered, and some one in recent years has driven a hole through the handle, probably for the purpose of hanging it up as a curiosity. The oaken base is somewhat thicker than usual and comparatively light in tint.

[1] The printed sheet only is shown.

History of the Horn-Book

In presenting to Dr. Croker this horn-book the donor, a lady, sent with it an imaginative little "history" sufficiently interesting to be transcribed in full : "You ask me, my Friend, for my History. The history of letters as of Men presents, I fear, but a series of ingratitude from poor to

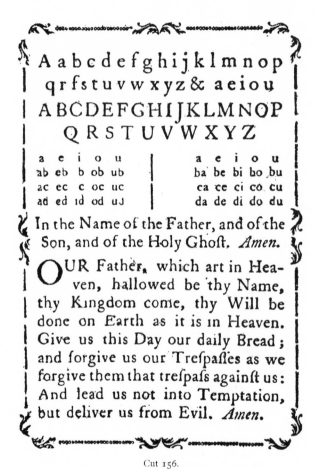

Aabcdefghijklmnop
qrfstuvwxyz& aeiou
ABCDEFGHIJKLMNOP
QRSTUVWXYZ

a	e	i	o	u		a	e	i	o	u
ab	eb	b	ob	ub		ba	be	bi	bo	bu
ac	ec	c	oc	uc		ca	ce	ci	co	cu
ad	ed	id	od	ud		da	de	di	do	du

In the Name of the Father, and of the Son, and of the Holy Ghoft. *Amen.*

OUR Father, which art in Heaven, hallowed be thy Name, thy Kingdom come, thy Will be done on Earth as it is in Heaven. Give us this Day our daily Bread ; and forgive us our Trefpaffes as we forgive them that trefpafs againft us : And lead us not into Temptation, but deliver us from Evil. *Amen.*

Cut 156.

rich, Elected to Electors, Whig to Tory, and Dunces to their good old Horn-Book. I am old and squalid—too old to reap any benefit from Dr. Crook and his Statistics. In my time there was plenty of Wisdom and less Learning—very much plodding—to be sure, nobody ever came back to simple I, to tell how much of profit ; in short, people were always

THE TASKMISTRESS.   *Celia A. Levetus.*

contented with what they knew, and that formed the grand secret of my reputation. You may talk if you please of the light of learning, but from experience I say that learning never looks so tempting as when surrounded by glorious dimness or in the uncertain perspective of lantern-horn. It is made too glaring now to be respected, it is too well dressed, and too frequently seen on the Trottoir like a Southernhay Belle[1] to be earnestly admired—and I guess, that to feel the ability to get to-morrow or next day at the learning of Centuries with the same ease and with the large addition of to-day's printed reflections, will keep many people much as idle and ignorant as it is the fashion to say my times' people were. Well, well, I ought perhaps to be more modest, but I remember when I was a pretty intelligent-looking thing, and when my Mistress, Mrs. Jane Speed-sure, bought me of the Huckster (who every six months frequented our village of Sandford) and laid me on the bright little round Table before she pronounced me fit for the young Squire, who, together with many others, came to reap the select extracts they might obtain from the united brilliancy of myself and Mistress. I could fancy myself young again—and I see the ancient Woman (who by the bye I would rather introduce to you on Monday morning, the preceding day having equally illuminated her mind and person) surrounded by her Table, her Cat, her Spinning Wheel and by twenty Scholars, holding as they sit their Horn-Books, close to their eyes, as if signs might be perfected by reflection, or standing at the Table whilst she, with the mighty Granny pin[2] then pointed at me —the disfigurement of which bad habit I shall carry with me to oblivion, and then at him who held me with less effect I trust—and oh! how often have I doubly suffered when my holder, between the anguish occasioned by the cause and effect, has dashed me to the ground. I had rest, it is true, for I reposed, occasionally, with Bunyan, Baxter, and Bishops on the Shelf, which to the admiration of our Neighbours adorned our Cottage wall. Ah! those good men had rest then!!! But, I have said I was destined to be the young Master's property: as he seemed to be licensed to learn less than the others, so in proportion he ill-treated my Person, perhaps he did not require to learn so much, as he was born to be rich,

[1] In the days before railways Southernhay and Northernhay were the Hyde Park and Regent's Park of Exeter city. A fashionable damsel of Devonshire was known as a Southernhay belle.
[2] "Granny pin," a pin of large size.

History of the Horn-Book

which was synonymous with learning—or he might, through my obscurity, have had visions of unknown Mathematical illuminations, examine me and mark the consequences. We were all but well acquainted, and he might have revealed the truth to me. When at twelve years old he was suddenly sent to a distant County to spread my fame, I fell into less worthy hands, but I eagerly anticipated the time when my old Master should return and claim me for his Children's use and put an end to my honorable sinecure. I wish I could possibly recollect the exact day on which I perceived by the ringing hearty laughter and the consequent stir about me that something very unusual had occurred. Trouble has almost driven memory of events and circumstances out of me. Mrs. Jane brightened and put off her worn expression, and prepared to set out at once with some of her riotous troop to welcome home my first object of curiosity and of attention. Now my joyous time I thought approached, and when I saw, a few days after, my ancient Ally enter our smoky room, I could do all but speak. He, how changed in every look and movement! Could I be changed? No, I had remained the same ; he had sped with years—and so in truth it proved. I have neither heart nor spirits to tell how he talked of ' barbarous ignorance,' how ungratefully he recommended me to be burnt, and how he said that reform would at some future year reach us : Happy has been the ignorance in which for many years I have reposed in my old chest, and happy am I now to find myself under the protection of a Friend to learning and a Friend also to the neglected

HORN-BOOK.

July 2nd, 1832."

The uncovered horn-book shown in cut 157, the property of Mr. F. Hockliffe of Bedford, is interesting for two reasons : (1) The printer, doubtless observing that the typographical border was generally either partially or wholly covered by the brass latten, has altogether omitted it. (2) Though probably made in the latter part of the first quarter of the present century, this horn-book, as to its lettering, is the same as cut 131 of the time of Charles II., the only difference being in the leading of the type. Some former owner has been at pains to cut away all the horn that was visible, but has left a narrow strip which is seen on lifting up the brass latten.

356

History of the Horn-Book

Four late horn-books, now in the collection of the writer, showing no signs of wear and quite perfect, one of which is reproduced in cut 158, were some time ago purchased from a dealer who buys job lots at sales.

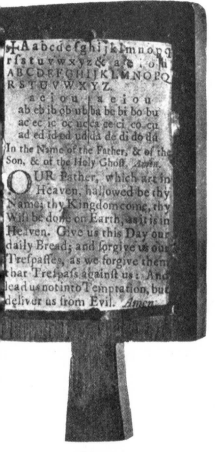

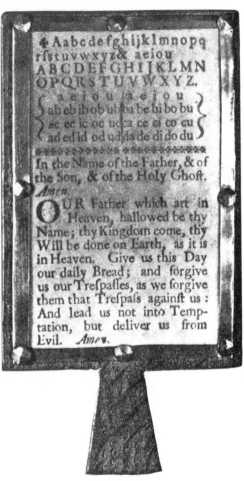

Cut 157.

Cut 158.

They are said to have been in a box of odds and ends not catalogued in detail ; they probably formed part of some long-forgotten old stock. As all four are of the same class, and in regard to typographical imperfections form two pairs exactly alike, they may have been printed in twos, which argues a small demand, rather than in the more usual fours, eights, or sixteens. The absence of border will be noted, and also the ornamentation between the syllabarium and invocation.

A curious horn-book—curious from the position of the handle and from the bordering of stout fibrous tape dusky with exposure—is depicted in cut 159. The owner is Mr. Arthur Pease of Darlington, in whose family it has been since it first saw light—probably about 1820. The horn, with the exception of a small crack, is quite perfect but much scratched and dulled by wear. The tape—in lieu of the ordinary brass rimming—is not a modern " repair " : the horn-book was so made. That it is narrow on two sides and broad on the other two points to little economies, or rather perhaps to the use of odds and ends in the way of material. Tape in lieu of the usual brass latten I have not before met with, and I should think that such a horn-book could hardly be of town manufacture. The numerous flat-headed nails are of brass. The Latin

Cut 159.

cross at the beginning of each alphabet will be noted.   The base is a
strong serviceable piece of oak a full quarter of an inch thick.

Cut 160.

A horn-book owned by Mrs. Hesketh-Gower is shown full size in cut
160.   The printed sheet of this interesting and very late example is in
modern type ; the typographical border and base vary from any I have

seen. The inner frame is of ebony and the outer of mahogany. The period can hardly be earlier than 1830.

A late horn-book, with lettering of the usual type, is the only

Cut 161.

example with a cedar-wood base that I have seen. The date may be about 1830. It was purchased by the writer from a lady correspondent.

A wooden block in the collection of the writer which not unlikely was used for illustrating a page in an A B C book, as well as for making horn-books, is shown in cut 161.

History of the Horn-Book

Report says that the horn-book (cut 162) was in the Great Exhibition of 1851. It has the distinguished honour of being, barring spuriosities, the very latest and most modern horn-book in existence. Sir Henry Peek, Bt., whose property it is, tells me that as a thing of price he "picked it up" in a jeweller's shop in the country, whence it found its way to his private museum at Rousdon. The type used, known as thin-faced Clarendon, first appeared about 1848. Hypercritical persons may say that Sir Henry's handleless horn-book is not a horn-book at all, but simply a specimen of type treated somewhat in horn-book fashion—that is, fixed on to the usual oaken slab, but rimmed instead of "stripped" with brass latten, and faced with a protective translucent material which, in this instance, is not horn but a plate of

Cut 162.

gelatine held with brass pins. It is quite evident, however, that whoever mounted this "sport" must have had practical acquaintance with the horn-book.

Halliwell laments that though horn-books continued in general use in England until the commencement of the present century, even specimens of the latest are procured with great difficulty. "I remember," says Hone in one of his unpublished notes, "the horn-book to have been generally used by mistresses of small schools in the metropolis until 1790 or later." The horn-book was not peculiar to the dame's school. "The third school is the horn-book school, where 30 children are taught by the mistress," writes the Rev. John Entick in his *New and Accurate History and Survey of London, Westminster, Southwark, etc.,* 1766. "Down to the time of George II.," says Robert Chambers in his *Book of Days* (vol. i. p. 47), "there was perhaps no kind of book so largely and

History of the Horn-Book

universally diffused as the said horn-book ; at present there is perhaps no book of that reign of which it would be more difficult to procure a copy."

Several correspondents tell me that the implement known as a spud (cut 163), roughly cut out of wood with a sharpened edge and rounded or squared where the lower part meets the handle, and used by navvies to

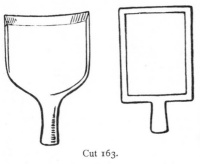

Cut 163.

scrape out concrete or earth adhering to the barrow after a load has been tipped, is in some parts of the country called a " horny-book," or " horny-buck." The little tool is usually fashioned by the workman himself who whittles it with his pocket-knife out of any handy bit of wood. It is suspended from the wrist of the barrow-man by a loop of string so as to be handy when wanted. It will be remembered that the making of English railways commenced about the time that the horn-books were finally discarded, and the term may have arisen from navvies getting hold of some and turning them to useful account. A gross or two of those despised horn-books would now be worth a small fortune.

Mr. Harry Praill, of Cannock, Staffs, writes that when in 1854 a large open fireplace in an old farm-house in the eastern counties was blocked up for the purpose of placing a stove in position, a horn-book was found in good preservation behind an oak mantelshelf. An old lady inquired about this horn-book, for she averred it belonged to her grandmother, and from it she was taught her letters. The old lady, who was nearly one hundred, said that she was not allowed to touch other books until she was able to read them fairly well. " While at Lewes some thirty years ago," continues Mr. Praill, " I showed the horn-book in my possession (see p. 341) to a very old and intelligent man, who said he remembered being taught his letters from a similar one, and that his parents could not afford to purchase a horn-book for his sole use. He further said that he was taught to form letters by writing with his finger on sand sprinkled or sifted on a level surface."

Mr. Edward Peacock, F.S.A., in *A Glossary of Words*, used in the wapentakes of Manley and Corringham, Lincolnshire (London, 1877), says :

A LIBERAL EDUCATION.

Ambrose Dudley.

History of the Horn-Book

'Horn-books were used here in dames' schools ninety years ago." The probability is that, in the more out-of-the-way places within Mr. Peacock's province, they were in use much later. Mr. Peacock writes : "My father, who was born in 1793, told me that he had never seen a horn-book, but when he was a boy he had heard them spoken of as old-fashioned things which had gone out of use. He advised me to make enquiries of an old yeoman of Yaddlethorpe—one Robert Lockwood, who was born in 1776. The old man, who was possessed of remarkable intelligence, said, 'They're all done away with now, but when I was a bairn everybody learned their letters from them.' Without my entering into details he described a horn-book exactly, and had he had an engraving of one before him he could not have done it better. From what he said, and from other scraps of information I have picked up, I think that horn-books were in use in this neighbourhood (North Lincolnshire) till about 1790—perhaps rather later in dames' schools."

Here is an extract from *What I remember about myself and old Merthyr*, printed for private circulation by the representatives of the author, Charles Herbert James, late of Merthyr Tydfil, Glamorganshire, deceased, who was born in Merthyr Tydfil on 16th June 1817 (M.P. for Merthyr Tydfil from 1880 to 1888) : "The next thing I remember with distinctness is my being at school at Mrs. Snelling's. Snelling was a blacksmith and lived in one of the houses now adjoining Biddle's Foundry. I was dressed, on some occasions at all events, in nankeen trousers, buttoned on to a little jacket, and my book was a horn-book about the size of the palm of my hand. The letters were engraved on it and coloured red. There was a hole at the top of the horn-book through which a string was run, and it went round my neck, and so I went to school, equipped with my indestructible book." A horn-book with its letters in red the writer has never seen, but that would be a poor reason for asserting that such a thing never existed ; the chances are all the other way. "Engraved" is presumably a slip for "printed," and by a hole in the top is probably meant a hole in the handle which, when the horn-book was suspended, would be the top.

A very aged Liverpool correspondent, whose memory would appear to be unimpaired, says that he well recollects the horn-books used in his early days, which he describes as being badly made, brown as to the horn, and the oaken slabs nearly black. Sheets of plain paper were wafered on to the backs, on which the children drew the a, b, c with soft lead plummets cut to a point. "I should think," he writes, "that the horn-books, or horn-gigs as we called them, used eighty-five years ago when I was at school in Portsea, must have been made at least fifty years before I was born."

Mr. Robert I. Jones of Tremadoc, North Wales, now in his eighty-first year, tells me that the Welsh horn-book was used in his schooldays. The printed matter consisted of the alphabets large and small, and mixed alphabet, with roots and the numerals. "The printing was on a sheet of white paper covered with transparent horn like that used in stable lanterns."

"More than seventy years ago," writes Mrs. Philp, "I had one of these horn-books in my hand, which I recollect being used in a school kept by some old people at Alford in Lincolnshire. The horn-book was very much like that represented in my sampler (see cut 203), and it was covered with a piece of clear horn like what was used for stable lanterns."

"When I was young, about sixty years ago," writes Mr. G. N. Maynard from Saffron Walden, "my first school was kept by an old dame who lived in the village where I was born, and it was here I became acquainted with this kind of book under the name of 'Horny Cracker,' made similar to the one I lend you (cut 146) but much larger and stronger. The horn-book," continues Mr. Maynard, "was frequently used as an instrument of punishment, and the children had cause to remember a crack upon their craniums administered with the idea of forcing an inlet for the mythical signs that so bothered the juvenile mind."

An esteemed Edinburgh correspondent writes me that he recollects maliciously destroying a horn-book when a boy at Haverfordwest. "I remember well," he says, "that the horn-book was a piece of plain deal and had the letters burnt in, and a thin sheet of horn nailed over the letters which opened with the cross and finished with the figures from 1 to 9. It would be about 10 inches long without the handle, and 6 or 7 inches broad, and there was a hole to hang it up by. In later years I have hunted for specimens when visiting remote villages, but I have never succeeded in getting one. A prominent Edinburgh curiosity dealer asked me about six months ago if I had any horn-books for sale. To test his

History of the Horn-Book

knowledge I said I might let him have half a dozen. He asked the price, and on my mentioning half a crown he immediately, with that inherent love a Scotchman has for bargaining, offered two shillings. A few questions showed that he had enquiries for horn-books, and I afterwards found that similar enquiries had been made in Glasgow, Aberdeen, and Dundee. I presume that your coming work on the horn-book is the 'milk in the cocoa-nut.'" The horn-book described in the foregoing paragraph is of a kind I have never seen.

Writing to Dr. Mackenzie from 20 Carlton Road Villas, Kentish Town, N.W., on 22nd February 1860, Miss Eliza Meteyard says : "Horn-books remained in use as far as regards the remoter districts of the country till late in the eighteenth century. I remember to have seen one when quite a child in a little country dame school in Shropshire, and at a date slightly later than this, I saw another, stuck in a farm-house plate-rack in the mountainous district of Clunbury, near Ludlow, Salop. This is now three-and-twenty years ago. You must, however, recollect that till the advent of railways, these western border counties were primitive indeed, and that in their more remote parts you stepped back as it were into usages and customs of the seventeenth and eighteenth centuries. So late as the past Autumn (1859) I saw in a school at Deare Row, near Wilsonstow, Cheshire, alphabets pasted on small handled boards, in fact, small square battledores, precisely after the fashion of the ancient horn-books.

"There can be no doubt that the Chapman's nursery literature—block printing of the coarsest kind—gradually superseded the ancient horn-books. The alphabet accompanied by a prayer—and the numerals, and printed on rich papers, as we do not see in our day—was sold by the single sheet at fairs and markets—just as a ballad or broadside might be —and carried home, was fastened by mother or schoolmistress to a piece of wood or parchment. Probably in the majority of cases these 'steps to learning' were sold ready pasted on to wooden battledores. To this succeeded the pasting of the alphabet on coarse brown paper,[1] and board, so as to be a book without leaves. The covering outside was generally of barbarous gaudiness, and the price one penny. I well remember such an one being brought into our nursery from a market hawker's stall, and from this I learnt my alphabet."

[1] Probably millboard.

367

History of the Horn-Book

Mrs. Linnæus Banks remembers the horn-book in use seventy years ago. The late Mr. S. Sandars, whose name is mentioned on other pages, told the writer that he remembered the horn-book being used in Yorkshire schools about 1845.

In writing about the horn-book in St. Asaph Cathedral Library, Archdeacon Thomas says : "The use of horn-books was continued down to within living memory."

Dr. Frederick George Lee, Vicar of All Saints, Lambeth, says : " Horn-books were issued and used in Oxfordshire until about 1832."

As the spelling-book cheapened, doubts may have arisen whether the horn-book served any useful purpose beyond slightly helping the infant intelligence—an intelligence easily discouraged by small print and words it failed to understand.

NEVER · TOO · OLD · TO · LEARN.

CHAPTER XXV

Horn-book affinities—Block-printed sheets for teaching children—Catechisms opening with the A B C—The Primer and A B C—Early specimens—" Absey " books—The Stationers' Company—Decree of the Star Chamber—The Dutch *hane-bock*—The wakeful cock—An extra feather in the cock's tail—A B C ballads—Abecedaria—A third-century Abecedarium—An interesting French *Abécédaire*—" Reading Madeasies "—Banbury books for children—The sand-tray—Indian children learning to write on dust—The triangular wooden bar—Hornless sheaths of iron—Grooved reading-boards—An alphabet and a mirror: a French notion—A penny tin plate with the Christ-cross-row and St. George and the Dragon—Wooden tablets in English schools—The " new invented " horn-book—The A B C battledore—The inventor of the card battledore—" Battledore " applied to reading and spelling books—Battledores and their makers—The Welsh battledore—Examples in the Bateman sale—When the battledore disappeared—Needlework samplers—The A B C on sign-boards.

|N the early days of printing, a block-sheet with some affinity, though on a larger scale, to the horn-book, titled *Propugnacula, seu Turris Sapientiæ*, the Bulwark, or Tower of Knowledge, was in common use for teaching children (see reduction, cut 164). To modern eyes the method seems clumsy enough. Sotheby, in his *Principia Typographica* (vol. ii. p. 164), gives a two-page facsimile of one which he says belonged to M. Libri, "one of the most learned and distinguished literary men

369

that France has produced during the present century. The impres-

Cut 164.

sion was sold at the sale of a portion of his library in 1849, whence it was obtained by the Trustees of the British Museum."

It is a broadside, $15\frac{1}{2} \times 9\frac{1}{2}$, much of the same character as the

THE ROAD TO LEARNING.

H. Isabel Baker.

Temptationes Daemonum, in the form of a battlemented tower, the foundation being "Humility, which is the mother of the Virtues." Upon this foundation are four columns—Prudence, Fortitude, Justice, and Temperance; and above are four windows—Discretion, Religion, Devotion, and Contemplation. Even with the windows is a door having two leaves—Obedience and Punishment—serving as an entrance to this Tower of Wisdom, attained by mounting the steps of Prayer, Compunction, Confession, Penitence, Satisfaction, and Almsgiving. Of the tower itself 120 stones are shown, such as Be benevolent, Fear God, Give God thanks, Honour the Saints, Despise the world, Fear thy father, Love thy mother, Be sober, Lie not, Be not disobedient, Honour, Faith, Hope, Constancy, etc. There are six battlements, which are Innocence, Purity, Fear of the Lord, Chastity, Continence, and Virginity—altogether, a highly moral and religious object-lesson.

THE A. B. C.
+ A B C D E F G H I K L M
N O P Q R S T U V W X Y Z.
A b c d e f g h i k l m n o p q r
ſ s t u v w x y z. Amen.
ſt ſſ ff ſi fi ſſi ffi ffl ſh ct &.
a. e. i. o. u.
A B C D E F G H I K L M N O
P Q R S T U V W X Y Z.
A b c d e f g h i k l m n o p q r ſ s
t u v w x y z. Amen.
ſt ſſ ff ſi fi ſſi ffi ffl ſh ct &.
a. e. i. o. u.
In the Name of the Father, and of the Son, and of the Holy Ghoſt: So be it.

Cut 165.

Catechisms for children are thought to be as old as the eighth or ninth century. It is quite possible that they had an opening page with the alphabet in the manner of the horn-book from the time they were first issued. In later (printed) examples (cut 165), the alphabet was given both in black letter and in Roman, and there are variations in the arrangement. The very latest edition of the *Shorter Catechism* appears to be that of a year or two ago, printed by John Cameron of Glasgow, entitled, *The A B C with The Shorter Catechism agreed upon at the Assembly of Divines at Westminster and appointed by the General Assembly of the Church of Scotland to be a Directory for catechising such as are of weaker capacity. Printed by Authority.* The Authority or License, signed J. Moncrieff and dated 1859, permits John Cameron

History of the Horn-Book

to print an edition of eighty thousand copies. Backing the title is the alphabet, set horn-book fashion in a variety of ways, followed by the vowels, diphthongs, marks of punctuation, and an extended syllabarium. A copy of an edition set forth in the same manner, "Printed for the Company of Stationers" in 1771, is in the South Kensington Museum.

In early days before the invention of printing, the primer, or little collection of devotions used in schools, opened with the criss-cross-row or alphabet arranged in horn-book fashion, and the terms "prymer" and "A B C"—the Middle English name for the alphabet—naturally came later to be applied to all elementary books for children's use. The teacher of religion and of the alphabet went always together, and some account of the early MSS. and books of instruction is almost necessary in a *History of the Horn-Book*. Copies of the primer (the earliest known is about 1400 A.D.) are scarce, but considering the efforts made to destroy them, the wonder is that so many have been preserved. Cut 166 shows the first page, slightly reduced, of a vellum MS., a fourteenth-century common prayer-book in English, now in the Glasgow Hunterian Library. The contents are of the usual order—The Hours, The Seven Psalms, The Fifteen Psalms, The Litany, The Office for the Dead, and The Commendations—with some additions before and after the usual text.

A B C was written in numerous forms—abc, a b c, apece, apecy, apcie, apsie, absee, absie, absey, abeesee, abce, abcy, abece, abice, abicee, abcie, abcee, a-bee-cee, a-pece, apecey ; in Welsh Yr'Abiec. The earliest reference given in the (Oxford) *New English Dictionary* relating to the use of one of the forms (abece) is 1297. Cotgrave gives "Abece, Abcee, the Cross-row, an Alphabet." Mätzner [1] gives several of the foregoing forms. Detailed references would occupy much space, and are unnecessary. Allusion to teaching the alphabet is made in Langland's *Piers the Plowman* : [2] "Abstinence the abbesse," quod Pieres, "myne Abc me tauȝte" (taught). A curious example of phonetic spelling occurs in *A Nominale* : [3] "Hoc Alphabetum, a nabse."

An early allusion to an A B C fixed on a wooden board is found in *Reliquiæ Antiquæ* (*circa* fourteenth century), and is set forth on page 105.

---

[1] *Altenglische Sprachproben nebst einem Wörterbuche.* Herausgegeben von Eduard Mätzner. Zweiter Band. Wörterbuch. Erste Abtheilung. Berlin : Weidmannsche Buchhandlung, 1878.

[2] *Piers Pl.* Text B, Passus VII., l. 132, p. 84 of the small edition (Oxford Press).

[3] Printed in Wright's volume of *Vocabularies*, ed. Wülcker (Trübner), col. 719, l. 40.

✠ a · a · b · c · d · e · f · g · h · i · k · l
m · n · o · p · q · r · z · ſ · s · t · u · v ·
x · y · z · ꝥ · eſt amen · Pater noſt͛
Pater oure þat art in heuenes hal
lweð be thi name · þi kingdom com
to the · þi wille be do in erthe as in he
uene · oure echedaies bred ʒife us to day ꝥ
forʒeue us oure dettes · as we forʒeue
to oure dettoures · and lede us noʒt in to
temptacioun · bot delivere us from iuel
Heil marie full of grace · Amen · aue
þe lord is with the · blessed be thou a
monge alle women Ꝣ blessed be þe fruit
of þi wombe iheſus Amen · Credo in
bileue in god fader almyʒti makere
of heuene Ꝣ of erthe and in ihu criſt
his ouliche ſone oure lord · Whiche is
conſeyued of þe holigoſt · Ꞇ borne of
þe maide mary · and pyned vndir pouce
pilatus on rood inailed dede Ꞇ buryed
þe alʒte in to helle · þe þridde day he
aros from deth to lyue · he ſtie in to

Sam; Woodeforde
1682

Cut 166.

History of the Horn-Book

The lines which follow are from a curiously-titled rare book, bought by Dibdin for thirty pounds for Earl Spencer at the Roxburghe sale, *Dives Pragmaticus :*—

" A booke in English metre, of the great marchaunt man called Dives Pragmaticus, very preaty for children to rede ; whereby they may the better, and more readyer, rede and wryte wares and Implementes, in this world contayned. . . . When thou sellest aught unto thy neighbour, or byest anything of him, deceave not, nor oppress him, etc. Imprinted at London in Aldersgate strete, by Alexander Lacy, dwellyng beside the Wall. The xxv. of Aprell, 1563."

> I have inke, paper, and pennes to lode with a barge
> Primers and abces, and bookes of small charge,
>   What lack you scollers ? come hither to me,
> I have fine gownes, clokes, jackets and coates
> Fyne iurkins, dublets, and hosen without motes ;
> Fyne daggers, and knyves, and purses for grotes,
>   What lacke you, my friend ? Come hether to me.

In the *Promptorium Parvulorum*, an early grammar, editions of which were printed by Pynson, Wynkyn de Worde, and others, occur the varying forms of *abse, apecy*, and *apcey*. Shakespeare has " And then comes answer like an Absey book " (*King John*, Act I. sc. 1). " An A B C book, or as they spoke and wrote it, an ' Absey ' book, is a catechism," says Johnson, a definition vaguely comprehensive but perhaps open to criticism. Baretti gives in his *Alvearie or Quadruple Dictionarie containing four sundrie tongues* (1580): " Abce for children to learne their crosrow. A young beginner, or a child that learneth but his abce." In the first edition of his *Survay of London* (1598, p. 26), Stowe says : " This streete is now called *Pater Noster* Rowe, because of Stationers and Text-writers that dwelleth there, who wrote and solde all sorts of bookes then in use, namely *A B C* or Absies with the *Pater Noster, Aue, Creede*, Graces, etc. There dwelles also turners of Beades, and they were called *Pater Noster* makers."

The Stationers' Company, which claimed amongst other works a monopoly in licensing the A B C in its various forms, allowed John Wallye in Foster Lane, and Mistress Toye to print a ballad of *The A B C*

History of the Horn-Book

of a preste called Huegh Sturmey, and another entitled *The Aged Man's A B C.* In 1558-59 John Tysdale was licensed "to prynt a a. b. c. in laten for Rycharde Jugge, John Judson, and Anthony smythe," the charge for the license being 4d., which, says Mr. Arber, is the first instance recorded in the Stationers' Register of one printer printing for another. In 1561-62 a license was granted "for an A b c for chyldren, iiij^d." R. Jones was licensed in 1588 to print the A B C for children " newly deuised with Syllables, the Lorde's Praier, our Belief, and the Ten Commandments." Two years later the license was renewed, coupled with the condition that no addition to the text should be made hereafter. In 1607 the Company inflicted a fine of twenty shillings on Edward White, senior, for having caused an impression of the *A B C for Children* to be printed, and they also mulcted the printer thereof in the mitigated penalty of ten shillings. In 1631 proceedings were ordered against Roger Daniel "concerning printing the A B C." In a list of books controlled by the Stationers Company made out in 1620 appear A B C with the Catechism, the Horn A B C, Spelling A B C, and Primers.

About three years before the venerable Court of Star-Chamber was finally abolished, or to be precise, on the 11th of July 1637, a decree was issued concerning printing.

" + *Item* that no Haberdaſher of small wares, Ironmonger, Chandler, Shopkeeper, or any other perſon or perſons whatſoeuer, not having been ſeuen years apprentice to the trade of a Book-ſeller, Printer or Book-binder, ſhall within the citie or ſvbvrbs of London, or in any other Corporation, Market-towne, or elſwhere, receiue take or buy, to barter, ſell againe, change or do away with any Bibles, Teſtaments, Pſalm-books, Primers, Abcees, Almanackes, or other book or books whatſoeuer upon pain of forfeiture of all ſvch books. . . ."

The oldest edition ·of the printed A B C is supposed to be that amongst the books of Archbishop Sancroft in the library of Emmanuel College, Cambridge. It is in Latin and English and contains sixteen pages, the first of which is reproduced full size in cut 167. A facsimile edition, with interesting notes by the Librarian of Emmanuel College, Mr. E. S. Shuckburgh, M.A., was issued by Elliot Stock in 1889, but the blocks are badly produced, and they labour under the disadvantage of being printed on coarse paper. The little book is undated, but it probably appeared in 1538. The text finishes: "Thus endeth the A B C translated out of Laten to (into) Englysshe with other deuoute Prayers," and finally "Imprynted at Londō in Paules Chyrche yarde at

The. B A C bothe in latyn and in Englysshe.

+ A a b c d e f g h j k l m n o p q r ʒ ſ s t v u x y ʒ ꝗ ꝫ eſt Amen.

a e i o u   a e i o u

ab eb ib ob ub   ba be bi bo bu

ac ec ic oc uc   ca ce ci co cu

ad ed id od ud   da de di do du

af ef if of uf   fa fe fi fo fu

ag eg ig og ug   ga ge gi go gu

In nomine patris ꝗ filij ꝗ ſpiritus ſancti. Amen.   In the name of the Father and of the Sone and of the holy ghoſt. Amen.
Pater noſter qui es in celis ſanctificetur nomen tuū. Adueniat regnum tuum Fiat voluntas tua ſicut in celo et in terra. panem noſtrum quotidianum da nobis hodie. Et dimitte nobis debita noſtra/ ſicut it

Cut 167.

the sygne of the Mayden's heed by thomas Petyt." The A B C opens with the alphabet followed by the vowels and syllabarium, *In nomine* and *Pater noster*. On the following pages are the Hail Mary! the Belief, a number of Graces before and after meals, prayers, and the ten commandments in rhyme. Mr. Shuckburgh remarks it is the earliest known specimen of this class of unauthorised primer, containing the alphabet

The A.B.C

fet fozthe by the Kynges maieftie
and his Clergye, and commaun=
ded to be taught thzough out all his
Realme. All other btterly fet a part,
as the teachers thereof tender
his graces fauour.

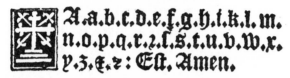 A.a.b.c.d.e.f.g.h.i.k.l.m.
n.o.p.q.r.z.f.s.t.u.b.w.x.
y.z.¶.z: Eft. Amen.

A.B.C.D.E.F.C.H.I.K.L.
M.N.O.P.Q.R.S.T.U.W.
X.Y.
A.B.C.D.E.H.G.H.I.K.
L.M.N.O.P.Q.R.S.T.
U.W.X.

In the name of the Father, and
of the Sonne, and of the holye
Ghofte. So be it.

Cut 168.

and the prayers and elementary religious formularies used in the teaching of children, and the daily life of home.

The first page of a scarce and early A B C of eight pages is shown in cut 168.   It was " Imprinted at London by Wyllyam Powell," probably

✠ A.a.b.c.d.e.f.g.h.i.k.l.m.n.o.p.q.
r.z.ſ.s.t.v.u.x.y.z.ẛ.ꝛ.⁹ ā.ē.ī.ō.ū.
In noīe p̄tis ⁊ filij ⁊ ſpirituſſctī. Amē.

a e i o u   a e i o u
[:::] ab eb ib ob ub   ba be bi bo bu [:::]
ac ec ic oc uc   ca ce ci co cu
[:::] ad ed id od ud   da de di do du [:::]
af ef if of uf   fa fe fi fo fu
[:::] ag eg ig og ug ga ge gi go gu [:::]

❡ Oꝛatio dominicalis.

Pater noſter qui es in celis: ſa=
ctificetur nomē tuum. Adue=
niat regnum tuū. Fiat volū=
tas tua: ſicut ī celo ⁊ in terra.
Panem noſtrum quotidianuȝ da nobis
hodie. Et dimitte nobis debita noſtra
ſicut ⁊ nos dimittimus debitoꝛibus no=
ſtris. Et ne nos inducas in tentationem
Sed libera nos a malo. amen.

Aue maria gꝛa plena, dñs tecum
bñdicta tu in mulierib⁹ : ⁊ bñdi=
ct⁹ fruct⁹ ventris tui Jeſ⁹ chꝛiſt⁹. amen
Credo i deū patrē oipotētē creato=
rē celi ⁊ terre. Et in ieſū chꝛiſtū fi=
liū ei⁹ vnicū dñm nꝛm. Qui conceptus
Say.

Cut 169.

about 1545-47, and the only known copy is among the Greville books
in the British Museum. Mr. Powell shows his loyalty by putting above

ILL-TIMED INQUISITIVENESS.   *Kenneth M. Skeaping.*

the imprint, "God save the Kynge, the Queene and the Realme, and send us peace in Christ. Amen." A great authority in these matters, the late Henry Bradshaw, has pointed out that though Powell was not the king's printer, it is clear from the wording of the title that all other books were to be set aside and this revised edition alone used. In Powell's edition the instructions for serving at Mass are omitted, and the commandments are given in full, while the Graces are simplified, and fewer in number. The Catechism, which had no place in Petyt's A B C, appears in brief.

A probably unique example in Latin, after the old liturgical Sarum use, is the A B C treasured in Lord Robartes's library at Lanhydrock. It is printed on four leaves of vellum, with rubricated capitals, and was found imprisoned as binder's waste in the covers of an old book, where it had remained undisturbed for something like three and a half centuries. The cut (169) shows the first page in facsimile, full size. The original is not quite perfect, and the open letters show the restorations in the reproduction. It will be noted that the first page consists of the alphabet, vowels, and short syllables, followed by the Lord's Prayer, *Ave Maria*, and part of the *Credo*, the remainder being prayer. The facsimile, of which but twenty-five copies were issued in June 1891, is prefaced with many valuable notes on the A B C and its history by Mr. W. H. Allnutt of the Bodleian Library, Oxford, which, had space allowed, I should have sought permission to here reprint in full. From its having the ecclesiastical sanction of the church of Sarum and not that of Royalty, the date of this interesting A B C may be assigned either to the reign of Henry VIII. or to that of Mary.

A rare eight-page A B C in Latin belonging to the writer is that printed by Jacob van Gaesbeeck at Antwerp, early in the eighteenth century. The first and last pages are reproduced in cut 170 in facsimile. In the alphabet, opening with an ornamental Greek cross, it will be noted that V precedes the U. The text is of the usual order. The double imprint at the end is unusual. The upper one—*Impr. F. G. Ullens Can. et Schol.* (Imprimatur F. G. Ullens, Canonicus et Scholaster)—is the authorisation to print granted by F. G. Ullens, Canon of the Cathedral and Ecolâtre— that is, Inspector of Education. To these functions he added that of Licenser of Books, and he authorised the publication of those containing nothing opposed to the Catholic religion. In regard to Jacobus van Gaesbeeck, about whom I have been unable to find out anything, Mr. Max Rooses, the chief of the Plantin-Moretus Museum, tells me that Van Gaesbeeck was admitted as master-printer into the Confraternity of St. Luke at Antwerp, 1714-15.

A common and later form of the Dutch primer or *hane-bock* is a sixteen-

✠ A. a. b. c. d. e. f. g. h. i. k. l. m. n.
o. p. q. r. f. s. t. v. u. w. x. y. z. Eſt.
A. B. C. D. E. F. G. H. I. J. K. L. M. N.
O. P. Q. R. S. T. V. U. W. X. Y. Z Æ.

Oratio Dominica.

PAter noſter qui es in cælis. San-ctificetur nomen tuum. Adveniat regnum tuum. Fiat voluntas tua ſicut in cælo & in terra. Panem noſtrum quotidianum da nobis hodie. Et dimitte nobis debita noſtra, ſicut & nos dimittimus debitoribus noſtris. Et ne nos inducas in tentationem. Sed libera nos à malo. Amen.

Salutatio Angelica.

AVe Maria, gratia plena, Dominus tecum, benedicta tu in

Quinque Præcepta Ecclefiæ.

STatutos Ecclefiæ Feſtos celebrato. Sacrum Miſſæ c cium diebus Feſtis reverenter dito. Indicta certis diebus jejun & à quibusdam cibis abſtinent obſervato. Peccata tua Sacer proprio, aut alteri cum ejus fa tate, ſingulis annis confitetor. croſanctam Euchariſtiam ut m mum ſemel in anno, idque ci Feſtum Paſchæ, ſumito.

Septem Sacramenta.

1 BAptiſmus. 2. Confirma 3 Euchariſtia. 4. Pœniten 5. Extrema Unctio. 6 Ordo 7 M trimonium. *Impr.* F. G. Ullens. *Can. & S*

Antverpiæ. apud JACOBUM VAN GAESBE

Cut 170.

page small octavo. The title-page is faced with a woodcut illustration of children being taught in school ; then on a page to itself—presumably that it may crow to its heart's content without disturbing anybody—is the effigy of the wakeful cock, which is commonly found in children's books published on the Continent. Sometimes the cock is displaced by a little bantam vignetted on the title-page. The alphabet and spelling exercises follow, and towards the end are the Lord's Prayer, the Articles, and the Commandments, the primer finishing with a series of alphabetically-arranged moral aphorisms.

History of the Horn-Book

The German *fibel* or child's first lesson book is probably a dialectic variation of *bibel*. Luther's *fibel*, printed in 1525, has, besides the alphabet, the Paternoster, Credo, and a selection of prayers. The first really German *fibel* was published by Valentine Icksensamer of Rothenburg, and was printed at Nuremberg, 1537. In regard to children's books issued in Germany, "improved" editions were so numerous that it became a mild Teutonic joke to say that an extra feather in the cock's tail was enough upon which to found a new one. A primer printed at Lübeck during the Reformation has on the title-page "improved by Johann Balhorn," who, say humorists, embellished the original woodcut of a cock which stood upon the title-page, by adding a nest of eggs for it to sit upon and hatch. One may suppose, however, that the words "improved by Johann Balhorn," which in Germany have long been a catchphrase or proverb, were applied to the editions of the Lübeck code of law published by Balhorn in 1585, which was "improved" or edited in an unsatisfactory manner. Balhorn's printing-house has been carried on under various names from 1470 to the present time.

Sheets known as A B C's assumed various forms. A few only need be mentioned. One is entitled, *An A B C to the Christian Congregation, or a pathway to the heavenly habitation.* It was "Imprynted at London by Rycharde Kele," probably about 1550. In 1557 appeared *A Ballet intituled an A B C, with a Prayer ;* and in 1587 was printed *The Battaile of A B C.* In the Roxburghe Collection of Ballads in the British Museum are three acrostic alphabet poems : *The Virgin's A B C, or an Alphabet of vertuous Admonition for a chaste, modeste and well-governed Maid. To the Tune of The Young Man's A B C ; The Young Man's A B C, or Two Dozen of Verses which a Young Man sent his Love, who proved unkind. The Tune is "The Young Man's A B C" ; and A right Godly and Christian A B C, shewing the duty of every degree. To the tune of Rogero.*

In describing an early and badly-printed child's primer in his *History of Printing*, Mr. Theodore L. de Vinne arrives at the opinion that it is printer's waste, because there is a large square space left for an opening initial which was evidently intended to be afterwards inserted in the forme of type. In the early days of printing it was quite common, however, to leave gaps into which initial letters were afterwards stamped, written, or coloured. There is not the smallest evidence to guide us as to whether

385

History of the Horn-Book

such wretchedly-executed work as this would have the initials added afterwards. The probability is that Mr. de Vinne is right in his conjecture.

The binding of primers was sometimes in boards—literally in boards, —veneers of pine about the substance used in making lucifer-match boxes, covered with tinted paper turned over at the edges. The boards were often stamped on the outside from blocks used for decorating the backs of horn-books. There is an example in the British Museum with

Cut 171.

Cut 172.

St. George and the Dragon. The late Mr. S. Sandars, of Kensington, owned half a dozen little primers thus bound of various dates. His copy of the 1775 edition (London : printed for the Company of Stationers) has on the front outside cover the effigy of William, Duke of Cumberland, of Culloden fame (cut 151), and on the back a crowned double-headed eagle (cut 171). Another copy printed two years later is stamped both back and front with a quaint old ship under full sail (cut 172). To the average child the Catechism could never have been delectable reading ; hence, perhaps, the attempt to entrap his vision by smearing the cover with blobs of gold and silver foil.

History of the Horn-Book

A letter in the writer's possession, dated 12th October 1832, addressed to "W. Hone, Esq., Gracechurch Street," from a correspondent in Edinburgh whose signature is undecipherable, says :—

"The Revnd. Doc' has informed me that the only thing on the 'a b broad' (horn-book) was the first page of the *Shorter Catechism* torn off and pasted on ; which was renewed when the other was worn. There was no covering of Horn or anything else. The *Shorter Catechism*, first page, contains as you will see the alphabet and the numbers."

A north-country correspondent writes me that within living memory schoolmasters used to tear out the alphabet from a penny Catechism and stick it on a handled board. When the printed sheet was so worn as to be no longer legible, it was topped with another, a practice thought to be more thrifty than teaching the A B C from the Catechism itself.

Abecedarium, a term elastically used, may denote a primer or a horn-book. Diderot, in his *Encyclopédie ou Dictionnaire Raisonné des Sciences, des Arts et des Métiers*, 1751, gives Abécédaire as an adjective derived from the names of the first four letters of the alphabet, A B C D, applied alike to books and persons. M. Dumas, the inventor of the type case, has compiled some very useful Abécédaire books—that is to say, books which treat of letters in relation to reading and which teach how to read with facility and correctness. Abécédaire is different from alphabétique (alphabetical). Abécédaire applies to the thing itself, whereas alphabétique denotes the sequence. Dictionaries are arranged in alphabetical order, but are not on that account Abécédaires. In Hebrew there are Psalms, Lamentations, and Canticles whose verses are arranged in alphabetical order, but I do not think for that reason they should be called alphabetical works. Abécédaire is also applied to a person who has not yet passed his A B C. An Abécédaire doctor is one who is just commencing, and is not yet well practised. Persons who give instruction in reading have also been called Abécédaires. But in this latter sense the word is less often used, says Diderot.

In the State Museum of Antiquities at Leyden there is a Greek Abecedarium of about the third century A.D., on papyrus, in which the vowels and their combinations with consonants in horn-book fashion are in columns, an arrangement suggesting a survival of the period when columnar writing was in vogue. A portion of this interesting papyrus is figured in facsimile (cut 173).

Pliny, who tells us that papyrus for writing purposes dates from the time of Alexander the Great, might have been mildly astonished had it been proved to him that it was made use of by the Egyptians 2300 years B.C. Pliny also tells us how papyrus was made, but he is rather

Cut 173.

vague. The plant (*Cypereus*) was cut into strips which were laid to the required width side by side on a board, and over this was placed another layer at right angles ; Nile water was used for moistening, and adhesion was probably aided by the use of some glutinous material. The sheets were afterwards pressed and dried. In part of an interesting papyrus fragment of the Greek Psalter, probably of the seventh century, lately acquired by the British Museum, the syllables are marked off by dots for the purpose of teaching scholars to read.

Abecedaria were commonly used long before the invention of printing

History of the Horn-Book

with movable types, and in the twelfth century when, according to Hallam, Latin, the language of religious and secular instruction, was more generally understood in this country and in Western Europe than it had been before, the text—if there were any text beyond the alphabet—would have been in Latin.

In a very old work, Higden's *Polychronicon*, Lanfranc shrewdly suspects from a man's first utterance that he is almost ignorant and places before him a copy of the Abecedarium (alphabet) to be explained.[1]

Mention is made of an Abecedarian in the *Life and Times of Anthony Wood*, antiquary of Oxford, 1632-95 (Oxford Historical Society, 1892), p. 284 : " Martock in com. Somerset, ever fruitfull in good Wits and happy in many worthy school masters, among which Thomas Farnabie (anagram 'Bainrafe') was one, who had his beginning here, but at that time went under the disguised name of Thomas Bainrafe for a reason not meet to be mentioned here. In the year 1646 when Mr. Charles Darby was called to teach the grammar schoole at Martock, he found many of his scholars ingenious men and good grammarians, even in their grey haires. It is a report there that when Mr. Bainrafe landed in Cornwall, his distress made him stoop so low as to be an A. b. c. darian, and several were taught their horn-book by him."

An interesting example of a late French *Abécédaire* or spelling-book is that by Madame Dufrenoy, published in Paris at the early part of the century. The text relates to a young gentleman, one Achille de St. Germain, and his cousins and brothers, each of whom for the reward of a covetable print improvises a short story. The chief charm of the book lies in the twenty-six designs by MM. Devilly and Leloi, painters to the Manufactory of Royal Porcelain of Sèvres. On Sèvres they would have been attractive, but unfortunately as book illustrations they suffer much from the method of production—lithography, then in its early days.

---

[1] Ranulf Higden, Hydon, Hygden, Hikeden, etc., died in 1364, and all that is known of him personally is that he was born in the West of England, and took vows as a Benedictine monk in 1299 at St. Werburg's, Chester, where he was buried. He was the author of several works, but the one by which he is best known, and in which is the reference to an Abecedarium, is his *Polychronicon* or universal history, which he brought down to his own time. The *Polychronicon* continued to be a text-book for nearly two centuries. There are numerous MS. copies, and two English versions, one of which was printed by Caxton in 1482 ; the other was printed for the first time in the Rolls Series. The original passage runs : "Tunc Lanfrancus ex prima hominis collocutione perpendens quod prope nihil sciret, *abecedarium* litterarum illi apposuit expediendum."

History of the Horn-Book

In a letter, under the heading "What did Shakespeare learn at School?" addressed to the *Athenæum* on 7th October 1876, Mr. F. J. Furnivall quotes from another written to him by Mr. J. H. Lupton, of St. Paul's School: "An A B C book, for which a pupil teacher or abecedarius is sometimes mentioned as having a salary."

John Florio, born of Italian parents in London, was partly educated in Germany, and settled at Oxford, where he taught French and Italian, and was appointed by James I. tutor to Prince Henry. In his *World of Words*, which appeared in 1598, he gives " Horne-Book, Abecedario, and A-bee-cee " book as synonymous.

Cotgrave gives " Abécédaire, that begins to learn his Abcee ; hence also childish, young, simple, ignorant." According to the *New English Dictionary*, Abecedarian is the usual term applied to a child learning his A B C. The *Athenæum* (No. 2801) has " Abecedarian (alphabetical) requirements have rendered the present volume the least interesting."

The most popular lesson book for children in the last century was known as the *Reading Made Easy*. More than one publisher of children's books claimed to be the originator of the *Reading Made Easy*, generally pronounced as one word—" Readingmadeasy " or " Redamadeazy," and known in the trade as " Reading Easies," a rudimentary spelling-book of moral tone, of which countless editions were printed retailing from twopence to a shilling. W. Rusher, of Banbury, took the lead with " Readingmad-easies," his first essay at sixpence appearing in 1786. The three-hundredth edition, when the title had changed to *Reading Made Most Easy*, appeared about 1830. It opens with the alphabet set out in a variety of ways on a leaf by itself. This leaf is repeated, for which an explanation is forthcoming. "One Alphabet is commonly worn out before the Scholar is perfect in his Letters ; I have therefore added another—W. R." The little book is prefaced with favourable opinions from learned pedagogues, and reference is made to a criticism in the *Gentleman's Magazine* for August 1787. Following the alphabet come words of two, three, four, and five letters, "so disposed as to draw on learners with the greatest ease and pleasure both to themselves and teachers." At the end are lessons taken from the Psalms in words of two divided syllables.

At the turn of the century, the phenomenal success of this little work led Rusher to publish the *English Spelling Book*, selling for eighteenpence,

390

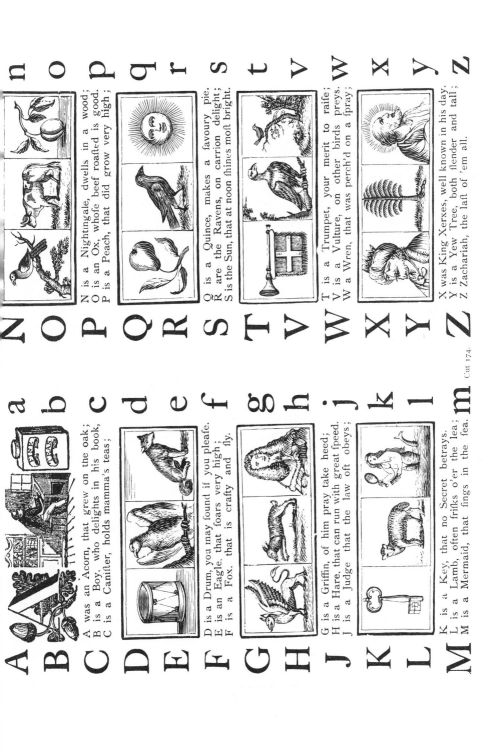

N is a Nightingale, dwells in a wood;
O is an Ox, whose beef roasted is good.
P is a Peach, that did grow very high;

Q is a Quince, makes a favoury pie.
R are the Ravens, on carrion delight;
S is the Sun, that at noon shines most bright.

T is a Trumpet, your merit to raise;
V is a Vulture, on other birds preys.
W a Wren, that was perch'd on a spray;

X was King Xerxes, well known in his day.
Y is a Yew Tree, both slender and tall;
Z Zachariah, the last of 'em all.

A was an Acorn, that grew on the oak;
B is a Boy, who delights in his book,
C is a Canister, holds mamma's teas;

D is a Drum, you may found if you please.
E is an Eagle, that soars very high;
F is a Fox, that is crafty and sly.

G is a Griffin, of him pray take heed;
H is a Hare, that can run with great speed.
J is a Judge that the law oft obeys;

K is a Key, that no Secret betrays.
L is a Lamb, often frisks o'er the lea;
M is a Mermaid, that sings in the sea.

Cut 174.

which ran into many editions. This opened with the alphabet set out as in his *Reading Made Easy.* Then came something more interesting to the juvenile eye—two pages with the alphabet in small and large letters running down the sides, and illustrations with verses underneath. These pages, which also did duty in the battledore, are shown in cut 174. The progressive spelling lessons take the form of " entertaining stories adapted to the capacity of youth." There are illustrated lessons in natural history and lessons in geography ; " Tables " are followed by illustrated fables, and an attempt is made to explain grammar. A page, " Poor Richard giving advice " (cut 175), is here reproduced in facsimile ; in the line following the cut—which, by the way, is from the original wood-block—will be noted the word " plow," a form of Old English spelling sometimes wrongly ascribed to American inventiveness. At the end of everything is the Church Catechism and some prayers.

The writer's copy of a sixpenny *Readingmadeasy*, published by Norbury of Brentford, is the fortieth edition, and is dated 1815. From a Licence, headed George R., granting to one Stanley Crowder, " who hath purchased the Copy Right," sole permission to publish this and other books mentioned therein, including a Treatise on the Use of the Globes, it would appear that the first edition was issued in 1766. Thomas Dyke, Gent., was the original author, upon whose work D. Fenning, whose name appears on the title-page, improved. There is a distinctly funny and highly laudatory testimonial or recommendation on a page to itself immediately following the title, commencing, " I have perused this Edition of Mr. Dyke's *Reading Made Perfectly Easy* "; it is funny, because signed D. Fenning. A noticeable feature of this *Reading Made Easy*, issued by Norbury, who may have held a share in the " Copy Right," are prettily-designed and nicely-engraved full-page cuts, headed " The Prince of Wales & Bishop of Osnabourg," " Her Majesty Queen Charlotte and The Young Princes."

Without the horn-book, or to be exact, without the alphabet on which the horn-book is founded, we are taught that the world could not have been civilised. With the other side of the question, as to whether we are not over-civilised, the reader need not be bored. Maybe the followers of Nicolas Pelargus Storch[1] who would have unlearned their A B C if they

---

[1] It will be remembered that Storch founded among the German Anabaptists in the sixteenth century a small sect known as the Abecedarians, whose aim it was to abolish all knowledge.

could, were right in believing that the world at large would have been the better had it never learned to read.

A Word to the Wife is enough !

God helps them that help themfelves.
Sloth, like ruft, confumes fafter than labour wears, while the ufed key is always bright ; if you love life, do not fquander time.
The fleeping fox catches no poultry.
Early to bed and early to rife,
Makes a man healthy, wealthy, and wife.

He that by the plow would thrive,
Himfelf muft either hold or drive.
Buy what thou haft no need of, and ere long thou fhalt fell thy neceffaries.
Fond pride of drefs is fure a very curfe,
Ere fancy you confult, confult your purfe.
What maintains one vice would bring up two children.
A fmall leak will fink a great fhip.

Cut 175.

Dr. Andrew Bell had a hand in driving the horn-book out of existence. He invented, or rather re-invented, writing on sand. About his sand-tray

History of the Horn-Book

or sand-desk he wrote a pamphlet in 1797, followed by another edition in 1805, entitled "An experiment made in the Male Asylum at Madras suggesting a System by which a School or Family may teach itself under the superintendence of a Master or Parent." Later on, the doctor's revival was largely adopted in this country. The sand-tray consisted of an edged board, about three feet long by ten inches wide, in which was placed some dry sand. A shake or two gave a level surface, on which the teacher, followed by the child, wrote with the finger-tip or a pointed stick. Popular education is largely indebted to Dr. Andrew Bell's almost costless method—a reversion to the oldest of old forms—of teaching bairns how to read and write. Of writing on sand in early times there are, we know, numerous records. The Buddha of ancient India is said to have worked out marvellous calculations with his finger on sand, and is it not written, "But Jesus stooped down, and with His finger wrote on the ground, as though He heard them not" (John viii. 6).

In the native schools at Surat, and elsewhere in our Indian possessions, the floor of the room where the children assemble is thickly strewn with dust swept up from the street. In lieu of a slate the pupil is provided with a wooden board and also a pointed stick. He scatters dust over the board, and on that traces letters or tasks in verses dictated by the master. Careless little Hindoo boys do not escape scot-free. The master looks at the work submitted to him on the dust-boards; if it is satisfactory, he strikes the board with the end of a rod, when the figures disappear; if he disapproves, he strikes again, but this time it is not the board. In the *Proceedings of the Society of Antiquaries of London* (vol. ii. first series, p. 312, Ap. 7, 1853) is the following note :—" Robert Cole, Esq., F.S.A., communicated copies of two letters which he had received from the Rev. Matthew Lowndes of Buckfastleigh, Devon, accompanying a specimen of the old Horn-Book for children in general use about 60 years ago in dames' schools, but which were extinguished by Dr. Bell's Sand-bag (*sic*). Mr. Lowndes considered the old Horn-Book to be more useful than any of the substitutes which have been allowed to supersede it " (see p. 329).

A late offshoot of the horn-book for teaching writing is a triangular wooden bar (cut 176). On each of the three sides, one of which, forming a base, must always be underneath resting on the table or desk, a written copy was pasted, and renewed as it got soiled. It will be noticed that

PLAYING AT SCHOOL.

Georgie Cave France (Mrs. Gaskin).

History of the Horn-Book

from the shape of the block the writing lesson is always at a convenient angle to be copied. I am indebted for the example illustrated (reduced to half its length) to Mr. Percy Kemp, of Horton Kirby National School,

Cut 176.

near Dartford, whose predecessor somewhere in the fifties had a number of them in use.

Closely akin to the horn-book were the arithmetical tables for the use of schools, published by the Society for Promoting Christian Knowledge in 1826. Little larger than an ordinary horn-book they were enclosed in an iron sheath similar to that in cut 6, but there was no horn. I am indebted for a sight of one of these interesting relics—found a few years ago in pulling down an old house in Sussex—to Mr. J. C. Stenning of Beckenham. The Rev. E. M'Clure, M.A., the Society's secretary, tells me that a reference to the old account-books shows that the little printed sheets were sold in series at fourpence-halfpenny per dozen.

Another offshoot of the horn-book (cut 177) is seen in children's reading-boards with grooves, in which slide cardboard letters to form words, and something considerably more remote is a horn-book fan of French make, purchased as lately as 1856, which is in the collection of Mr. H. Syer Cuming, F.S.A. It is small, of cheap make, and no doubt intended for the use of little demoiselles both at school and at home. The boldly

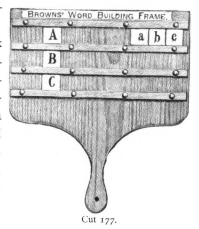

Cut 177.

designed alphabet in capitals is divided into four groups ; the numerals from 1 to 5 and from 6 to 0, designed with equal boldness, run down the two side sticks. The spaces between the lettering are occupied with conventional ornaments. The reader will guess that our gay neighbours are

also responsible for the toy (cut 178) in which vanity and learning join hands
—an alphabet on one side and on the other a mirror. This also is owned
by Mr. Cuming.

The tin plate (cut 179), with a stamped alphabet encircling the rim,
was bought for a penny in London streets some fifteen years ago. The
alphabet and opening cross formed by four dots, and the device of St.

Cut 178.

George and the Dragon, point unmistakably to an origin connected with
the horn-book. The diameter of the plate is six and a quarter inches.

The Sunday School Union issued about 1827 a small wooden tablet
with alphabet exercises pasted on both sides. These are shown slightly
reduced in cuts 180 and 181. The full size is two and seven-eighths in
width by six and a quarter inches in length. For the use of this interesting relic, an offshoot of the horn-book, I am indebted to Mr. A. Sindall.

Amongst the last wooden tablets used in English schools was the small
handleless deal slab with alphabet and figures on one side and syllabarium
on reverse, also published by the Sunday School Union, and known as
Freeman's Lesson Board, which sold for a penny. It appears in a catalogue dated 1835, and only a couple of years ago the dustman cleared
away the discarded stock.

Handleless wooden tablets on a large scale, measuring some fifteen by
twelve inches, with a boldly-printed alphabet pasted thereon and varnished,
are still in use in some of the Cornish Sunday Schools and may be in other
counties.

The printed cardboard battledore, sometimes called a battledore book, is an offshoot of the horn-book. It served a double purpose. In school it was used for teaching children who, between times, played the game of battledore and shuttlecock with it. A " Battledore-boy" was a boy learning his letters. To obtain sufficient stiffness to bear knocking about, the battledore was printed on a double fold of stiff card, with an extra piece lapping over one edge in the old pocket-book fashion.

Cut 179.

Before the advent of cardboard battledores—about which more presently—wooden ones, meant primarily for playing the game of battle-dore and shuttlecock, sometimes had the alphabet painted, impressed, or cut on the front. " To know B from a battledore" was a cant phrase generations before the cardboard battledore came into use, and, says Nares, " it implies a very slight degree of learning."

The later battledore that figures herein, an exact imitation of one in

399

History of the Horn-Book

the collection of Mr. Edward F. Shepherd of Staines, was printed by
J. G. Rusher of Banbury at the early part of the century, and, as can be
seen from the cuts, is obviously a very late edition.

T	U	V	W	X	Y	Z

Left cut (Cut 180):

```
T  U  V  W  X  Y  Z
t  u  v  w  x  y  z
W  z  Y  t  U  v  X
x  V  w  Z  y  T  u
S  l  R  k  Q  j  P
i  O  h  N  g  M  f
```

```
L  s  N  p  W  a  J  u
w  Y  f  G  q  O  z  A
R  i  Q  h  M  k  H  c
e  B  v  S  g  E  o  U
Z  n  K  d  C  m  P  r
b  X  j  V  y  T  l  D
      I  t  F  x
```

These Exercises, containing all the Alphabet, are not to be used as Reading Lessons.

BE LIKE JESUS: PRIZE HIM.
be like Jesus: prize him.
FIX YOUR JOY QUITE ON GOD:
fix your joy quite on God:
SO WILL YE HAVE PEACE.
so will ye have peace.

Cut 180

Right cut (Cut 181):

```
A  B  C  D  E  F
a  b  c  d  e  f
C  d  A  e  B  c
f  E  b  F  a  D

G  H  I  J  K  L
g  h  i  j  k  l
K  j  L  l  G  h
i  I  g  H  k  J
F  e  D  c  B  a

M  N  O  P  Q  R  S
m  n  o  p  q  r  s
P  q  S  r  O  p  M
o  R  m  N  s  Q  n
L  f  K  e  J  d  l
c  H  b  G  a  F  g
```

Sold by R. Davis, at the Sunday School Union Depository. No. 5, Paternoster Row, London.

Cut 181.

Wooden battledores with the alphabet may still be made, for within
living memory was a toy-shop in Queen's Head Row, Newington Butts,
kept by an old widow named Alder, where such battledores were sold.
The less shaded of the two cuts (182) is from a sketch by Mr.
H. Syer Cuming, F.S.A., who says he remembers that the battledore was

400

History of the Horn-Book

of plain solid wood and the letters were in glossy black paint. The more finished sketch is by an artist friend, who would fain see such things again in children's hands.

About half a century ago, when commencing business as a stationer and printer in Portmadoc, Wales, Mr. E. Jones came into possession of a few roughly-made wooden battledores like that depicted back and front

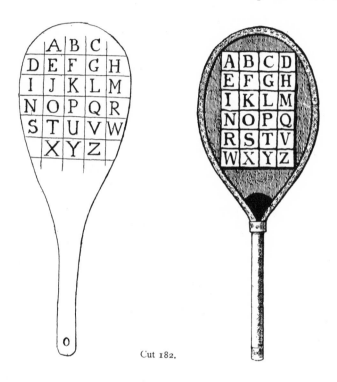

Cut 182.

in cuts 183, 184, shown nearly full size, but he cannot recollect selling any of them. Before his time they were in use in Welsh Sunday Schools. "Local printers," says Mr. Jones, "made such things themselves. The wood was shaped by a neighbouring carpenter and the printer provided the alphabet. The picture at foot varied, and was cut from the coloured penny toy books of the period and stuck on. Pictures of any kind were not so plentiful in those days, and these decorations were very attractive for children, daubs as they were."

"I strongly conjecture," says Hone, " that before the use of the horn-

A B C Ch D
Dd E F Ff G
Ng H I L Ll
M N O P Ph
R S T Th U
W Y

Cut 183.

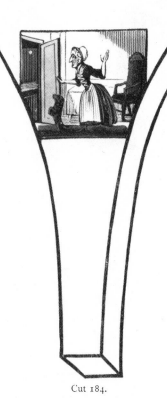

a b c ch d dd
e f ff g ng h
i l ll m n o p
ph r s t th u
w y
1234567890

Cut 184.

book, the alphabet for teaching the letters to little children was often placed upon a battledore. I remember to have seen some years ago at a country church—I think in the West of England—an old battledore used for putting notices on, which it was the duty of the parish clerk to read to the congregation. The Horn-Book is frequently termed the battledore, because it is shaped like a battledore, which is properly a stout piece of board squared, with a short handle of the same piece, much used formerly

Cut 185.

by women, and still used by them in some country places to beat clothes in washing." Such a battledore (O.E. batyldoure) or batlet is figured in cut 185, copied from one of a pack of playing cards drawn perhaps half a century ago.

George Fox printed in 1660 an exceedingly curious "battledore" divided into thirty-five parts in as many languages, with the opening or titled pages mostly outlined in the form of a horn-book. On account of the great number of characters required, it is said that several printers had to be employed in its production, which is perhaps one reason for the scarcity of complete copies. There is a fine example, enshrined with other Quaker literature in contemporary covers with brass clasps, in the library attached to the Friends' Meeting-House in Bishopsgate Street. George Fox was assisted in the compilation of this wearisome and not very convincing scold—the object being to prove the correctness of friends "theeing" and "thouing" each other (" *If thou thouest him thrice, it shall not be amiss.*"—*Twelfth Night*)—by two learned friends, John Stubs of Bishoprick, the author of some half-dozen works, and Benjamin Furley of Colchester, a still more prolific writer of Friends' literature. The first titled page—reproduced in cut 186, one-third the size of the original—is perhaps as much as the reader will care to see.

The honour of inventing the folding cardboard battledore is claimed for Benjamin Collins, and the date 1746 is fixed by his still preserved

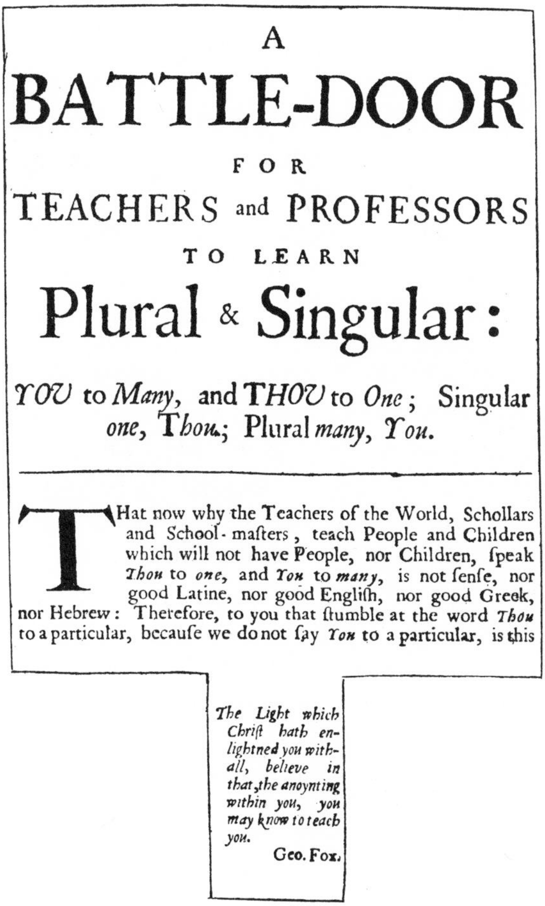

A

BATTLE-DOOR

F O R

TEACHERS and PROFESSORS

T O   L E A R N

Plural & Singular :

YOU to *Many*, and *THOU* to *One*; Singular one, *Thou*; Plural *many*, *You*.

That now why the Teachers of the World, Schollars and School-mafters, teach People and Children which will not have People, nor Children, fpeak *Thou* to *one*, and *You* to *many*, is not fenfe, nor good Latine, nor good Englifh, nor good Greek, nor Hebrew: Therefore, to you that ftumble at the word *Thou* to a particular, becaufe we do not fay *You* to a particular, is this

The Light which Chrift hath en- lightned you with- all, believe in that the anoynting within you, you may know to teach you.

Geo. Fox.

Cut 186.

account books.   He speaks of it as "my own invention," from which he deservedly drew kudos and cash.   In ten years—that is, between 1770 and 1780 when they had become popular—Collins sold considerably over a hundred thousand battledores, which he records cost him three pounds ten per thousand, and he sold them at twelve shillings per gross. The selling price was twopence. The earliest battledores were covered with the highly-coloured gilt embossed Dutch paper—amongst noted last-century makers are Marx Leonhardt Kauffmann and Paul Hinzberg— precious in the eyes of children in the time of Newbery and other long since defunct publishers of juvenile literature. The manufacture of this attractively gaudy paper long ago ceased, and what is left is carefully preserved in the cabinets of the curious. Such paper was largely employed in Holland for the covers of university speeches, and for enshrining wedding poems and invitations of a festive character.

The term battledore was at times applied indiscriminately to the horn-book, the battledore, and to reading and spelling books. A most interesting horn-book named *The British Battledore* is illustrated in cut 94. In the British Museum is a little book of six pages dated 1835, containing the A B C Arabic and Roman numerals and words of two and three syllables, entitled *The Battledore, or First Book for Children.* A correspondent tells me that in a little village in the Isle of Wight he heard an old dame scold her grandchild for leaving her battledore on the grass all night. The battledore turned out to be a child's ordinary first lesson book. The old lady said that she had never heard of a horn-book.

Writing to William Hone in 1831, William Bateman says in a letter hitherto unprinted :—

" In reference to these little affairs the result of my enquiries is, that for the last sixty years, in this neighbourhood the horn-books have usually been called ' Battledores,' when probably the folding pasteboards now in use (one of which is enclosed) and authoritatively inscribed battledore were beginning to supersede their prototypes, the genuine horn-books— that is, that both the one and the other were in use in the same dame school, and called Battledores—but I think no horn-books have been recollected in use within the last thirty years or more."

" At this time " (1830), says Hone in an unpublished note, " there is sold with the alphabet, etc., printed upon it for the teaching of young children a stiff piece of paper. It is folded to make two leaves and a flap. This bears the title of *The Horn-Book or Battledore*, but the title is improper, for it is not either in shape or substance what it is called (A Horn-Book). Bailey, in his *Dictionary*," continues Hone, " calls *Battledore*

LESSONS.

Ambrose Dudley.

History of the Horn-Book

a horn-book, because it has the same shape ; it may be conjectured—perhaps reasonably—that as the use of letters increased, the battledore was reduced to a more portable size, covered with horn, and thenceforth called either the horn-book or battledore."

Very many printers produced battledores. There were *The Battledore, The Royal Battledore, The London New Battledore, The New Improved Battledore, The New Royal Battledore, The Imperial Battledore, The British Battledore, The Pretty Battledore, The New Battledore, The Good Child's Battledore, The Infant's Battledore*, and countless others. Some of the later examples bore no titles at all. Rusher of Banbury, Richardson of Derby, Leighton of Nottingham, Wright of the same town, Toller of Kettering, Kendrew of York, Fordyce of Newcastle, Stark of " Gainsburgh," Mozley of Gainsborough and Derby, Whitehorne of Penryn, the celebrated Newbery, and the great Catnach himself, often placed their name before the title, as *Mozley's Royal Battledore*. Battledores were issued singly and in sets. The writer has a set, " Published by J. and C. Mozley, Derby, and Paternoster Row, London," all of the same size and numbered from 1 to 8. They vary much in the cuts and in the wording, but in all the alphabet is the leading feature. The lessons are not progressive, and the numbers would seem to have been principally intended for the guidance of the dealer in ordering assortments.

The inner printed side of the earliest examples was generally varnished, and as before mentioned, they were backed with gaudily coloured Dutch paper, which gave way to a tinted and later to white paper ; both sides were then printed upon and the varnish was omitted. The selling price was now reduced to a penny. J. M. Mozley, of Gainsborough, issued both penny and twopenny battledores. An example in a parcel of odds and ends (which also contained the horn-book shown in cut 154), purchased by the writer at Sotheby's Sale Rooms in January 1894 for £3 : 16s., is covered with highly-coloured Dutch paper, and was probably printed late in the last century. It is entitled *The Royal Battledore, or First Lesson for Children*, and sold for twopence. The left-hand page contains the alphabet in small and large letters, vowels, compound letters, syllabarium, and the Invocation, which is followed by a child's prayer : " I pray God to blefs my Fa-ther and Mo-ther, Bro-thers and fif-ters, all my good friends, and my Ene-mies. *Amen*." Then

409

comes the Lord's Prayer divided into syllables, and at foot the figures 1 to 0.

The right-hand page has a series of crude cuts, one to each letter—Apple, Bird, Cat, etc. There is an admonitory verse, divided so that a line comes at top and bottom of each page :—

> He that ne'er learns his A B C
> For ever will a Blockhead be,
> But he that learns thefe Letters fair,
> Shall have a Coach to take the Air.

But this was really copied from another (cut 187), with slight varia-

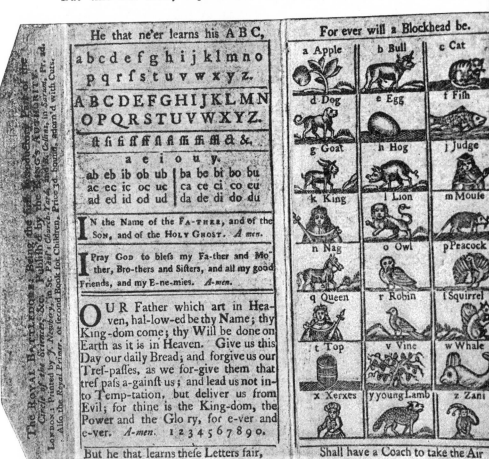

Cut 187

History of the Horn-Book

tions published by the celebrated Newbery of St. Paul's Churchyard, in conjunction with the inventor of the battledore, B. Collins of Salisbury. A copy in facsimile reposes in the cover of this volume, and if by any chance the reader should come across a twopenny original, he might do worse than invest a shilling or sovereign in its acquisition.

Harvey and Darton issued amongst others *The Child's Own Battledore*, printed from engraved copperplates, " Published as the Act Directs, January 1, 1798," at "threepence plain, fourpence coloured." A copy is in the South Kensington Museum.

Mrs. Field, in *The Child and his Book*, speaks of a battledore with this verse :—

> These little girls do dumb-bells use,
> But wherefore do you ask ;
> Why 'tis to make them walk upright,
> Oh, 'tis a pleasing task !

The *Prince Arthur Battledore*, issued by G. R. Barber, Eastwood, Notts, has some simple-looking sentences, one or two of which seem calculated to stagger the infant intelligence :—

Do we go	As I go
Ye go up	Be it so
So be I	So do I.

In later years battledores were made in countless variety, and there must have been very many kinds of which not a single example is now existing. Type-founders kept in stock for the use of printers *clichés* of battledores with letterpress complete. Two examples from the Caslon Foundry are shown in cuts 188 and 189. Some of Rusher's (of Banbury) original battledore blocks have been preserved ; impressions are given in cuts 190, 191. Several pictorial battledore blocks of the Bewick school were sold in a miscellaneous collection of engraved wooden blocks dispersed at Sotheby's rooms on the 19th and 20th of April this year (1895).

There are in the British Museum a couple of Welsh battledores—one printed at Carnarvon by W. Humphreys of Castle Square, and the second by William Spurrell of Carmarthen. They are not dated, but were probably issued between 1830 and 1840. Spurrell's battledore is called a horn-book (Llyfr corn). Spurrell and Son are still in business as printers in Carmarthen. Mr. Spurrell, junior, writes that the English battledores which ceased to be published by his firm some fifty years or more ago were all sold out, and that the stock of the Welsh battledores was sold off as waste-paper some six or seven years ago during an alteration of the premises.

Routledge's *Child's Illustrated Cloth Battledores*—rather a mouthful of

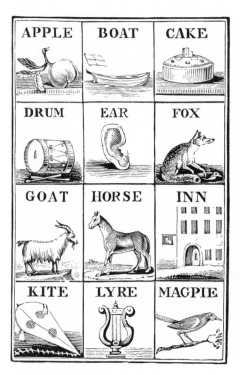

Cut 188.   Cut 189.

a title—appeared in series about 1830. The " cloth " is covered with paper on both sides. Letterpress and pictures are both commendable. One of the latest was that issued in 1845-50 in progressive series by Messrs. Chapman and Hall of the Strand, price threepence, entitled Gaffer Goodman's *Picture Horn-Books*. The size is somewhat larger than usually prevailed. The illustrations are well engraved and carefully printed, and

History of the Horn-Book

the text is appropriate. Red lines divide letterpress and cut into blocks. On the inside flap are the following directions to the teacher :—" The great advantage of the Instructions Card is that instead of placing before the child a large amount of learning, the work of a twelvemonth, nothing

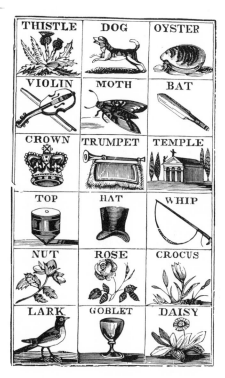

Cut 190.   Cut 191.

here is given but what may be learned in a few days. As Horn-Book succeeds Horn-Book, it has all the allurements of a new plaything ; it is well therefore not to place a fresh card in the child's hands until it is thoroughly well acquainted with the lessons in that preceding, otherwise the delight in the new possession will prevent it returning with pleasure to the lessons in the old card.

413

History of the Horn-Book

No. 1. The Alphabet & Words of Two Letters.
No. 2. Words of Two & Three Letters.
No. 3. Words not exceeding Four Letters.
No. 4. Words of One Syllable.
No. 5. Words not exceeding Two Syllables.
No. 6. Words not exceeding Three Syllables."

The writer is fortunate in possessing a perfect set; he understands that the publishers have not a single example.

One by Salter of Welshpool had printed on the flap—

> Those that will not learn their A B C
> Will Blockheads all their lifetime be,

an altered and curtailed prophecy pointed with the cut of an ass. Of a couple of late battledores disposed of at the dispersal of the Bateman collection (see p. 39) one was "Printed and sold by G. Nall, Bakewell," the other, "Published by Thomas Richardson, Derby." The first is interesting as tending to show that with printers, both in large and small towns, the battledore was at one time an article of regular production.

A paper on the horn-book in Willis's *Current Notes* for October 1855 thus opens: "Horn-Books are now so completely superseded by the Battledore and the various forms of Reading made Easy that they are rarely met with, and few persons believe that such was formerly the means adopted to teach the infantine ideas how to shoot."

The battledore began to fail in popularity between the thirties and forties, but it lingered on until about the time of the Great Exhibition of 1851 or a little later.

The letters A B C would naturally be used on sign-boards by publishers of children's toy-books. Edward Raban printed in 1620 at the sign of the A B C in Cowgate Port, Edinburgh. In a paper on Old Traders' Signs in St. Paul's Churchyard, Mr. Cuming tells us that the A B C was thus used by one Richard Fawkes, a bookseller. Hone says: "I remember to have seen for many years on the east side of Drury Lane at a printer's a carved sign of the letter A." A late example is the A a B, which was interpreted "great A, little a, and a big bouncing B," the sign of a printer named Bailey of Bishopsgate Street, who flourished

History of the Horn-Book

in the early years of this century. Until quite recently there was a sign-board in Amsterdam, "'t Vergult A B C. Anno 1659," but now the house is demolished. In Utrecht there is yet in the Choorstraat a house with a similar signboard.

The specimens of needlework known as samplers, and earlier as sampleths and sam-cloths, painstakingly worked by our foremothers— "And in a tedious sampler sewed her mind,"—generally opened with the alphabet. The sampler nearly always "contrives to pay the double debt" of teaching letters and stitches at one stroke. It served, in fact, the purpose of a horn-book to many generations of little girls.

Samplers worked on a ground of canvas in brightly-coloured silks or wools, at times enriched with gold and silver thread, spangles of talc, and discs and strips of metal, were worked at an earlier period than that from which any specimens survive. Perhaps we do not thereby miss much, and frankly, the decorations on those which do remain to us are always im-possible—impossible trees, impossible houses, impossible birds, beasts, and fishes, impossible men, women, and children, and not good convention even at that. At foot was the name of the proud, painstaking little sempstress, followed by her age and the year of achievement. The dimensions of samplers varied very much indeed. In late times the most usual size was that of a pocket-handkerchief—a description sufficiently elastic perhaps to escape criticism. The earliest samplers preserved to us are mostly long and narrow ; later, they broadened out. The old narrow samplers—samples of the most intricate and beautiful broidery over which years were spent and young eyes half ruined—were sometimes made in two or more pieces, afterwards skilfully joined. There are tiny samplers measuring but an inch or two either way. Moths and damp—Thackeray speaks of "a mouldy old sampler"—have been their enemies-in-chief. Shakespeare, Sidney, Pope, Milton have not disdained mention of them, and Anglo-Saxon women, centuries before Milton's time, were famed for the beauty and excellence of their needlework tapestry, known and admired on the Continent as *Opus Anglicanum*.

Puritan mothers carried with them to America their inherited love of fine needlework, and at dames' schools girls were well taught how to spin, weave, embroider, and knit. One child on record knitted the alphabet and a verse of poetry on to a pair of mittens, and many quaint samplers

which have been preserved testify to the industry and cleverness of our young cousins.

Artists, too, have recognised the sampler. In Wheatley's many-figured picture of "The Schoolmistress," engraved in stipple by Coles in 1794, a sweet-faced mite is working on one. A bigger girl, holding a larger sampler, on which appears an incomplete alphabet, is waiting her turn to interview the old dame, who at the moment is engaged in helping over the stile a youngster perplexed with the abstruse mysteries of C A T.

The oldest sampler I have—the handiwork of Rebekah Fisher—measures $34 \times 7\frac{1}{2}$ inches, and is reproduced in miniature in cut 192. To describe the variety of stitching in this super-elaborate piece of broidery is utterly beyond my masculine mind. It is exquisitely worked in coloured silks, and the date is 1648. The South Kensington Museum contains some fine samplers, the earliest 1654. The latest in my collection is dated 1863. I have also a so-called sampler in fine preservation (which has been shown at the South Kensington Royal School of Art Needlework), whereon birds, beasts, and trees are most intricately and beautifully worked. There is no lettering on the needlework itself, but on the frame is an inscription : "Opus Domina nobili *Strafford* acu pictum, cui maritus vir illustrissimus A.D. 1641 *Carolo I.* Rege ultimo supplicio affectus est."

The "reading" on samplers—very often a verse from a hymn—is nearly always in a moral, minor, or miserable key. But there are exceptions :—

416

History of the Horn-Book

Young ladys fair, whose gentle minds incline,
To all that's curious, innocent and fine,
With Admiration in your works are read,
The various Textures of the twining thread.
Then let your fingers with unrival'd skill,
Exalt the needle, grace the noble quill.

Compleated by Ann Luty in her 13 year, 1788."

An unframed, undated—probably about the middle of the last century —and somewhat slovenly piece of needlework (cut 193—the full size is 7 × 10½ inches) has a redeeming irony :—

This is my Work so
you may see · what
care my mother as
took of me · ann bell.

A nameless and dateless sampler (*circa* 1780-90), elaborately decorated with birds, beasts, and bushes, has the following variant :—

When I was young
And in my Prime,
You see how well
I spent my time.
And by my sampler
You may see
What care my Parent
Took of me.

The needlework on another nameless and dateless sampler, probably of about the same period, is better than the versification or the spelling :—

Jesus permit thy gracious
Name to stand
As the first effort of her
Infant hand
And while her fingers o'er this
Canvas move
Engage her youthful heart to
Seek Thy love
With thy dear children let her
Shear A Part
And Wright Thy self thy law
Upon her heart.

Cut 193.

History of the Horn-Book

By the omission of a full stop or of a capital, a girl like Miss Higgins might give her verse a rendering unconsciously profane :—

> Elizabeth Higgins is My Name England is
> My Nation Fetter Lane is My Dwelling Place
> And Christ is My Salvation
> ended in the 8th year of my age June the 13
> Anno Domini 1790.

From a sampler by Mary Ann Dawson, " her work, aged 11 years 1818," may be gathered something of the British school-dame's erudition :—

> Our Father eat forbidden
> Fruit and from is glory fell
> And we is children thus were brought
> To death and near to hell.

Sarah Pelham " Finished this sampler Nov. 8, 18 ," the absent figures being represented by a blank space. Both she and her mistress were apparently befogged as to the exact year they were living in, but it was between 1800 and 1805. Miss Pelham, who seems to have looked upon herself as quite old, breaks into a weak-ankled couplet :—

> When I was young
> And in my prime,
> Here you may see
> How I spent my time.

Two samplers are interesting as being the work of a couple of little girls who afterwards came together as mistress and maid. Kitty Harrison, who " ended this sampler Sep. 12 in the ninth year of her age, 1770," was the widow of Sir Thomas Carr when Eliza Petett entered her service. Tradition says that 'Liza proved a good and faithful servant, and one intuitively knows that when children the mistress must have been pretty and bashful, the maid modest and demure. 'Liza's sampler, " 1823 aged 12," is creditable, while my Lady Kitty's, in finer material, is exquisitely wrought.

Mr. Edward Peacock tells us that in the will of Margaret Thomson of Freston, in Holland, proved at Boston, 25th May 1546, a sampler, probably of price, is specially devised : " I give to Alys Pynchebeck my syster daughter my sawmpler with semes."

History of the Horn-Book

There is a footnote on samplers on p. 9 of Sir Arthur Mitchell's *Past in the Present : What is Civilization ?* (Edinburgh, David Douglas, 1880): "Dr. George W. Balfour has furnished me with an interesting illustration of the dying out of a practice by a process of degradation. It is supplied by the Sampler, which was worked by nearly every little girl in the country forty years ago, and for a hundred years and more before that time, but which is now rarely, if ever, worked by any one. Dr. Balfour has given me five of these samplers—the work of five generations of ladies in one family. They are all dated at the time of working them ; but no one need consult the dates in order to arrange them according to age. The oldest shows by far the most careful work and the best taste. As they come down to the latest they get ruder and ruder, till we reach those wonderful tubs with inconceivable fruit trees or flowers in them, or those still more wonderful and less conceivable peacocks, worked with coarse thread on coarse canvas, and not in any respect superior either in taste or execution to the paintings or sculpturing of the lowest savages we know. All the young ladies who worked these five samplers belonged to a chain of families living in affluence and refinement, and it was assuredly not a want of culture or taste in the later of them, for the parents of some of the workers were among the appreciators and patrons of Raeburn. Sampler-work was a practice dying out, and death came to it in the usual way, by a process of degradation. This is the only explanation."

In *Midsummer Night's Dream* (Act iii. sc. 2), Helena exclaims to Hermia—

> We, Hermia, like two artificial gods,
> Have with our neelds created both one flower,
> Both on one sampler,—

which, as a correspondent in *Notes and Queries* points out, opens up a new question, "Was it the custom—as Shakespeare, who observed everything, hints—for more than one girl to work upon one sampler ? Has, in fact, any one ever seen a sampler signed by two workers ?" I have a sampler dated 1690, the work of Mary Thicket, aged thirteen years, and Ann Thicket, whose age is not given.

Another sampler is curious because apparently worked by an infant in arms. After the name comes "aged 1 years," but an examination

A TRIPLET OF SAVANTS.

shows that a figure has been removed. It would look as though the little needlewoman, although in her teens, did not know her own age, but told her teacher what she thought it was. The mistake was probably not discovered until the sampler reached home, when the second figure was picked out.

In a collection of Old Ballads, printed for J. Roberts, near the Oxford Arms in Warwick Lane, 1725, is a copy of "A Short and Sweet Sonnet made by one of the Maids of Honour, upon the death of *Q. Elizabeth*, which she sewed upon a Sampler of Red Silk." The tune is, "*Phillida flouts me.*"

> Gone is *Elizabeth*
>> whom we have loved so dear,
> She our kind Mistress was
>> full Four & Forty year.
> *England* she govern'd well,
>> not to be blamed.
> *Flanders* she govern'd well,
>> and *Ireland* famed.
> France she befriended,
>> Spain she had toiled.
> *Papists* rejected,
>> and the *Pope* spoiled,
> To Princes powerful,
>> to the World vertuous,
> To her Foes merciful,
>> To subjects gracious
> Her Soul is in Heaven,
>> The World keeps her glory ;
> Subjects her good deeds,
>> and so ends my Story.

A correspondent of *Notes and Queries* refers to a sampler which, when he wrote (23rd September 1871), was framed and glazed in the back parlour of an old farmhouse on Coniston Water, calling itself the Lake Bank Hotel. The sampler is described as of Charles II.'s time (1660-85), which is sufficiently determined by the workmanship and costume : "A hunting scene, lord and lady in the foreground with hawk on wrist ; dogs behind ; ancestral castle in the distance ; trees and flowers everywhere. The needlework elaborate and (so far as untutored man can judge) exquisite ; the principal figures wrought in high relief, so that the lady's dress, which

History of the Horn-Book

is of satin embroidered with mock pearls, stands out in a half cylinder from the canvas, and the gentleman's off-leg is worked 'in the round,' and only holds on by the hip to the plane of the picture. Apropos of sampler-making, I myself within the last few months have done something towards a revival of that homely but excellent art. I offered prizes of a few shillings to the girls of one of the parish schools in Paddington. How the malapert schoolmistress did sniff and stare! But twelve girls came forward as champions, and that eagerly, with our grandmothers' samplers as patterns they went to work and produced in a few weeks twelve new and happy combinations of old designs; with trees, and golden apples, and red flowers, and a Cris-cross row and Adam and Eve, and Noah's Ark, and the robin, and the cock that crew. Poor things, you will say, poor benighted creatures; but will they not prize those samplers, they and their children after them? All I know is that they worked with a spirit and delight beyond the reach of crochet; that the malapert mistress surveyed the result with wonder and respect; and that even the school inspector, that austere critic of hemstitch (don't you call it?) and Berlin wool, is said to have been almost persuaded."

Those interested in such matters may keep a look-out for *A Manual of the System of Teaching Needlework in the Elementary Schools of the British and Foreign School Society.* In the second edition (and presumably in the first), published in 1821, rules are specifically laid down for teaching children the use of the needle. Monitors are directed to see that the little girls take their work out of their bags and that their hands are clean. The classes are thus divided:—Girls in the first are to fix a hem on waste-paper (to save material); the second class is to hem (paper is now discarded); the third is to fix a seam for sewing and felling; the fourth is to sew and fell; the fifth is to draw threads and stitch; the sixth is to gather and fix on gathers; the seventh is to make button-holes; the eighth is to sew on buttons; the ninth is to do herring-bone stitch; the tenth is to darn; the eleventh is to mark; and the twelfth is to tuck, whip, and sew on a frill. In sampler-making, the girls are practically taught how to mark the capital and small letters of the alphabet, and the figures from 1 up to 10. "The first sampler is marked with red cotton, the second is composed of finer materials" (silk). At the end of the book is a wearisome series of questions and answers for each class in the manner

History of the Horn-Book

of the *Shorter Catechism.* To this generation the most interesting part of the Manual is that devoted to practical illustrations of needlework on the materials themselves—on bits of paper for the earliest, and on linen, cotton, flannel, and canvas—specimens, evidently the work of the little girls themselves, of the needlework taught in the whole of the classes. Cut 193*a* shows one of these specimens full size.

There must have been, in earlier days, illustrations of lettering and

Cut 193*a*.

ornamentation for the guidance of little fingers engaged in sampler-making, but trifles so ephemeral would pass away. As to the mysteries of stitches —the satin, the knotted, the stem, the feather, the cushion, and others still more complex—they have been described at length in the Countess of Wilton's *Art of Needlework*, and in treatises still more abstruse.

A sampler worked in coloured silks, nearly 27 inches long by $2\frac{1}{2}$ wide, is interesting because it is one of the few specimens known containing

a cross. The letters are arranged (cut 194) in higgledy-piggledy fashion in a division evidently intended to be filled up with ornament. Underneath is a cow with crumpled horn, and an animal the like of which mortal eye hath not beheld alive. The name of the sempstress does not appear ; the time is probably the early years of the last century. The only other sampler known to the writer which contains the cross is one begun and never finished by a clever but incorrigibly lazy member of his own family when a child ; the cross, however, does not precede the alphabet, but follows the letter z, and immediately afterwards are the figures 1 to 10.

If it were not for the needlework inscription on a sampler elaborated in silks of many hues (cut 195), " Elizabeth Clarke February the 12, 1692," it might be more properly described as a piece of embroidery. The inscription looks as if it had been let in, but I have taken the sampler for examination from its contemporary frame and find that the inscription forms part of the original work. The subject may be left for the ingenious reader to puzzle over. The size of the original is 10 × 9 inches.

Samplers of oval shape were the exception. A nicely-worked one measuring 12 × 16 inches is reproduced in cut 196.

Important as regards size and painstaking workmanship is the large map sampler (cut 197), measuring 20 × 23 inches. The ornamentation, outlines of counties, and elaborate lettering are all the work of the needle in the finest possible stitching. The scroll at the top is inscribed : " The Map of England and Wales, with part of Scotland and Ireland, by me Ann Hope finishd 1777." It would be interesting to know when it was begun.

426

History of the Horn-Book

In some samplers architecture is the strong point. A representative example about 14 × 17 inches is shown in cut 198. The samplers shown in cuts 199 (9 × 16 inches) and 200 (8¼ × 18 inches) are chiefly remarkable for beautifully minute and elaborate workmanship. The same

Cut 195.

remark applies to cut 201 (11 × 16 inches): "SUsanna neWham WOrKt This in the Ashby HOSPITAL in the year 1760." The reader may perhaps spare a moment to con the inscription and its accessories on the prettily-worked sampler (cut 202), which seems to be a love letter from one Debby to another Debby: "Preserve in your bosom," says

ABCDEFGHIJKL
MNOPQRSTVUWXYZ
1234567891

abcdefghijklmnopqrft
vuwxyz

From all that dwell below the Skies
Let the Creators praise arise
Let the Reedeemers Name be sung
Thro every Land by every Tongue
His Praise shall sound from Shore to Shore
Till Suns shall rise and set no more

Judith Spanton 1809

Cut 196.

History of the Horn-Book

Debby No. 1 to Debby No. 2, "a Remembrance of your Affectionate Deborah Jane Berkin, Bristol May 1st 1778." I am not up in biting beasts and fail to recognise the insect so earnestly commended to be cherished.

Cut 197.

A most interesting sampler, thirteen inches square, begun in 1826, and—impossible as it may at first appear—finished in 1894, is shown

History of the Horn-Book

Thrice welcome to my Op'ning eyes
The morning Beam which Bids me rise
To all the joys of youth .
For thy protection Whilst I slept
O Lord my humble Thanks accept,
And Blefs my lips with Truth .

Louisa
Le page
her work
in the year
1806

Cut 198.

—Mrs. Susanna Philp of Erith-on-Thames, whose maiden name was

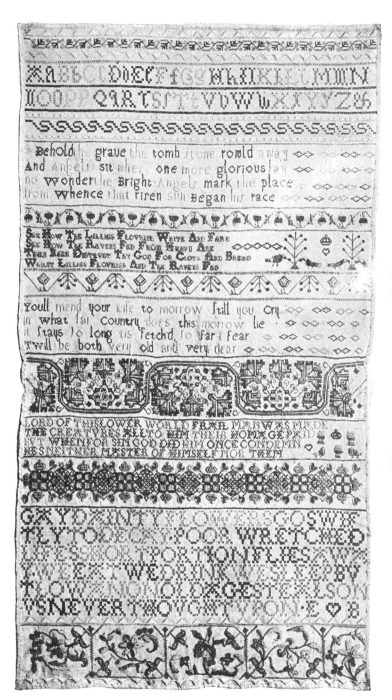

Cut 199.

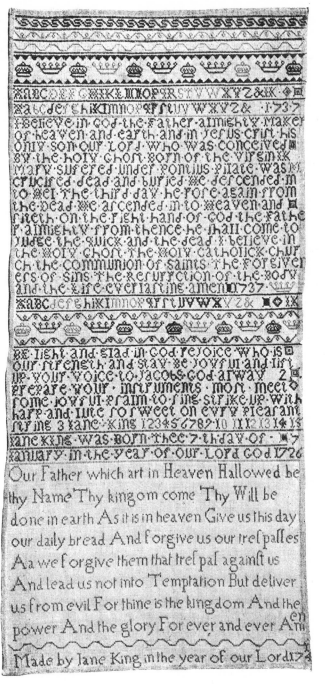

Cut 200.

Leake. The mistress of the little girl gave her Metz's picture of

Cut 201.

"School" (see p. 175) to broider in coloured silks. While minutely and painstakingly carried out, the reader will notice that the print has not been followed in all its details. This is owing to the slovenly laying out of the mistress. To the same reason is due the omission of the final " e " in the maiden's name—the planning left no room for it. When the sampler reached the writer it was unfinished, the right arm of the school-mistress with the hand grasping the handle of the horn-book being

Dear Debby
I love you sincerely
My heart retains a grateful sense
of your past kindness
When will the hours of our
Separation be at an end
Preserve in your bosom a Remembrance
of your Affectionate
Deborah Jane Berkin
Bristol
May 1st 1778

Cut 202.

entirely absent. It seems that, after spending two years over it, little Miss Leake had to leave sampling for studies more important. Consent was kindly given to my employing the services of a lady skilled in the use of the needle, who has in a fashion added the missing arm and hand ; there was insufficient space to put them in properly.

Bargain-loving hobby-hunters, like myself, in want of a mild pursuit may note that at present there are beautifully-worked old samplers, which framed are interesting and decorative, to be had at fairly reasonable prices. I have given sixpence for a sampler—a rare bargain that—and five pounds for one not so good. An amateur collector in a far-

Cut 203.

away village sent me a capital assortment at a shilling apiece, begging me to keep as many as I could. He thanked me warmly for being so obliging, and I fondly cherish the hope of another deal. We each thought that we had the better bargain, and we each had, or the transaction would have been savourless.

435

CHAPTER XXVI

IN the fourteenth century gingerbread was made of rye dough spiced with ginger, cloves, or cinnamon, and sweetened with honey or sugar. Shakespeare has, "An I had but one penny in the world, thou shouldst have it to buy gingerbread" (*Love's Labour's Lost*, Act V. sc. 1), and " pepper (hot spice) gingerbread," *First Part of Henry IV.*, Act III. sc. 1. Shenstone has " Gingerbread y-rare." We know that gingerbread with raised devices was sold on stalls in the open market in the fourteenth century, and for anything that can be proved to the contrary, slabs of it, impregnated with spice and impressed with letters of the alphabet, were eaten by little people before ever the horn-book disturbed their peace of mind. Gingerbread Fairs, which survived until recent years, were at one time common and always popular. The fair maids of Taunton—Taunton was one of the early homes of gingerbread-making—bought alphabetical slabs of gingerbread which were offered as bribes to little people clever enough

AGAINST THE GRAIN.

Marion M. Reid.

History of the Horn-Book

to master their A B C, the letters being devoured as they were correctly named.   Matthew Prior [1] has :—

> I mention'd diff'rent Ways of Breeding :
> Begin We in our Children's Reading.
> To Master John the English Maid·
> A Horn-book gives of Ginger-bread :
> And that the Child may learn the better,
> As he can name, he eats the Letter :
> Proceeding thus with vast Delight,
> He spells, and gnaws from Left to Right.
> But shew a Hebrew's hopeful Son,
> Where We suppose the Book begun ;
> The Child would thank you for your kindness,
> And read quite backward from our *Finis :*
> Devour the Learning ne'er so fast :
> Great A would be reserv'd the last.

In an exceedingly scarce child's book entitled *Fortune's Foot Ball* (Tabart and Co., 1806), the text being an autobiography of Isaac Jenner, a mezzotint engraver who achieved some notable work, the author speaks of having learned the alphabet by " feasting on my gingerbread book with my associates only on condition of performing well my task."   And later we find in *Poems by a Bard at Bromsgrove* (J. Crane), 1835 ?—

> The bakers to increase their trade
> Made alphabets of gingerbread,
> That folks might swallow what they read.
> All the letters were digested,
> Hateful ignorance detested.

Hone [2] was humorously inclined when he wrote :—" Among my recollections of childish pleasures I have a vivid remembrance of an alphabet called the Horn-Book, price one farthing, published by the Gingerbread Bakers and sold by all dealers in gingerbread in town and country.   There was a superior edition with a wider margin, handsomely gilt, price a halfpenny.   I formerly purchased for my own use several copies of different editions of this work, but have not preserved one.   It was rather larger than the common horn-book, and made of dark brown gingerbread."

[1] Prior's " Alma," Canto II., in *Poems on Several Occasions*.   London : printed for J. Tonson in the Strand, and J. Barber upon Lambeth Hill.   MDCCXXI. p. 64.
[2] Unpublished notes.

History of the Horn-Book

In his *Poem in Praise of the Horn-Book* (see p. 47) Tickell says :—

> Or if to Ginger Bread, thou shalt descend,
> And Liquorish Learning to thy Babes extend ;
> Or sugar'd plane, o'er spread with beaten Gold,
> Does the sweet Treasure of thy Letters hold.

Hot spiced gingerbread, sometimes called "book gingerbread," impressed with the alphabet and sold at a halfpenny a slice, was cried in London streets until early in the present century ; and to this day may be bought, not only at fast-dying-out English fairs but in the shop of the Kensington confectioner, squares of gingerbread marked from A to Z. In times when the horn-book was in general use, a large trade was done in its gingerbread counterpart. The wooden moulds used for stamping it were in the form of short planks about two inches thick, on which were cut series of devices with others on the reverse side. The long brown slabs were impressed, and after being baked were cut up. The making of gingerbread was looked upon as an art requiring not only instruction but special aptitude. Unless the ingredients were properly mixed, the oven at a proper temperature, and the baking properly timed, the confection instead of eating short came out like leather. Gingerbread was held in repute by great and small. Swift says : "'Tis a loss you are not here, to partake of (participate in ?) three weeks' frost and eat gingerbread in a booth by a fire upon the Thames."

The Dutch gingerbread horn-book mould figured, with an impression, in cuts 204, 205, was courteously sent to me from a Rotterdam correspondent, Mr. G. van Rijn. The date 1778 will be noticed, and the figures at foot of a boy and girl reading.

The lettered moulds for gingerbread horn-books were of course cut in reverse, otherwise impressions would read backwards ; cuts 206, 207, 208, and 209 show English moulds and ha'porths of gingerbread stamped therefrom. The mould or matrix (cuts 208, 209) for a horn-book signed "Chadwick,"—the name of a celebrated maker of gingerbread sold at fairs —was kindly given to me by Mr. R. H. Woodruff, who procured it from Mr. Edward Jeboult (now deceased) of Taunton, from whom I afterwards acquired a goodly collection of moulds. Before they reached Mr. Jeboult's hands, some unregenerate person had sawn the moulds right through, reducing the two-inch thickness to one, and had further divided the planks

Cut 206.

so as to leave but a single design on each piece of wood, the intention being to nail them on to pieces of furniture as ornamentation. However, this bit of well-intentioned iconoclasm, while exposing innumerable worm burrows, has not injured the moulds themselves, for which their owner is duly thankful. Mr. Jeboult told me that this collection of moulds was used by a Mr. Stagg of East Street, Taunton, the successor of a long line of gingerbread-makers who supplied the markets and fairs of Somerset. Mr. Stagg has long been defunct.

The halfpenny gingerbread was made of flour, sugar, and treacle. In a white variety of cake stamped from the same moulds there was more sugar and the treacle was omitted. Pieces of gold foil were dabbed on both sorts, and if tradition is to be credited, a lick of the tongue preceded the application of the foil. The white cakes being sweeter and dearer—they sold for a penny—were considered the better and were often given to bairns as rewards for good conduct. It may be noted here that confectioners sold a white gingerbread of a better

Cut 207.

Cut 209.

Cut 208.

class made of flour, butter, ground ginger, lemon rind, nutmeg, and loaf-sugar.

Mr. Jeboult, whose grandfather carved gingerbread moulds or stamps

Cut 210.

more than a hundred years ago, ingeniously opined that the old saying, "Taking the gilt off the gingerbread," arose from the custom of selling

Cut 211.

damaged or broken bits at half the ordinary prices, an explanation which goes a stage further than that generally accepted.

In regard to the age of these moulds, it is hazardous to be too precise, but from the general character of the designs one would think that they ought to have been carved about the middle of the last century. But makers of gingerbread moulds, as well as makers of moulds for stamping the backs of horn-books, had an exasperating habit of using, and perhaps repeating, designs

Cut 213.

Cut 212.

without much regard to period, consequently they may possibly be forty or fifty years later. In fact, if we are to accept the example pictured in cut 210 of the *Royal George*, wrecked in 1782—lamented by Cowper in deathless memorial stanzas—we may approximately fix the date of the moulds as between that year and the end of the century. The horn-book (209) and its matrix are full size; the other moulds, selected for illustration, 211, 212, 213, and 214, are all somewhat reduced.

445

Cut 214.

The subjects, with the exception perhaps of the sign of " The Cat and Fiddle " (cut 215)—

> Sing hey diddle, diddle,
> The Cat and the Fiddle—

which is faint from much wear, are mostly self-explanatory. A word, however, may be said of cut 216, "The Cock in Breeches," a favourite device. Gingerbread thus impressed—

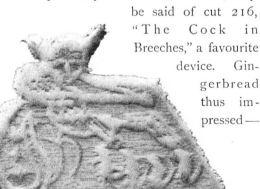

Cut 215.

Cut 216.

vended also at Bartholomew Fair, and in fact at fairs generally—was often given as a sort of make-weight to good customers. So acceptable a gift naturally lent itself to small jokes ; for since the world was young who is to wear the breeches and rule the roast has afforded a theme for mild pleasantries. It will readily be seen why gingerbread impressed with the "Cock in Breeches" should form a sort of fun of the fair, of which our progenitors never grew tired. No doubt other devices bearing an emblematical or political significance, which might now be difficult to understand, were stamped on gingerbread in days when newspapers were not, or were only seen of the few.

SINCE these pages[1] were printed, five more horn-books have been found.

A black-letter example, uncovered (cut 217, *vide* pp. 312, 313), faced with much-worn talc, and the oaken base and text ravaged by worms, was recently advertised for disposal by some one in Cardiff, "the best offer over seventeen pounds accepted." The writer became its purchaser for the sum of six pounds ten shillings. It was found under the flooring-boards of an old house at Packlechurch, near Bristol, about forty years ago. The nails for securing the brass rimming—part of which has disappeared—have long shanks which are turned over on the other side of the wood. The period may be Elizabeth's.

An uncovered hornbook, quite perfect but for the disappearance of

Cut 217.

a piece of latten on the upper left-hand side, was advertised in the *Athenæum* by some one at Doncaster for the sum of five pounds, and was purchased by the writer. It is like that shown in cut 148. The base is of very roughly split oak without pretence to finish.

[1] These notes, ending on page 450, appeared in the two-volume edition.

Another appeared in a sale at Sotheby's on the 20th of February this year (1896), and was catalogued No. " 709, HORN-BOOK containing alphabet and the Lord's Prayer, of the early part of the 18th century, in perfect preservation, size $4\frac{1}{2} \times 2$ inches." The face is identical with that in cut 146. The back is covered with Dutch gilt-paper, bleached by age, but otherwise this horn-book is in excellent preservation. The purchaser was Mr. Quaritch of Piccadilly, who secured it for ten guineas.

A very nice and perfect horn-book, in general appearance like cut 142, was recently acquired by a resident in Northampton for half-a-crown. An American visitor afterwards offered three guineas for it, but he was outbidden by the writer. This horn-book is covered with faded red paper, a little scorched in one place, and had probably been thrown on the fire as rubbish, a happy change of mind resulting in its rescue. The paper covering appeared to be undecorated, but further examination disclosed the faintly embossed effigy of Charles II. on horseback. As to antecedents, nothing is known.

A very large horn-book, shown much reduced in cut 218, has the alphabet carved (see p. 5) in bold relief. It measures $6\frac{3}{4}$ inches wide by $13\frac{3}{4}$ inches long, with an average thickness of a quarter of an inch. This horn-book was recently obtained from a Newport Pagnell correspondent, who writes : " I have known the old alphabet for a very considerable period. It was originally covered with white paint which I had picked off. If I hear anything further I will let you know." Traces of white paint still remain. Some portions of the lettering, as the lower part of the short " and," and the letters E and O, are slightly damaged, otherwise it is well preserved. The eight nicks seen in the cut are probably the work of a boy consumed with a desire to try the temper of a new jack-knife. I thought at first that they might have been intended as guides for a pair of strings running across to direct attention to the letters contained in a particular line, but the nicks bear no relation to the letters, and although repeated on the other edge, they do not correspond in position or distance. There are no nicks at the top or at foot. The oak from which this horn-book or tablet is made is undoubtedly old, but the deep and uniformly regular grooves extending downwards on both sides of the hole in the handle may possibly indicate the over-zealous touch of the spuriosity maker. On the other hand, they may have resulted from ordinary wear. However, whether genuine or not, I was glad to become the possessor of this fine tablet for a sovereign, a sum which in these days would not pay for the labour of making.

Cut 218.

SOME FURTHER NOTES

Cut 219.

OF horn-books unnoted in the two-volume edition of this 'History' I have since heard of some twenty examples.

One of the earliest references to "a boke of horn" is mentioned on p. 283, where 1450 is given as a date when the horn-book was known to be in use. A large-sized horn-book, or, what is more probable, a hornless alphabetical wooden tablet (cut 219), appears in a small panel in one of the borders of a richly illuminated vellum manuscript, dated 1326, *Liber de Officiis Regum*, by Walter de Wilemete, clerk. This manuscript, which is in the library of Christ Church College, Oxford, is full of quaint odds and ends.

I am indebted to the courtesy of an antiquarian correspondent, Mr. Thomas R. Beaufort, who has supplied me with several references, for the sight of an early black-letter horn-book recently discovered beneath the flooring of an old house in Dorking, or rather of what is left of it. It is similar to that shown in cut 129, but in regard to the oaken base on a somewhat smaller scale, with the handle much shortened. What little remains of the rimming—affixed to the outer edge by ten instead of the usual eight tacks—is in the original condition, and of iron instead

453

of brass. The woodwork is perfect, but the horn has entirely disappeared, and of the printed sheet nothing is left but a scrap or two on which a couple of words only can be deciphered. My correspondent has been good enough to negotiate with the owner of this interesting old wreck, which has since become mine at an outlay of a guinea.

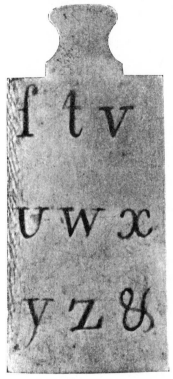

Cut 219a.

A lady has shown me two small ivory horn-books of a kind not before met with. In the first the lettering—an alphabet of capitals—instead of being engraved on the ivory, is printed on paper which is stuck on and varnished, the reverse side being blank. The second example is similar to an ivory horn-book in the pocket of this volume : the lettering is sunk and filled in with black composition.

Cut 219a represents a curiously incomplete ivory horn-book with a portion only of the alphabet written on one side, the other being blank, in ink which age has faded to a dull brown. It would seem that ivory tablets or horn-books were vended plain as well as lettered, the example illustrated, on which the writing is upside down, apparently belonging to a series designed to not unduly tax the infant eye and mind.

The large ivory horn-book reproduced quarter size in cuts 220 and 221 is the only perfect one of its class I have seen.[1] It measures from top to bottom of handle 8 inches, and across $6\frac{3}{8}$ inches. The thickness of the ivory is one-sixteenth of an inch. The pointer used with it is of polished mahogany, and is shown much reduced (the full length is $11\frac{3}{4}$ inches) in cut 222. Both date from the closing years of the last century. This horn-book and pointer were acquired by the writer from Mr. W. F. Grace, in whose family they have been from the time that one of his female progenitors taught with their aid the A B C to

[1] There is a portion of a similar horn-book, a mere slip, shown in cut 45, p. 117.

ABCDE
FGHIJK
LMNOP
QRSTV
UWXYZ

Cut 220.

And

Lord. Lady. Mr Mrs

Miss. To day. To morrow

Yesterday. Read

Very well. Bateman

Fire. Dogs. Chaise Walk

Ride. Glass. Rain. Dry

Cut 221.

the children of the great Duke of Marlborough. The name " Bateman "
in the exercises would have been puzzling had not an explanation been
handed down. It appears that it was the name of a favourite nurse,
and the conclusion follows that such horn-books were engraved to order.

A horn-book of ivory, like that depicted in cut 48, is in the possession of Mr. H. Pollard of Bengeo, Hertford. Nothing is known of
its antecedents.

An interesting ivory horn-book, which recently became mine by
purchase, is reproduced back and front, full size, in cuts 223, 224. It will
be seen that on the front is engraved an alphabet of capitals, followed by
the small letters and vowels, and that on the reverse is the Lord's Prayer.
The silver collar indicates a breakage in the handle. The date is about
1770.

Lord Rosebery has been credited with the possession of a fine
collection of horn-books. He has one only, a small one of ivory.

A very fine and perfect silver horn-book, probably of Dutch origin,
with engraved back (cut 225), has been shown to me by Mr. Frederick
E. Daniel of Barrow-in-Furness, in whose family it has been for many
years. At the end of the handle, in front, the maker's initials, W. P., in
Roman letters, have been stamped in with a punch, and at the back, just
above the heart-shaped hole for suspending, the same initials are repeated
in black letter. The lettering on front is practically the same as that in
cut 37.

Mrs. M. G. Letchworth, of St. Peter's Vicarage, Maidstone, is the happy
possessor of a very beautiful silver horn-book, similar to that in cut 37,
except that the treatment of the engraved subject on the back varies
somewhat in details.

A very nice and quite perfect horn-book of the standard type is owned
by Mr. Septimus C. Gurney, of Saunderton, Princes Risborough, which
came to him from his grandfather, who found it in the drawer of a piece
of furniture purchased at a sale held in the neighbourhood of Aylesbury.

Some Further Notes

Another horn-book of the middle period, perfect but that the horn is cracked in one or two places, I recently purchased from a person who

Cut 223.

Cut 224.

had seen it knocking about at home for years, until his eyes were opened to its value from reading a review of this ' History.'

History of the Horn-Book

An uncovered, bedraggled-looking, standard type horn-book, the text worm-eaten and about one-half of the horn and latten missing, was disposed of in Sotheby's salerooms (lot 854) on 22nd June 1896. It was stated to be the property of a well-known antiquary, and the purchaser was

Cut 225.

Mr. Quaritch, to whom it was knocked down for £4 : 10s. In the same rooms, in sale beginning 31st July, a similar horn-book in good condition was purchased by Mr. Quaritch for £10.

Mrs. Alldin Moore has shown me an almost perfect uncovered horn-book of the standard type. The middle tack on the right-hand side, together with the brass in its neighbourhood, is corroded, and there are

Some Further Notes

signs of corrosion on the lower slip of latten. It has now passed into the possession of her son, Captain W. N. Moore, R.N.

Mr. Morgan S. Williams, of Aberpergwm, has long owned an interesting horn-book closely resembling that depicted in cut 146. It shows signs of much wear. The brass latten remaining is of extreme thinness, and little more than one-sixteenth of an inch in width. It was found by a carpenter under the floor-boards of an old house in the neighbourhood. Mr. Williams frankly confesses that he had it in his possession for several years without knowing what it was.

A nearly perfect horn-book, with Roman lettering, covered with leather originally brown, but now much faded, and embossed with the device of St. George and the Dragon, is owned by Mr. George R. Harding of St. James's Square. Of its antecedents nothing is known.

An uncovered horn-book of the late period, quite perfect, has been shown to me by its owner, Mr. Jeffrey Whitehead, of Newstead, Wimbledon.

In Sotheby's rooms, on the 25th of February this year (1897), two horn-hooks of the middle period came up for sale. The first example (lot 881) is covered in faded red leather, stamped in black with the device of an eagle in its eyrie in the act of making a meal upon something which looks uncommonly like a swathed baby. It was bought by Mr. Pearson for £6. The second (lot 882), covered with faded brown leather, is stamped on the back in silver, much oxidised, with the device of St. George and the Dragon ; on the front, portions of the printed sheet and horn have been eaten away by insects. The brass rimming and tacks are wanting, and the little that remains of the printed sheet and horn is loose —that is, entirely separated from the wooden tablet. It was purchased by Mr. Tregaskis for thirty-six shillings. Both these horn-books were wrongly catalogued as having a "talc frontispiece." In the same sale (lot 880) the black-letter horn-book delineated in cut 138 came up for sale, and was purchased by Mr. Maggs for £10 : 5s. All three buyers are well-known second-hand booksellers.

A leather-covered horn-book similar to that in cut 131 (p. 304), with the effigy of Charles II. on horseback, was recently heard of by Sir Walter Besant, who secured it for the modest outlay of £3.

The Raban horn-book sheet mentioned on p. 130, until recently belonging to Mr. N. Q. Pope, of Brooklyn, N.Y., has been purchased by

History of the Horn-Book

Messrs. Dodd, Mead, and Co., of New York, who are asking two hundred dollars for it. It will be remembered that an exactly similar horn-book was sold at auction in 1878 for three shillings.

Two notable horn-books changed hands in Sotheby's salerooms on 16th July 1896. The catalogue entries are as follows : "(717) Horn-Book, Roman letter containing the Alphabet, words of two letters, and the Lord's Prayer, protected by a thin pane of horn, with brass rims, the back covered with leather, having stamped thereon the effigy of Charles II. on horseback (size $3\frac{1}{2} \times 2\frac{1}{2}$), in fine preservation (described and illustrated in Tuer's *History of the Horn-Book*, p. 147, vol. ii.). (718) Horn-Book, black letter, the horn covering deficient, secured to a piece of oak, with part of the brass rimming, very rare (described and illustrated in Tuer's *History of the Horn-Book*, p. 119, vol. ii.)." They were both bought by Mr. Quaritch: lot 717 realised £32 : 10s. ; and 718, £10.

In regard to some horn-books described in earlier pages, the owner, Mr. S. Richards, of Nottingham, writes me an amusing letter—

> I was bereft of my horn-books in a most extraordinary fashion. A collector called one day and coaxed me to shew them. I told him that I would not sell, but immediately he got them in his hands he slipped them into the inside pocket of his coat which he buttoned up, saying, "You may bid good-bye to your horn-books—put your own price on them!" And although I protested sharply, I have never seen them from that day to this. I tried to get them back, but it became evident that nothing short of assault and battery would help me. In despair I eventually consented to let him have them at a tremendous price, which I have ever since regretted doing.

Mr. John Bohn, a Brighton bookseller, has sent me for inspection an interesting octavo sheet measuring some $4'' \times 7''$, described by him as "a true horn-book." On one side are engraved lettered pictures of the deaf and dumb alphabet inscribed at foot "A good Method to teach Deaf and Dumb Persons to converse with one another and with all who are willing to learn this Secret and Silent way of Conversation. Sold at the Print Shop in Grays Inn, Pr. 1 Peny." The date would seem to be the early part of the last century. It is just possible that such a sheet may have been mounted on card-board or wood, horn-book fashion, but there is no evidence that it was published with this intent.

460

LOST AT SEA

Tristram Ellis

Some Further Notes

The accompanying illustration (226) of a child being taught its letters by the aid of a horn-book or tablet is reduced to quarter size from a pen-and-ink drawing by Hendrik Goltzius (1558-1617). The reader will note the imposing length and knobbiness of the wit-sharpener.

Cut 226.

I am indebted to the courtesy of Messrs. Joh. Enschedé en Zonen, of Haarlem, for *clichés* from a couple of old wooden blocks (cuts 227, 228), in both of which the horn-book is shown. Impressions probably formed frontispieces to children's primers, but how the blocks came into the possession of the great Haarlem foundry is unknown.

Illustration 228*a* (reduced to one quarter size), representing an itinerant vendor of tablets and books for children, forms No. 44 of a set of eighty Italian etchings of the *Cries of Bologna*, by Simon Guillain, from drawings by Annibale Carracci, first published at Rome in 1646. It will be noticed that, as in some other Continental examples, the lettering on

463

the principal horn-book slung from the man's basket reads sideways.

To the chapters on the horn-book in literature I am able to add several allusions.

That licentious lawyer, Thomas Morton, a "gentleman" of Clifford's Inn, who went to America in 1622, and was twice deported to his native country as an incorrigible blackguard, has mention of the horn-book in his *New English Canaan* (chap. xix. p. 153): "*Of the silencing of a Minister in New Canaan.* A silenced Minister

Cut 227.

Cut 228.

out of courteousness, came over into New Canaan to play the spie: he pretended out of a zealous intent to doe the Salvages good, and to teach them; hee brought a great Bundell of Hornebooks with him, and carefull hee was (good man) to blott out all the crosses of them, for feare least the people of the land should become Idolaters" (*New English Canaan or New Canaan. Containing an Abstract of New England, composed in three Books. The First Booke setting forth the originall of the Natives, their Manners and Customs, together with their*

Some Further Notes

tractable Nature and Love towards the English. The second Book setting forth the naturall Indowments of the Country, and what staple Commodities it yealdeth. The third Book setting forth what people are

Cut 228a.

planted there, its prosperity, what remarkable accidents have happened since the first planting of it, together with their Tenets and practise of their Church. Written by Thomas Morton of Clifford's Inne gent., upon tenne yeares knowledge and experiment of the country. Printed at Amsterdam by

465

History of the Horn-Book

Jacob Frederick Stam in the Yeare 1637). Lowndes speaks only of this edition, but in vol. ii. of *Tracts and other Papers relating principally to the Origin, Settlement and Progress of the Colonies in North America from the Discovery of the Country to the year* 1776 : *Collected by Peter Force, Washington,* 1838, an exactly similar text is given which purports to have been " printed by Charles Green 1632."

The horn-book is mentioned in the *Poetical Works of the Rev. Samuel Bishop, A.M., London,* 1796, two volumes. In vol. i. p. 229, in " Poems on Occasional Subjects," we find—

> Some frivolous gentry of the present day
> In *Alphabetic Buckles* shine away,
> But language needs not fashion's flimsy aid ;
> Its elemental base is deeper laid :
> Your children living, and your grandsires dead,
> Lov'd, while they thumb'd, and *tasted* as they *read*,
> The HORN-BOOK'S best edition, Gingerbread.

And in vol. ii. pp. 163, 164, epigram 3—

> If by " Plus, Minus " I express
> This paradox, that *more* is *less*,
> No rule of grammar I transgress,
>   Nor dogmatize at random.
> The veriest horn-book scholar knows
>   That *half* round O (C) an hundred shows
> While *whole* round O for nothing goes
>   Quod erat demonstrandum.

In an ancient account book in the old muniment room of Wollaton Hall we find—

12th July. 6th of Edward VI. : For my nephew Francis, for a pound of sugere-plate and greete comfettes to make hym larne his booke.   2od.

For twoe A. B. Sez.   1d.

For halfe a pounde of Counters for my niece Margaret contayning in number XL. to lerne to caste with all 8d.

The " Francis " here alluded to was the celebrated Sir Francis Willoughby, and " Margaret " afterwards became Lady Arundell.

In *Humphrey Clinker* (2nd edition, London, 1772), vol. ii. p. 82, Winifred Jenkins writes to Mary Jones : " You will also receive a horn-buck for Saul whereby she may learn her letters, for I'm much consarned

about the state of her poor sole"; and in vol. i. p. 232 we find:
"Remember me to Saul—poor sole! It goes to my heart to think she
don't yet know her letters—But all in God's good time—it shall go hard,
but I will bring her the A B C in gingerbread; and that, you nose, will
be learning to her taste."

Speaking of the villager's taste in reading, Richard Jefferies, in his
Life of the Fields (new edition, Chatto & Windus, 1892), says: " First,
the idea that he would require something easy and simple like a horn-
book or primer must be dismissed."

The writer—Mr. W. E. Garrett Fisher—of an amusing paper in the
National Observer (18th July 1896), entitled " Authors at Fault," records
that—

The Author of one of those more or less historical novels which have recently
thronged in such profusion from our presses has fallen into a mistake which, unlike
the rest of his work, is worth recording. His scene was laid somewhere in the
vague centuries in which knights wore armour, and one affecting chapter introduced
the hero in the act of drawing his trusty horn-book from his pocket, in order to jot
down a few memoranda in its pages.

Allusion to the horn-book is made in some lines by Mr. John
Leighton, F.S.A., which accompany the prospectus of his Book-Plate
Annual for 1897. They are printed in black letter within a border
shaped like a horn-book.

> When the horne-boke was the lanthorne of lernynge,
> . . . . . .
> Blythe youth wyssht the horne-boke a battledore.

Something in the manner of the horn-book may be seen in our own
days in Westminster School, Little Dean's Yard. For the use of monitors
the psalm and prayers, etc., in Latin, for the six days are printed on a
couple of octavo sheets, which are mounted on the front and back of a
handled wooden tablet.

In the cemetery attached to the old—eleventh or twelfth century—
roofless church at Kilmalkedar, Ireland, there was until recent years (it
has been stolen) a pillar-stone inscribed with the letters of the alphabet.

Let into the outer walls of the old church of Stratford St. Mary,
Suffolk, are stones—probably ninth or tenth century—separately carved
with the letters of the alphabet, the whole forming a complete series, the

object of which the vicar, the Rev. J. G. Brewster, M.A., seems to think has never been satisfactorily explained, but he leans to the opinion that they indicated a wish to educate the people in a popular and national way. The Kilmalkedar pillar-stone and the Stratford St. Mary stones have sometimes been described as "horn-books," which seems to be stretching the meaning of the term to breaking point. Both alphabets may have been used as abecedaria, but it is equally likely that they were intended as charms to keep away evil spirits and things uncanny.

Cut 229.

In cut 229 is shown full size a most flagrant spuriosity, on the face of it the work of the same bungling hand which achieved the imitation pictured in cut 101. The origin of these spuriosities is given in Chapter XIV. In regard to the one under notice, the base is of oak stained to a dark tint, but a morsel whittled out with a penknife exposes the under-lying, light tinted, modern wood. The tacks, of which there are a dozen, and the rimming are of iron, artificially rusted. This horn-book was recently sent to Messrs. Sotheby, Wilkinson, and Hodge to be disposed of, and I was asked to value it with a view to its sale. The price I put on it was eighteenpence. In replying to the letter of Messrs. Sotheby refusing to sell, the owner wrote: "While I respect the opinion of Mr. Tuer and yourselves, you must remember that there are experts and experts."

Some Further Notes

Charity suggests that there must be something congenitally wrong about a person who rejects the evidence under his nose.

In regard to certain spurious horn-books in the form of a cross mentioned on p. 179, it is there stated that the alphabet is lithographed on modern paper. This is a mistake, the letters and ornamentation being drawn in ink of a light hue. Another spurious horn-book, $4\frac{1}{4}$ inches in height (shown reduced in cut 230), was bought for the sum of two pounds

Cut 230.

in October 1895 by a Fellow of the Society of Antiquaries from Signor Chanteri, a Folkestone dealer whose name is mentioned·in other pages.

The age of the horn-book belonging to Lord Egerton of Tatton (see p. 43) has again been questioned, this time by a scholarly writer in *Bibliographica*, who points out that in a horn-book of Elizabeth's time we might look for spelling of the period as "giue," "deliuer," for "give," "deliver," etc. But the value of the U and V being known, and the tendency to modern spelling admitted, the horn-book might not unnaturally be expected to lead the way. French type was imported into this country, and it was certainly known here that in the model Roman letters made by Geoffrey Tory which appear in his *Champ Fleury* of 1529, there are shown a well-formed capital V and capital U. The omission of contraction signs for *et* and *con* after the alphabet in this and other

469

horn-books proves nothing except that they are not there. The same critic points out that unless both the cuts of the Bateman horn-book agree in misrepresenting it, this famous example—of the genuineness of which there is no doubt—is printed from a block and not from type. His inference is unsound, for the Bateman horn-book *is* printed from type. The principal cut (p. 34) is from a *cliché* taken from the original block engraved many years ago by order of Mr. Bateman, and the smaller cut (p. 36) is a copy of it; what is wrong in the drawing rests with the draughtsman whose name appears at the foot of the larger cut.

In regard to the alphabet block (see p. 283) which I think may have been cut for Wynkyn de Worde, the same authority points out that the cipher and initials at foot do not exactly agree with any of the known varieties used by De Worde. It would be singular if they did. The block is of the roughly cut Catnach class, and there are eccentricities throughout. As to the suggestion that it may possibly be the work of the eccentric John Bagford (see p. 309), sufficient motive would seem to be wanting.

Returning to the Tatton horn-book, another writer has pointed out that in an early part of its career it may have been injured and the printed sheet replaced by one of a later date. With this supposition I do not quarrel, but it is outside the argument.

It may be mentioned here that a feeble imitation of the Tatton horn-book in base metal has lately appeared in a West End toy-shop, for which five shillings is charged. As there is no intent to deceive, purchasers will not be prejudiced at finding the words " Printed at Nuremberg " at the foot of the Lord's Prayer.

A critic who complains of the indexing as inadequate, good-naturedly takes me to task for adding " irrelevant illustrations." He refers to the full-page pictures. With deference, I would suggest that when a thing has been forgotten, pictures illustrating its use are helpful and therefore permissible. The indexing has been considerably extended.

In the Preface to the two-volume edition I mentioned that I had pestered countless people for information about the horn-book, and it may be remembered that Mr. Gladstone's reply was unexpected but to the point ; he said that he knew nothing at all about it. In due time a copy of this ' History ' was sent to Mr. Gladstone. He writes—

Some Further Notes

I thank you very much for your highly interesting gift. It has already disabled me from repeating the confession which I formerly made with perfect truth, but I hope not in the terms given in your Preface, for they seem to convey disparagement, and it is a gross and vulgar error to disparage that which one does not know.

Writing from Oxford in February of this year (1897), Dr. Murray, who, it will be remembered, kindly placed at my disposal his "Horn-Book" notes collected for the *New English Dictionary*, says: "I do not know that a single quotation for *Horn-Book* has come in since I shewed you what we had, but no special work can be done at any word until we reach it—*Horn-Book* will be reached in about twelve months."

LATE NOTE.

IN referring on page 450 to a wooden tablet (cut 218) it is suggested that "the deep and uniformly regular grooves extending downwards on both sides of the hole in the handle may possibly indicate the over-zealous touch of the spuriosity-maker." I have come to the conclusion that this horn-book is a thing of yesterday. Since these pages were printed a bookseller has sent me another and a larger oaken alphabet tablet (shewn much reduced in cut 231) without doubt by the same hand. The length, including handle, is eighteen inches, and the width six-and-a-quarter inches. How the word "Amen" and the ornamentation above it came to appear in a horn-book illustration is set forth on page 180.

Cut 231.

INDEX

Index

Index

Index

Index

Index

Index

Sugere-plate and greete comfettes, 466.
Sunday schools, wooden tablets in, 398.
Surname of Crisscrosse, 66.
Swearing upon the horns, 212.
Swedish equivalent for horn-book, 162.
,, reading boards, 165.
"Swift, Dick, Thief-taker, etc.," 246.
Swindells (A.), chap-book printed for, 202.
Syllabarium added to horn-book, 286.
Symbolical meaning of letters of alphabet, 221.

Tabellæ, Greek and Roman, 279.
Table Book, advertisement for horn-book in, 255.
Tablets, continental, 6.
,, Egyptian, 276.
,, from Pompeii, 280.
,, inscribed leaden, 110.
,, used at Jewish burial service, 167.
,, with numerals, 9.
Tacks used for horn-books, 89.
Talc, horn-book faced with, 106.
Tape-bordered horn-book, 358.
Tatham's *Fancies Theater*, 74.
Tattling stick, 134.
Tatton horn-book, age questioned, etc., 469, 470.
,, horn-book imitated in a toy, 470.
Tatton's (Lord Egerton of) horn-book, 321.
Taunton gingerbread-makers, 442.
Taylor's (Dr.) Work on the Alphabet, 45.
,, *Works*, 24.
Taylor, Wm., of South Weald, 230.
Tell-Trothes New yeares Gift, 72.
Temple of Knowledge, 150.
"Thief-taker, Dick Swift," 246.
"Thieves like a horne-booke," 24.
Thirty trades employed in the making of a horn-book, 194.
Thistle on back of horn-book, 324.
Thomas's (Archdeacon) history of the St. Asaph horn-book, 316.
Thompson's (Sir E. M.) *Greek and Latin Palæography*, 276.
Thomson's (J. H. S.) pedigree of horn-book, 50.
Thorne, horn-book exhibited at Great Dunmow by Mr., 173.
Tickell's *Poem in Praise of the Horn-Book*, 223.
Tickell, Thomas, 221, 223.
,, on gingerbread, 441.
Tiles with alphabets, 274.
Timbs, *Things not Generally Known*, 23, 92, 173.
Times correspondents' references to horn-books, 28.
Tin as a rimming, 89.
Tindale on *crosserowe*, 71.

Tin plate with St. George and the Dragon, 398.
,, rimming in a horn-book, 190, 295.
Tirocinium, or a Review of Schools, 201.
Tittles or dots on the horn-book, 301.
Tokens, Nuremberg, 27.
Tomkins's *Lottery of Pictures*, 159.
Tory's (Geoffrey) *Champ Fleury*, 469.
Tower of Knowledge, 369.
Trades, thirty, in making of horn-book, 194.
Tragicall Raigne of Selimus, 75.
Triplet of dots in horn-books, 62.
,, of stories, 42.
Tristram Shandy, Christ-cross-row in, 79.
Tudor Exhibition, New Gallery, 19.
,, ,, portrait of Lady Petre in, 292.
Tuer (Andrew W.), horn-books belonging to, 31, 332, 341, 345, 357, 449, 450, 453, 454, 457.
Tupper's *Proverbial Philosophy*, 133.
Type-founders, early, 99, 304.

U as a capital, 45, 320.
U in place of U, 106.
University Library, Cambridge, 6.
U, omission from alphabet, 105.

VARIATIONS in text of Lord's Prayer, 183, 189.
Vatican, Greek terra-cotta ink-bottle in, 280.
Vellum or parchment horn-books, 230.
Verse on a battledore, 411.
,, on A B C, *Melancholike Humors*, 1600, 71.
,, on *cros-rowe* in Drayton's *Ideas Mirrour*, 73.
,, on *crystes crosse*, fifteenth-century, 70.
,, on the horn-book by H. M., 50.
Vertical columns, writing in, 275.
View of the Beau Monde, 232.
"Village School," by Jan Steen, 142.
Villette, Charlotte Brontë's, 204.
Virgin teaching the Infant Jesus to read, 161.
Vocabulary of East Anglia, 54.
Volpone, Ben Jonson's, 192.
Vorsterman's device of double-headed eagle, 50.

WALARICH, Saint, 148.
Walpot horn-book, 141.
War, A B C of, 193.
Warburton, Bishop, on *Christ-row*, 204.
Ward's *Dale and its Abbey*, 274.
,, *Reformation*, 203.
Warren (the Rev. F. E.), fescue belonging to, 25.
Warren's (Rev. F. E.) ivory horn-book, 121.
Warrington Museum horn-book, 327.
Warr's (Earl de la), collection of MSS., 28.

485